REACHING YOUR FULL POTENTIAL
Success in College and Life

REACHING YOUR FULL POTENTIAL

Success in College and Life

Willie Claiborne Brown
University of California at San Diego

Prentice Hall, Upper Saddle River, New Jersey 07458

Library of Congress Cataloging-in-Publication Data

Brown, Willie C. (Willie Claiborne)
    Reaching your full potential : success in college and life /
Willie C. Brown
        p.   cm.
    Includes bibliographical references and index.
    ISBN 0-13-956814-X (pbk.)
    1. College student orientation—United States.   2. College
students—United States—Life skills guide.   3. College students—
United States—Attitudes.   4. Success.   I. Title.
LB2343.32.B763   1999
378.1´98—dc21   98-16690
                                                               CIP

Acquisitions editor: *Sue Bierman*
Publisher: *Carol Carter*
Development editor: *Katie E. Bradford*
Production editor: *Trish Finley*
Production liaison: *Barbara Marttine Cappuccio*
Director of manufacturing and production: *Bruce Johnson*
Managing editor: *Mary Carnis*
Manufacturing buyer: *Marc Bove*
Creative director: *Marianne Frasco*
Cover design: *Joseph Sengotta*
Cover art: *Normand Cousineau/Stock Illustration Source*
Chapter opening art: *Normand Cousineau/Stock Illustration Source*
Chapter 1 photos: *"Early socialization," Michelle Bridwell/PhotoEdit;
"Friends," Dratch/The Image Works; "Teachers," Kagan/Monkmeyer
Press; "Media," Court Mast/FPG International; "Religion," SuperStock,
Inc.; "Parents," SuperStock, Inc.; "Culture," SuperStock, Inc.;
"Daydreams," Gala/SuperStock, Inc.*
Author photo: *Charles Lundy*
Marketing manager: *Jeff McIlroy*
Editorial assistant: *Amy Diehl*
Page make-up/formatting: *Clarinda Company*
Printer/Binder: *Webcrafters*

©1999 by Prentice-Hall, Inc.
Simon & Schuster / A Viacom Company
Upper Saddle River, New Jersey 07458

Printed in the United States of America

10 9 8 7 6 5 4 3 2 1

ISBN 0-13-956814-X

Prentice-Hall International (UK) Limited, *London*
Prentice-Hall of Australia Pty. Limited, *Sydney*
Prentice-Hall Canada Inc., *Toronto*
Prentice-Hall Hispanoamericana, S.A., *Mexico*
Prentice-Hall of India Private Limited, *New Delhi*
Prentice-Hall of Japan, Inc., *Tokyo*
Simon & Schuster Asia Pte. Ltd., *Singapore*
Editora Prentice-Hall do Brasil, Ltda., *Rio de Janeiro*

CONTENTS

2

PERSONAL CHANGE: HOW YOU CAN IMPROVE YOUR THINKING AND BEHAVIOR   31

3

OUTLOOK: PROACTIVE STUDENTS CHOOSE OPTIMISM OVER PESSIMISM   63

6 HEALTH AND WELLNESS: PROACTIVE STRATEGIES FOR NOW AND THE FUTURE   207

7 RELATIONSHIPS: CONSTRUCTIVE INTERACTIONS WITH PEERS AND AUTHORITY FIGURES   251

8 FINANCES: UNDERSTANDING AND MANAGING YOUR MONEY   305

EXERCISES

4 PERFORMANCE: HOW TO MAKE THE MOST OF YOUR ABILITIES   101

5 LEARNING STRATEGIES: YOU ARE RESPONSIBLE FOR YOUR EDUCATION   143

6 HEALTH AND WELLNESS: PROACTIVE STRATEGIES FOR NOW AND THE FUTURE   207

7 RELATIONSHIPS: CONSTRUCTIVE INTERACTIONS WITH PEERS AND AUTHORITY FIGURES   251

8 FINANCES: UNDERSTANDING AND MANAGING YOUR MONEY   305

PREFACE

TO INSTRUCTORS

As an instructor, you might wonder why you should consider *Reaching Your Full Potential* for your course when there are already many good texts on the market. In the next few pages, I hope to convince you that this book is different from other texts, and offers many benefits to both you and your students.

Reaching Your Full Potential is about student responsibility. Often, this issue gets slighted in debates over education reform. Throughout the history of this nation, educators and policy makers have focused on what *we* can do for students. The issues often discussed are:

- Better schools

- Better teachers

- Longer school days

- More school days per year

- More resources and better facilities

These issues are important and necessary. But we need to give equal attention to what students can do for themselves. A key question is, "What will make students better students?" We hear little about creating better consumers of education. Where are the plans that will help students help themselves? What will help students motivate themselves to learn? By failing to address these questions, we treat students as bystanders while we discuss issues that greatly affect their lives.

Today, themes of personal responsibility resonate in our society. Perhaps this is the best time in our recent history to introduce books that tell students *what* they can do for themselves and *how* to do it. This is what *Reaching Your Full Potential* is all about. This book forms the basis for a plan that defines student responsibility, and thereby addresses a missing item in the debates over how to best educate our youth.

Reaching Your Full Potential draws from my experiences of almost thirty years of working with students at a major university. I have spent most my career as a biology professor with a deep concern for students—those who took my classes as well as those who did not. I have worked with students who were biology majors and almost as many who were not. Most of the latter student contacts have come from my student success course. This course focuses on thinking and learning strategies for use not only in academic matters but in all segments of life. I have observed students' behaviors, and I have listened to students' concerns. I have learned much about how to succeed from successful students. On the other hand, I have learned much about how not to succeed from less successful students. Specific habits of thoughts and behaviors apply to both types of students. In some cases, I have helped successful students fine-tune their good habits and get even better. In other cases, I have helped less successful students replace bad habits with those that help them succeed.

Some clear messages have come out of my experiences with students. For example, many students:

- Spend little or no time thinking about why they think in certain ways and how these patterns largely determine their success or failure.

- Are not aware that they can improve their chances of success by changing the way they think.

- Do not know how to change their thought patterns.

- Are willing to change self-defeating thoughts and behaviors when they see a need and have a proven set of tools.

The rationale for this book is straightforward. Students encounter complex circumstances during college life, some of which are beyond their direct control. But there are other circumstances that they can control through choices and personal judgment. On these, they *can* do the following: identify specific tasks, prioritize, evaluate options, make decisions, take action, and expect results. Students who follow this pattern on a consistent basis are proactive. Proactive students can be positive role models for other students and thereby contribute to a more productive and healthy campus environment. Based on the landmark book *The Seven Habits of Highly Effective People* by Dr. Stephen Covey, many people now understand the value of being more proactive. *Reaching Your Full Potential* is the first book to adapt these concepts to student audiences. The following paragraphs describe the contents and some of the important features of this text.

Chapter 1 asks readers to understand and analyze their thinking and behavior via an exploration of beliefs, values, and attitudes, and takes a look at the influences that lead to these aspects of one's approach to the world.

Chapter 2 presents a method for changing the beliefs, values, and attitudes discussed in Chapter 1 that can lead to a reactive stance and counter-productivity. Chapter 2 begins by distinguishing self-defeating thoughts and beliefs from productive thoughts and beliefs. The chapter discusses the benefits of changing one's thinking process, and identifies and describes a variety of thinking problems. The chapter then introduces a cognitive approach as a tool for improving the quality of one's thinking. At the end of all subsequent chapters in the book, readers are asked to apply this tool to exercise scenarios related to the chapter topics.

Chapter 3 contrasts optimistic and pessimistic attitudes and the likely results of these opposing attitudes with regard to student success.

The remaining five chapters offer a fresh approach to the typical topics of performance/goal setting, learning strategies, health and wellness, relationships, and finances by examining these areas from a proactive versus reactive perspective.

The following list describes some of the features of *Reaching Your Full Potential* that might appeal to students and at the same time help them make the most of the opportunities available on your campus. For example, this book:

- **Encourages Excellence.** Many student success books focus on survival—how to survive the first year or a specific course. This book is a prescription for excellence! *Reaching Your Full Potential* encourages students to be their personal best.

- **Engages the Reader.** *Reaching Your Full Potential* is "reader friendly." Anyone with a high school education should be able to read it and understand the concepts. Each chapter starts with a preview of the chapter's contents and a list of key terms. Headings and subheadings divide the chapters into manageable units for easy reading. Numerous illustrations highlight the main points. The book also provides exercises, journal activities, and vivid examples through stories and models. These tools help students identify their strengths and weaknesses. Students can address their fears, faults, hopes, and aspirations through the eyes of vicarious peers. Students find out not only where they are, but also where they can be.

- **Fills a Void.** This book will help students adapt to change. The world is in a constant state of change. Some of these changes improve our society while others threaten our survival. A major driving force of these changes is the transition from an industrial to an information-based economy. Many people are finding it hard to adapt. The skills they have are no longer adequate, and they find it difficult to maintain a decent standard of living. Some people see a decline in the overall quality of life, and are confused about how their own efforts might make a difference. The people who will survive and thrive under these conditions are those who improve their thinking skills, yet no systematic process is available to help people meet this challenge. Neither schools, nor the private sector, nor government has focused sufficiently on *how* to think and learn. Individuals must become more self-reliant in this area. *Reaching Your Full Potential* provides students with a personal guide for growth and constructive change. This book will help them improve their academic performance, manage their personal lives more effectively, and adapt quickly to changes that affect their lives and careers.

- **Promotes Self-monitoring.** Chapters 3 through 8 contain pre-chapter self-assessment questionnaires to help students assess their levels of proactivity in six areas of focus. Through this instrument, students can see where they are and how far they need to go. The corresponding post-chapter self-assessment questionnaires at the end of the text can be used at any point during the course for students to assess how much they have improved.

Clearly, students will benefit from a book that will help them improve their levels of proactivity, but there are benefits to educators as well. For example, professors can be more productive and efficient in the use of their time. When more students become proactive, they will think and behave like scholars. This development will improve the communication and interaction between students and faculty. Teachers will be able to more effectively transfer their enthusiasm for their disciplines, and thus enhance the development of young scholars.

Everybody wins when teachers and students collaborate on improving the academic system. Students experience a sense of involvement and receive valuable mentoring. Teachers perceive a greater sense of accomplishment, and the whole system is enriched.

Willie Claiborne Brown

A SPECIAL

MESSAGE

TO STUDENTS

What kind of person are you? How would you describe your behavior? Do you wait for something to happen, or do you seize the initiative? Do you often see problems and become a problem yourself, or do you focus on solutions? Do you expect someone to take care of you, or do you assume responsibility for your own behavior? If you are like most students, you are so busy with the day-to-day struggles of academic life that you haven't thought much about why or how you do what you do. Your concern right now might be how to do well on your next exams. You might wonder how you will be able to get all of the reading done, and how to write your term paper and turn it in on time. Perhaps you are worrying about not being able to capture all of the major points of your professor's lectures. Or, maybe your most important concern right now is to how develop friendships and have some fun.

The purpose of these questions and this message is to encourage you to think about how you conduct your life. In my almost three decades as a professor at a major university, I have worked with thousands of students. In my experience, most students tend to be more reactive than proactive. The reactive students are usually not at the top of their classes, nor do they end up with the most productive careers.

You often can distinguish reactive students from proactive students by their language. Note the different language patterns in the table below:

REACTIVE LANGUAGE	PROACTIVE LANGUAGE
I see problems.	I see opportunities.
My classes are boring.	I look for points of interest and relevance in all of my classes.
I don't like my teachers	I will find ways to work with my teachers.
This is the end of our relationship.	How can we resolve this conflict?
I can't handle this situation.	I will find a way to work around this situation.

(continued)

REACTIVE LANGUAGE	PROACTIVE LANGUAGE
I'm not comfortable living in this small college town.	I can adapt.
I have to . . .	I choose to . . .
I need . . .	I prefer . . .
I give up.	I will find a way.
It's your fault.	We both might have made some mistakes; let's move on.
My performance is good enough.	How can I improve my performance?
I'll try.	I will do my best.
Mistakes were made.	I am responsible.

Perhaps you might examine your own language for a clue for how you might behave. If you tend to be reactive, now is the time to take action. This book will help you become more proactive. If you are already proactive, *Reaching Your Full Potential* will help you get even better.

The focus of *Reaching Your Full Potential* differs from that of many student success texts. This book asks you to put forth extra effort in exchange for short- and long-term benefits. Whereas many books focus mainly on study skills, *Reaching Your Full Potential* helps you refine your study skills and at the same time correct thinking and behavior patterns that might hinder your success. If you master the concepts in this book, you can expect to succeed as a student and also in life.

Here are some of the important features of this book:

- **Focuses on the Total Person.** *Reaching Your Full Potential* stresses the point that learning involves more than just going to class, taking notes, and taking exams. Learning involves the total self and is a direct reflection of your overall attitude, beliefs, values, goals, confidence, source of motivation, emotions, habits, and quality of relationships.

- **Builds on and Expands Natural Thinking Skills.** *Reaching Your Full Potential* goes beyond positive thinking—the theme of many self-help books. It focuses on non-negative thinking as the most practical and effective pathway to growth and change. The book outlines proven cognitive strategies to help you avoid or overcome self-defeating thoughts and behaviors in the shortest period of time. Through cognitive strategies, you exploit your natural ability to think rationally and solve problems— the same skills needed in the classroom. You might find it easier to improve when you can focus on a single approach. Cognitive strategies let you address academic issues as well as those relating to your career and personal life.

- **Helps Students Perceive a Level Playing Field.** Some students believe that they will face hardships in college because of gender, race, ethnic background, religion, or special challenges. They often feel intimidated by professors, administrators, or seemingly more competent students.

While the challenges might be real, this book will help students gain confidence in their abilities, and thereby feel less threatened by these concerns.

- **Emphasizes Proactivity.** Proactive individuals have a distinct advantage in a highly competitive, global marketplace. Any student can become more proactive. There are only two requirements: (1) a set of viable tools, and (2) a commitment to change and growth. This book provides the tools. You provide the commitment. The result will be a greater control over your attitudes and behaviors.

- **Promotes Self-monitoring.** *Reaching Your Full Potential* contains questionnaires that will help you assess your level of proactivity in six areas of focus. You will find the questionnaires at the beginning of Chapters 3 through 8 and at the end of the text. Through self-monitoring, you can determine where you are, how far you need to go, and how much you have improved.

- **Provides Strategies for Current and Long-term Needs.** Unfortunately, many students stop using a textbook after a course ends. *Reaching Your Full Potential* is designed to be both a textbook and personal guide that you can use for the rest of your life.

The proactive/reactive framework and the strong emphasis on non-negative thinking sets this book apart from other books in preparing students for the future. For example, many people are finding it hard to adapt to the rapid changes in our society because there are no programs available to help them meet these new challenges. *Reaching Your Full Potential* provides you with a personal guide for growth and constructive change. It will help you improve your academic skills as well as achieve personal growth and career success.

As you pursue your education, you can expect that your teachers and administrators will play a major role in providing the instruction and resources that you need. But as a student, you cannot afford to be a bystander while others act on your behalf. **Take the lead!** *You* are the only person who can motivate yourself to learn. *You* can overcome challenges and setbacks. *You* can manage your emotions and choose to resist peer pressure. *You* can improve your interpersonal skills and find ways to resolve conflicts. *You* can control how you adapt to a rapidly changing world. *You* can avoid bad habits and choose to live by sound principles and ethical values. *You* can modify your thoughts and beliefs.

You have the most important role to play in *your* education and development, and this book will show you how. You will learn how to be a good student and at the same time be a good person. When you master the concepts in this book, you can expect to have a productive career, have a satisfying personal and family life, and be a valuable member of society.

ACKNOWLEDGMENTS

I am grateful for the contributions of many individuals who directly or indirectly helped me write this book. Special thanks go to:

- Dr. Stephen Covey for writing *The Seven Habits of Highly Successful People,* the book that stimulated my interest in proactive and reactive behavior.

- Dr. Gerald Kushel for his research and his book *Effective Thinking for Uncommon Success,* which shows how positive changes in thinking can lead to success in three dimensions: high job performance, a high level of job satisfaction, and a high level of personal satisfaction.

- The faculty, students, and parents of students at Compton Community College, Los Angeles, whose enthusiasm for my talk on proactive and reactive students inspired me to write this book.

- My mentor and writing coach, David Engler, for helping me gain the confidence and skill to complete this project.

- My colleague and friend Richard Engler for leading me to his father, David, and for his constructive feedback and support throughout the project.

- The hundreds of students who took my student success course, and especially the students who after completing the course worked with me to help monitor the progress of other students.

- The many students who kept me on task by asking, "How's the book going?"

- My colleagues and friends in the San Diego area for their encouragement and support.

- My colleagues who reviewed the material: Jerry Bouchie, St. Cloud State University; Jan Norton, Missouri Western State College; Elizabeth Davidson, Passaic County Community College; Rusty Belote, Florida International University; Mary Bixby, University of Missouri-Columbia; David DeFrain, Central Missouri State University.

- My Prentice Hall team: Todd Rossell for having the vision to see the value of my approach, and for taking a chance with me as a new author; Katie Bradford for her extraordinary efficiency and effectiveness as an editor; and Carol Carter, Sue Bierman, Amy Diehl, Barbara Cappuccio, Mary Carnis, Marianne Frasco, Mark Bove, and Trish Finley (Clarinda Publication Services), who worked diligently behind the scenes to help bring this project to completion.

■ My sons Marvin and Vincent for their support; and to Manuelita, my wife, best friend, and intellectual companion.

REACHING YOUR FULL POTENTIAL
Success in College and Life

"The key to success lies in your particular manner of thinking. . . ."

Walter Doyle Staples, psychologist[1]

Influences, Values, and Beliefs: Why You Think and Behave the Way You Do

HIS CHAPTER FOCUSES on the factors that shape your life. Three major factors have the most impact on the way you think and behave: genes, environment, and behavior. Of the three, you have the most control over your behavior. Behavior stems from the interplay between emotions, thoughts, and motivation. You influence behavior by the way you think. Thinking is a reflection of your mental activities and involves ideas, concepts, expectations, and interpretations of your beliefs, attitudes, and values.

When you master the concepts in this chapter, you will understand:

- The different levels of thinking

- The relationships among the components of the thinking apparatus

- How your patterns of thought influence your life

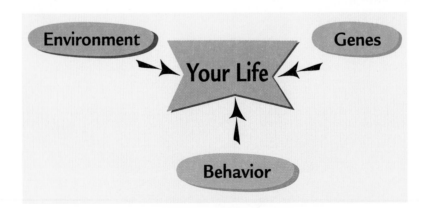

attitude   conscious thinking   motivation   total belief system

behavior   emotions   preconscious thinking   unconscious thinking

belief   genes   subconscious thinking   values

cognition/thoughts/thinking habit

Factors That Shape Your Life

Genes: basic units of heredity that reside on the chromosome.

Behavior: observable activities that you carry out as you interact with your environment.

The major factors that shape your life fall under the broad categories of (1) genes, (2) behavior, and (3) environment (Figure 1.1). You inherit a set of genes from your biological parents, and these genes define traits such as height, bone structure, and hair and eye color. Behavior describes the observable activities that you carry out as you relate to your environment. Examples of behaviors include activities such as driving a car, taking a test, talking to classmates, eating, dancing, and exercising. Your *environment* includes the effects of climate, geography, relationships, culture, government, politics, and media sources.

Some of the factors that shape your life are beyond your control (see Chapter 3 for more details). For example, there is nothing that you can do about the genes that you receive from your parents. Other factors allow you some control. For example, you have some degree of control over certain environmental factors: You might be able to choose where you live or attend college. You can pay attention to some media-based programs and ignore others. You can have an indirect impact on politicians and government policies through your vote. Other environmental factors, however, are out of your control, such as the weather and other people's behavior.

The purpose of this chapter is to help you focus on the factor over which you have the most control—your behavior. Of the three factors, behavior fits most closely with the basic theme of this book.

FACTORS AFFECTING BEHAVIOR

As Figure 1.2 shows, how you behave depends on your emotions, thoughts, and motivation. In the following sections, we explore each of these concepts.

FIGURE 1.1
Factors that shape your life.

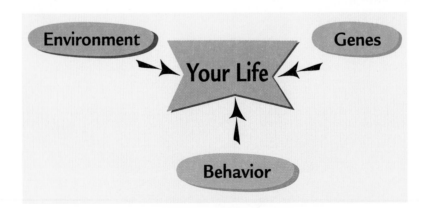

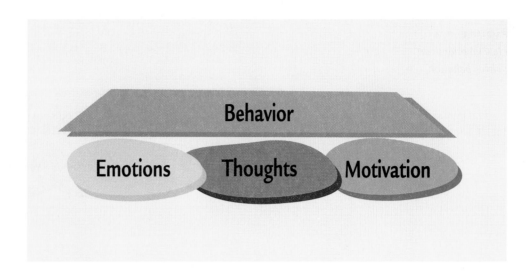

■ EMOTIONS

Emotions are basic feelings we experience as we relate to our environment. For example, if a person makes an A on an exam, he might feel happy. If he barely missed being in a car accident, he would feel relief. Here are some examples of emotions.

■ Fear	■ Love	■ Empathy
■ Joy	■ Surprise	■ Sympathy
■ Anger	■ Anticipation	■ Relief
■ Disgust	■ Hate	■ Anxiety
■ Sadness	■ Boredom	■ Frustration
■ Excitement	■ Happiness	■ Jealousy
■ Grief	■ Distress	■ Rage

Emotions can be mild or intense. We often can detect intense emotions by their effect on our bodies. For example, fear and anger might cause the following:[2]

■ Blood pressure and heart rate increase.

■ Respiration becomes more rapid.

■ Pupils dilate.

■ Perspiration increases; secretion of saliva and mucous decreases.

■ Blood clots more quickly when wounds occur.

■ Movement in the gastrointestinal tract increases.

■ Blood gets diverted from the stomach and intestines to the brain and skeletal muscles.

■ Blood sugar levels increase, leading to a greater supply of energy.

■ Hairs on skin become erect due to goose pimples.

In addition to their effects on our bodies, emotions can bolster (Figure 1.3) or impede (Figure 1.4) behavior. For example, if you feel happy about

FIGURE 1.3

How emotions can bolster behavior.

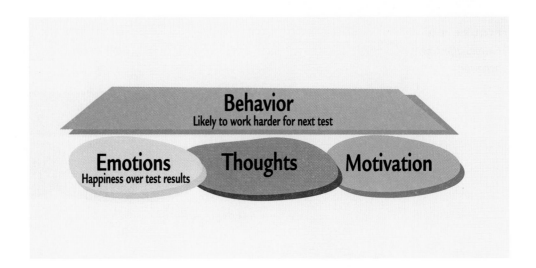

your test results, you are more likely to work hard to perform well on the next test. Or you might feel angry and fail to do your homework if your significant other falls in love with someone else.

■ MOTIVATION

Motivation: attempts by the body or mind to satisfy certain basic wants and needs.

A person's level of motivation has a strong impact on her behavior. Motivation results from the drive of the body or mind to satisfy certain wants and needs. Body needs might relate to survival issues such as hunger or thirst. Needs of the mind center on three basic issues: self-determination, connectedness, and competence.[3]

- *Self-determination*—most people do not want someone else to control their lives. Self-image is at the highest level when people feel that they are making the critical choices that determine the direction of their lives. For example, you love your parents, but you do not want them to tell you how to live your life.

- *Connectedness*—people have a need to interact with others in ways that convey love and caring. When a person loves someone and someone loves him, he feels good about himself. People who feel connected have a more positive outlook and tend to strive more and work harder. For example,

FIGURE 1.4

How emotions can impede behavior.

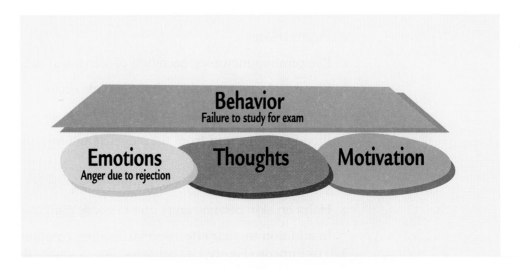

Journal Activity

Describe how emotions might have affected your performance in the past month. For example, if you were angry with your roommate, did the anger enhance, hinder, or have no effect on your ability to do your homework? If you were happy about some good news from home, did your happiness enhance, hinder, or have no effect on your ability to do your homework?

Monitor your emotions for two weeks to assess their impact on your performance. If you find that emotions hinder your performance too often, you might want to consult with a counselor.

_____

_____

_____

_____

_____

_____

_____

you probably find it easier to work through the challenges of college life if you have some close friends whom you know will always be there for you.

- *Competence*—people need to be effective, to take on meaningful tasks, and to complete them to the best of their abilities. For example, suppose the editor of the school newspaper asked you to write an article about your first month on campus. You would feel good if several students congratulated you on your well-written article.

Motivation provides the direction and energy for behavior. High levels of motivation enhance success while low levels hinder it (Figures 1.5 and 1.6).

FIGURE 1.5
Impact of high motivation on behavior.

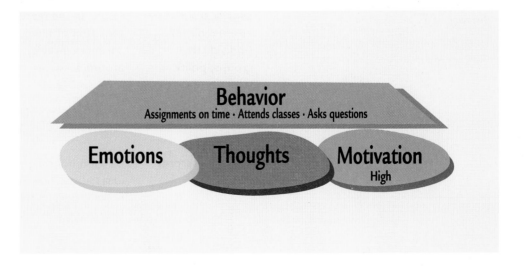

FIGURE 1.6

Impact of negative motivation on behavior.

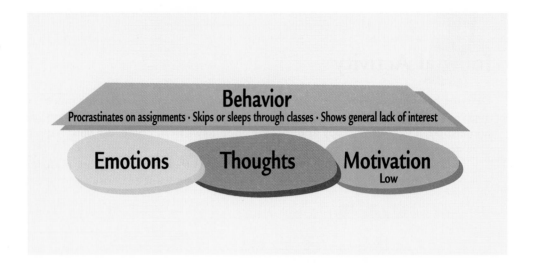

When the three basic needs of the mind are met, we are likely to have more drive and direction in achieving our goals. We will cover self-motivation in more detail in Chapter 4.

■ THINKING

Cognition/thoughts/ thinking: mental activities such as conceptions and ideas, meanings, images, beliefs, expectations, and attributions.

Most of what you do in life will largely depend on how you think. Thinking, or cognition, refers to all of your mental activities, such as conceptions and ideas, meanings, images, beliefs, expectations, and attributions. We will cover this topic in more detail later in the chapter.

DISTINCTIONS AMONG THE THREE FACTORS AFFECTING BEHAVIOR

Table 1.1 compares the definitions and gives examples for the three factors affecting behavior: emotions, thoughts, and motivation. These three factors often overlap, as represented in Figure 1.7.

TABLE 1.1

Distinctions among the Three Factors Affecting Behavior

	EMOTIONS	THOUGHTS	MOTIVATION
Definition	Feelings that are usually aroused by external objects (individuals, groups, politicians, television programs) and are directed at those objects	Mental activity that results in the representation of ideas, concepts, beliefs, attitudes, values	Feelings based on the drive of the mind or body to satisfy certain wants and needs
Example	Fear, joy, surprise, anger	Belief in honesty; ideas about how to make classes more interesting	Hunger, thirst, survival, self-determination, competence, connectedness

FIGURE 1.7
Overlap of the three factors affecting behavior.

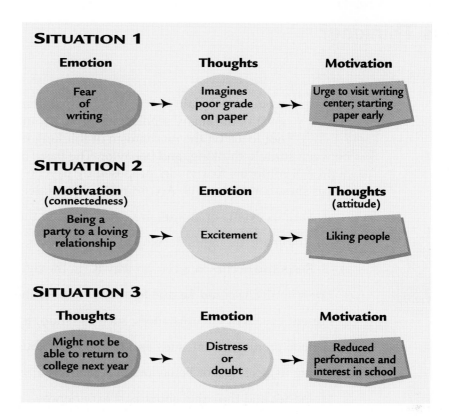

SITUATION 1

Emotion	Thoughts	Motivation
Fear of writing	→ Imagines poor grade on paper	→ Urge to visit writing center; starting paper early

SITUATION 2

Motivation (connectedness)	Emotion	Thoughts (attitude)
Being a party to a loving relationship	→ Excitement	→ Liking people

SITUATION 3

Thoughts	Emotion	Motivation
Might not be able to return to college next year	→ Distress or doubt	→ Reduced performance and interest in school

PROFILE FOR SUCCESS

Parvathi Aarthi Myer

My professional goals have always been present as a result of the influences of my parents and grandparents, but these goals have been further developed as a result of a Student Success course I took during my second year in college. One of the primary things I learned is to be a proactive learner by asking questions —questions about why I am doing what I am doing, about what I do not understand, about why I agree or disagree with certain things, and about why I learn what I learn. This process has helped me take ownership of my education. The professor helped me to analyze my study habits, my time management, and my ability to set goals, write, read, and problem solve. What I thought was a class on note taking evolved into this beautiful class on life management. I asked myself, "What type of person do I want to be, what do I value, and does the way I live reflect those values?" Where my actions were not consistent with my values, I was urged to think of ways to make my actions and values parallel one another.

Over the past three years, I have worked to translate my values into action. Practicing this parallelism has been the most empowering thing I have learned. Using the tools from the Student Success course has helped me achieve consistency in my work habits and live a balanced life. Being proactive has allowed me to align my personal and professional goals so that they are in harmony with one another and rest on the foundation of the things that I truly value.

What Is Thinking?

No one can explain exactly how human thinking occurs (the mechanism), but many scholars are working in this area. This text does not focus on the mechanism of thinking but on the key links between stimuli, thinking, and behavior. The basic framework for this approach conforms to a model proposed by psychologist R. S. Woodworth[4] and is shown in Figure 1.8. According to this model of human behavior,

1. Various events or stimuli are detected (A in the figure).

2. Automatic thoughts develop about the events (B in the figure).

3. Response occurs in a certain way (C in the figure).

The stimuli (A) could be due to one or more of the following:

- Present events or circumstances, such as failure to pass a test

- Genetic predisposition, such as a tendency to abuse alcohol

- Thoughts, feelings, or behaviors that occur as a result of these events

- Memories and thoughts about past experiences

The types of responses (C in Figure 1.8) may be emotional, motivational, physiological, or behavioral. We show the model as cyclical in that thoughts can trigger events, and responses can trigger thoughts.

Your thinking (B in Figure 1.8) is central to this model; it is the segue between what you detect as stimuli and how you respond. Consider the following example:

A. (event): You are expecting an A in math, but you receive a B.

B. (thoughts): "I was cheated out of an A—that's not fair."

C. (responses):

Emotional—you feel sad, disappointed, angry, and less confident about what you know.

FIGURE 1.8
Relationships among stimulus, thoughts, and corresponding human responses (adapted from R. S. Woodworth and H. Schlosberg, Experimental Psychology, *New York: Holt Rinehart and Winston, 1954, ch. 1).*

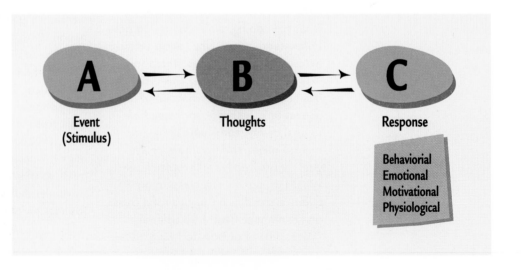

Event (Stimulus)   Thoughts   Response

Behaviorial
Emotional
Motivational
Physiological

TABLE 1.2

Example of Thoughts and Responses to Negative Stimulus

NEGATIVE STIMULUS	THOUGHT	RESPONSE
Failed a test	**Negative:** The professor made the test too hard.	**Negative:** Student makes cruel remarks about the professor to other students.
Failed a test	**Positive:** That was a challenging test. How can I be better prepared next time?	**Positive:** Student seeks feedback from the professor and teaching assistant.

Physiological—you get an upset stomach.

Motivational—you feel that you need to do something to ease your pain.

Behavioral—you go out and have a drink to drown your sorrow.

Note that the negative responses occur only because you thought you would get a better grade than you did. If you had expected a C grade, you would have been happy about the B.

This example shows that your thoughts determine whether you respond in a positive or negative manner. Regardless of whether the stimulus is positive or negative, negative thoughts lead to negative responses, and positive thoughts lead to positive responses. Table 1.2 presents an example. This example shows how your thoughts play an important role in shaping your behavior. In a later section, we will discuss how patterns of thought can ultimately shape your life.

The Different Levels of Thinking

You think along four different levels, as shown in Figure 1.9.[5]

CONSCIOUS THINKING

Conscious thinking: reflects your ability to be aware of events taking place in your body and in the surrounding environment and to be able to guide your actions.

Conscious thinking reflects a person's ability to be aware of events taking place in her body and in the surrounding environment and to be able to guide her actions. To *guide* means to plan or to solve problems. Conscious thinking takes place at the level of awareness. In other words, you can sense what is going on around you. Through conscious thinking, you do the following:

1. *Perceive*—events taking place in the environment through your senses of sight, hearing, touch, taste, or smell.

FIGURE 1.9

Levels of thinking.
Source: Adapted
from *Introduction to
Psychology,* Tenth Edi-
tion by Rita L. Atkin-
son, Richard C.
Atkinson, Edward E.
Smith, and Daryl J.
Bem, copyright ©
1990, pp. 196–198,
by Harcourt Brace &
Company, reprinted
by permission of the
publisher.

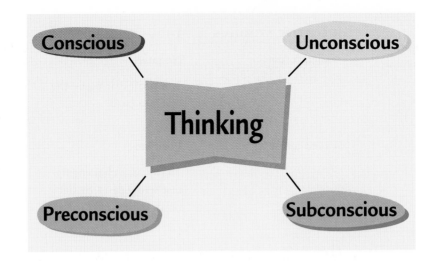

2. *Compare*—the current events with past experiences.

3. *Assess*—the relevance of the new events; you form thoughts, ideas, and opinions about these experiences. You also form opinions about yourself, that is, how you think and react to various events.

4. *Decide*—if and how you should use the new information.

Through this process you form your own picture of the world. Your picture, or "reality," of the world around you stems from your combined experiences and interpretations. Thus, your picture differs from that of any other person.

SUBCONSCIOUS THINKING

Subconscious thinking:
reflects your ability to
detect and analyze stim-
uli that you do not con-
sciously perceive.

Subconscious thinking is based on our ability to detect and analyze stimuli that we do not consciously perceive. The process is sometimes referred to as *peripheral attention.* For example, you are talking to a group of students in a crowded cafeteria. You ignore the other voices and noise until someone mentions your name. Then you pay attention to the other conversation.

UNCONSCIOUS THINKING

Unconscious thinking:
involves memories,
impulses, and desires
that are not available to
the conscious mind.

The process of unconscious thinking involves memories, impulses, and desires that are not available to the conscious mind. Though outside the stream of awareness, unconscious thoughts can still influence attitudes or behavior. Unconscious thoughts sometimes show up as dreams, "slips of the tongue," and bizarre behavior. A somewhat extreme, but not unusual, example of the latter case is when a man stalks a woman.

PRECONSCIOUS THINKING

Preconscious thinking:
involves thoughts that
you can access but that
are not part of your
consciousness at the
moment.

Preconscious thinking involves thoughts that you can access but that are not part of your consciousness at the moment. Preconscious thoughts involve a large number of functions. Among them are long-term memory, creativity, and mental stability.

■ LONG-TERM MEMORY

Your preconscious mind is like a giant computer with unlimited memory. Your memory stores all of the real and imagined events that you perceive at the conscious level as conditioned patterns of thought. Other names for these patterns are *programs* or *scripts.* Scripts govern your conscious thoughts and behaviors. The basis for your present and future behavior depends on these programs. When you face a new situation, you automatically refer to your scripts before you respond.

Habit: learned stimulus-response patterns.

Basic habits are the result of programs stored in your preconscious mind. Habits are learned stimulus-response patterns. For example, you consciously learned how to walk, tie your shoes, ride a bike, or cross the street. These events became a part of your long-term memory and now require little conscious thinking on your part when needed.

Habits can also steer people off track, as the following example shows: Ann had a habit of using a certain route to go to the cafeteria. She started out one day to visit a friend in a dorm that was on the same route as the cafeteria. However, instead of getting to the dorm, Ann ended up at the cafeteria. Habitual thinking had steered her away from her chosen destination that day.

There is both a good side and bad side of preconscious thinking. The good is that you do not have to reinvent yourself every day. You have a consistent pattern of thinking that allows you to function normally with reduced stress. The bad side of preconscious thinking is that the old programs dictating much of what you think and do are often negative. Psychologist Walter Doyle Staples explains this situation in *Think Like a Winner:*

> By the time you were eighteen, you were told 'No!' about 150,000 times. Eighty-five to ninety-five percent of all the programming you received from external sources was negative, while most of the remainder was neutral. The few hundred "yes's" you received hardly made any impact. In this purposeful way, you have been force-fed and conditioned to perceive and believe in a manner consistent with the experiences you have had and the people you have associated with. You ended up adopting the opinions and beliefs your primary reference groups acquired during their own upbringing.[6]

Given the choice, most people would not intentionally rely on outdated or negative scripts to govern their lives. But they do so by default. Most people know little about the process that led to the development of their programs. Perhaps they have seldom if ever thought about what to change in their thinking or how to change it.

■ CREATIVITY

The preconscious mind is the major resource for your natural creativity. You display your creative talent when you use the known (whether real or imagined) to come up with something new. The starting point for this process is when you attempt to solve a problem, resolve a conflict, or generate a new or original idea. These events trigger the preconscious functions of the mind to find the missing parts of the puzzle and put them together. To achieve this task, the mind scans the years of stored experiences in your memory, looking for the answer. Once the mind puts all of the pieces together, the solution will surface to the conscious level. You have probably heard this event referred to by the following terms: "bright idea," "illumination," or the "aha" phenomenon (see Chapter 5). Figure 1.10 illustrates this event.

FIGURE 1.10

Development of a "bright idea."

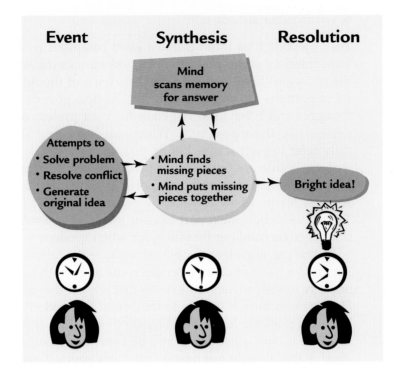

Journal Activity

Keep a record of when and where your "bright ideas" occur most often. Do you see a pattern—in the shower, while you are taking a walk, just before you are fully awake, just before you fall off into deep sleep, during a short nap, in the early morning or late night? For example, you might realize that most of your ideas surface during short naps, just before becoming fully awake, or while working in the garden. When you discover your pattern, you can use it to your advantage by being prepared to take notes as soon as possible after you perceive the "bright idea."

If you had to change your picture of reality every time you faced a new situation, you would get confused. In an extreme case, you would lose your sanity. Your preconscious mind ensures that your thoughts and actions conform to your stored programs. Thus, the mind often provides you with an automatic response to new situations rather than forcing you to go through a complex analysis each time. This process saves you time and in many cases might save your life. For example:

- If a big dog charges at you, you quickly get out of the way.

- You make quick judgments about the distance between you and the student coming toward you on a bike.

- You raise your hand when you want to ask a question in class.

- You cover your face when you cough or sneeze.

- If a stranger approaches you on a dark street at night, you assume that he is a foe rather than friend and try to protect yourself.

- If you have lived in a storm region, you get away from a tree or tall building when you see lightning.

These judgments stem from your programs of past experiences and interpretations. Even so, the assumptions people make are not always correct and can lead them astray, as you will see in Chapter 2.

Major Components of the Thinking Apparatus:
Total Belief System

Total belief system: a person's complete sphere of how he views himself and the world around him.

As the previous section showed, much of your thinking depends on scripts stored in your preconscious mind. These scripts reside in your total belief system, which is the complete sphere of how you view yourself and the world around you. This system contains three subsystems: beliefs, attitudes, and values (Figure 1.11).

FIGURE 1.11

Components of the thinking apparatus.

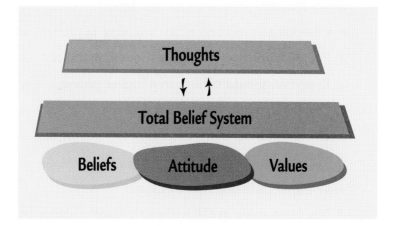

Belief: what a person thinks is true or is likely to be true.

A belief describes what a person thinks is true or is likely to be true. Beliefs cover your own view of what the world is like, what people you like, how events occur, and what you yourself are like.

Each person can have thousands of beliefs. Following are some examples of typical belief statements. One point to remember as you study this list is not to confuse beliefs with facts. For example, a person might believe that the world is flat, but this view is inconsistent with known facts.

- The world is flat.

- African-Americans are the best basketball players.

- Hard work does not pay off anymore.

- The campus library is user friendly.

- Women are terrible drivers.

- Loud music can damage your hearing.

- My Mom and Dad are good parents.

- Good people will go to heaven when they die.

- Republicans favor business concerns over the welfare of individuals.

- Rules were made to be broken.

- Books are too expensive.

- People who break the rules should be punished.

- Eating vegetables is good for your health.

- The Pope is the ultimate authority on birth control.

- There are twenty-four hours in a day.

- Media sources report only negative news.

- I am not good at math.

- Schools should spend more time teaching people how to think.

- The illegal immigrants are taking our jobs.

- All students should use computers.

- Campus administrators are too busy to interact with students.

- People will help you if you show that you care about them.

- Everyone should believe in a higher power.

- Democrats raise taxes and spend lots of money on social programs.

- Using condoms takes the fun out of having sex.

- Professors are boring.

- Going to class is a waste of time.

- You learn more in classes with a small number of students.

Sam Fereidouni

Some of my most basic beliefs and values are as follows: I believe that most people are "nice people" deep down inside, honesty is the best policy, everyone is 100 percent accountable for his or her actions and behaviors, people should always treat others as they would want to be treated, everyone should think globally and act locally, and one should "maintain an even strain." Some of these beliefs may seem a little like clichés, but I think they are simple truths that have held up through the test of time.

My values are consistent with my career goals, with the kind of person I am, and with the type of person I want to be because I discipline myself to align my actions with my values. For me it is not a question of whether my values are aligned with my career or any other part of my life—it is more a question of whether my career is aligned with my values. I have learned from my parents' lives that practically everything can come and go except for who you are because of your values and education. For example, my parents used to be wealthy and now they are not so wealthy, they used to live in a different country and now they live in the United States, and they used to have different careers than they do now. Practically everything is different for them now than it was 20 or 30 years ago, when they had no choice but to immigrate to the United States. Throughout all of this, the only things that haven't changed are their values and beliefs.

I believe our values are tested daily, if not constantly, and the result shows itself in the way we conduct our lives. What I try to do in these testing situations is to review my values and remember why I have chosen them. I then try to align my actions to be consistent with my value system and "do the right thing."

- Engineering students are nerds.
- I am a good and kind person.
- The sun rises in the east and sets in the west.
- The earth turns on its axis.

ATTITUDES

Attitude: a persistent cluster of beliefs that primes a person to lean toward or away from certain people, objects, or situations.

Attitudes are another component of a person's total belief system. An attitude is a persistent cluster of beliefs that primes a person to lean toward or away from certain people, objects, or situations. Each attitude reflects the following:

- Beliefs about certain people, objects, or situations
- Leanings toward or away from those people, objects, or situations
- Inclinations toward certain actions because of those leanings

For example:

- "Professor X is boring" (thought).
- "I dislike boring professors" (leaning).
- "I will not take Professor X's class because he is boring" (action).

Table 1.3 shows some beliefs and their corresponding attitudes.

Remember that patterns of attitude dictate certain responses or behaviors. Through your behavior, you act out many of your attitudes. Take a moment to complete Exercise 1.1. Based on your responses, do you think your attitudes will help or hinder you from being a successful student? Keep this question in mind as you work through the rest of this text.

TABLE 1.3

Examples of Beliefs and Possible Attitudes Associated with the Beliefs

BELIEF	ATTITUDE
I am not good at math.	I hate solving math problems.
Loud music cannot damage your hearing.	I like to listen to loud music.
Loud music can damage your hearing.	I avoid loud music whenever possible.
Republicans favor the concerns of business owners over those of employees and consumers.	I prefer Republican candidates.
Eating vegetables is good for your health.	I include plenty of vegetables in my diet.
Media sources report only negative news.	I ignore the negative news presented by the media.
Books are too expensive.	I buy used books whenever possible.
Campus administrators are too busy to interact with students.	I avoid campus administrators.
Engineering students are nerds.	I avoid interacting with engineering students.
Democrats raise taxes and spend lots of money on social programs.	I support candidates of the Democratic party.
Using condoms takes the fun out of having sex.	I don't use condoms.
You learn more in classes with a small number of students.	I prefer small classes.
Professors are boring.	I dislike boring people and situations.

Examples of Your Attitudes

List some of your prevailing attitudes in the categories listed.

CATEGORY	PREVAILING ATTITUDES ABOUT THIS CATEGORY
People	
Learning	
Work	
Intimate relationships	
Food preferences	
Study habits	
Health and wellness	
Type of music	
Money	
Types of movies	

VALUES

Values: a subset of one's total belief system that prescribes (1) ideal patterns of conduct (how a person ought or ought not to behave) and (2) states of being that a person sees as important.

In addition to beliefs and attitudes, your thinking is influenced by your values. **Values** form a subset of your total belief system that prescribes the following:[7]

1. Ideal patterns of conduct—how a person ought or ought not to behave. For example, a person might value, or think it is good to, show respect, be honest, be patient, and demonstrate courtesy.

2. States of being that a person sees as important, such as prestige, self-reliance, security, or fame.

Values reflect a list of linked attitudes. Therefore, a value describes a general condition not tied to a specific attitude and consisting of more than one attitude. For example:

Attitude: I do not like boring professors and will not take their classes
Value: I prefer situations that excite me and make me happy.

This value might reflect the person's attitudes about classes, books, presentations, plays, concerts, people, or places, as well as boring professors.

Here are some examples of values.

▪ Kindness	▪ Happiness
▪ Uncertainty	▪ Self-reliance
▪ Success	▪ Confidence
▪ Friendship	▪ Cooperation
▪ Perseverance	▪ Quality
▪ Reliability	▪ Resiliency
▪ Respect	▪ Responsibility
▪ Self-centeredness	▪ Discipline
▪ Service	▪ Tact
▪ Thrift	▪ Courage
▪ Courtesy	▪ Initiative
▪ Integrity	▪ Elitism
▪ Excellence	▪ Fidelity
▪ Honesty	▪ Justice
▪ Loyalty	▪ Maturity
▪ Patience	▪ Optimism
▪ Fairness	▪ Generosity
▪ Health	▪ Greed
▪ Excitement	▪ Adventure

Journal Activity

In Chapter 4, you will complete an exercise to identify your values. Prior to that exercise, however, do a preliminary check on your values by writing down your top ten values. Use the previous examples of values as a guide.

_____

_____

_____

_____

_____

_____

Note that the values may be positive or negative. Generosity is positive, greed is negative. In addition, a value such as adventure might be safe (+) in some situations and risky (−) in others.

A COMPARISON OF BELIEFS, ATTITUDES, AND VALUES

Table 1.4 compares the three subsystems of a person's total belief system. Exercise 1.2 will help you identify the origin of your values. As you master the concepts in this text, expect to assume greater control over which values enter or remain in your total belief system.

TABLE 1.4
Examples of Beliefs and Possible Attitudes and Values Associated with the Beliefs

BELIEF	ATTITUDE	VALUE
I am not good at math.	I hate math.	Excellence; success
Loud music cannot damage your hearing.	I like to listen to loud music.	Self-reliance
Loud music can damage your hearing.	I avoid loud music whenever possible.	Health
Republicans favor the concerns of business owners over those of employees and consumers.	I vote for Republicans.	Self-reliance
Eating vegetables is good for your health.	I like vegetables.	Health
Media sources report only negative news.	I avoid negative news.	Happiness
Books are too expensive.	I buy used books as much as possible.	Thrift
Campus administrators show little interest in students.	I dislike campus administrators.	Approachability
Engineering students are nerds.	I avoid interacting with engineering students.	Friendliness; approachability
Democrats raise taxes and spend lots of money on social programs.	I vote for Democratic candidates.	Generosity
Using condoms takes the fun out of having sex.	I don't use condoms.	Excitement; uncertainty
You learn more in classes with a small number of students.	I like small classes.	Quality; excellence
Professors are boring.	I dislike boring people and situations.	Excitement

Identifying Your Values and Their Sources

To the fullest extent of your memory, list the values you acquired from the sources listed here. Refer to your list of values that you made in the previous journal activity to do this exercise.

SOURCE	VALUES
Parents	
Teachers	
Peers	
Religion	
Television	
You	

Which source had the most impact on shaping your values? Which source do you expect to have the greatest impact on you in the future?

From the discussions above, you should now understand the relationships among the components of your thought processes. We now turn our attention to the impact of thinking on your behavior and your life.

How Patterns of Thought Can Influence Your Life

Figures 1.12 and 1.13 show how your total belief system shapes your thinking and how thinking, in turn, can shape your behavior, and ultimately your life. Focus on the role of thoughts in these figures. For example, in general, patterns of positive thoughts and behaviors lead to positive life outcomes (see Figure 1.12). Conversely, if you follow patterns of

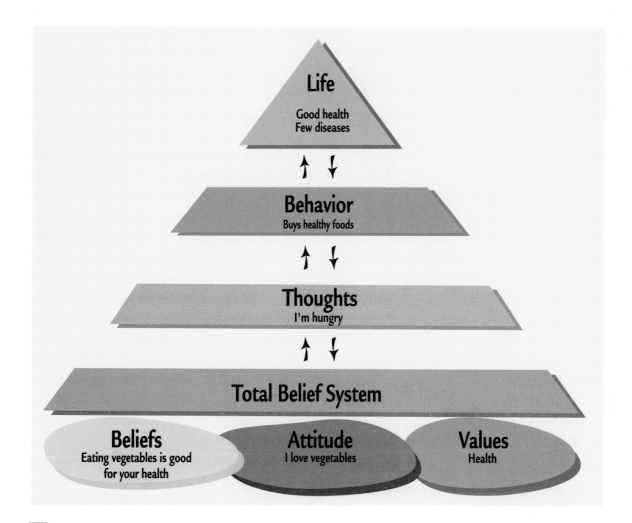

Life
Good health
Few diseases

↑ ↓

Behavior
Buys healthy foods

↑ ↓

Thoughts
I'm hungry

↑ ↓

Total Belief System

Beliefs
Eating vegetables is good
for your health

Attitude
I love vegetables

Values
Health

FIGURE 1.12

Relationships among total belief system, thoughts, behaviors, and life—positive example.

negative thoughts and behaviors (Figure 1.13), you can expect negative life outcomes.

In summary, your belief system leads to thoughts, which lead to behavior, which leads to life outcomes. In the next section we will explore the factors that influence the development of your total belief system.

How Patterns of Thought Are Acquired

Figure 1.14 is a model that shows how various influences have helped shape your picture of the world. Both internal and external factors have combined to make up your system of beliefs.

Internal factors consist of your ability to ask questions, discover, and daydream. For example, as a young child, you might have imagined yourself as a teacher, doctor, lawyer, singer, pilot, police officer, firefighter, banker, or business owner. You might be preparing for one of those careers now because of those early visions. In addition, you asked questions and used the answers to form a mental picture of what you and the world are like. Finally, you discovered things on your own, such as the sounds that certain animals make.

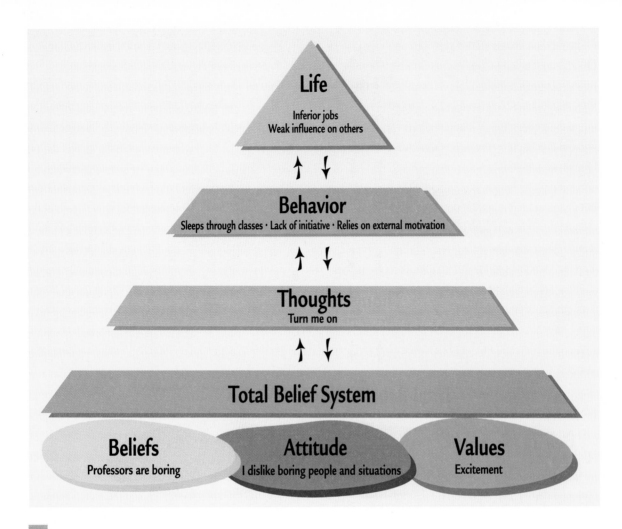

FIGURE 1.13

Relationships among total belief system, thoughts, behaviors, and life—negative example.

Among *external factors,* your parents had the greatest influence on the development of your mental makeup. You have their genes, and they were the source of most of your beliefs and values. Other external factors also played a role in your development:

- **Relatives**—some people have relationships with relatives that are as strong as or stronger than their relationship with their parents. These people will acquire some of the beliefs and values of those relatives.

- **Friends**—people adopt many beliefs just to gain acceptance by their friends. This practice is the basis of peer pressure.

- **Religion**—people develop beliefs about a higher power and how to interact with other humans as a result of religious teachings.

- **Country of origin**—if you grew up in the United States, you expect certain freedoms. But if you grew up under a dictatorship, democratic freedoms might be a strange concept to you.

- **Television**—this medium now plays a very strong role in shaping people's lives. If you grew up watching television, your beliefs and values might reflect what you saw and heard during those years. For example, this source might have shaped your views about politics, people, how you look, how you dress, what you eat and drink, or how you dance.

Over a period of time, you have built up a large bank of thoughts based on your interpretations of what you have learned from these varied sources.

How the Pieces of Your Life Fit Together

The purpose of this chapter was to lay the groundwork for how your thoughts and behaviors help shape your life. In one sense, this task was similar to looking at your life as if it were a large puzzle with many pieces (see Figure 1.14). The next step is to assemble the pieces and see how they fit together. For example, think of this puzzle as a pyramid with five major parts. First put the individual parts together, and then combine them to make the complete structure.

1. *Part one—major influences.* Both internal and external factors combine to form the base of the pyramid (Figure 1.15).

2. *Part two—total belief system.* These influences become the reference source for your total belief system (Figure 1.16).

3. *Part three—thoughts.* Your total belief system provides the basis for your thoughts (Figure 1.17).

4. *Part four—behavior.* Thoughts, together with emotions and motivation, are the major factors affecting your behavior (Figure 1.18).

FIGURE 1.14
Life viewed as a large puzzle with many pieces.

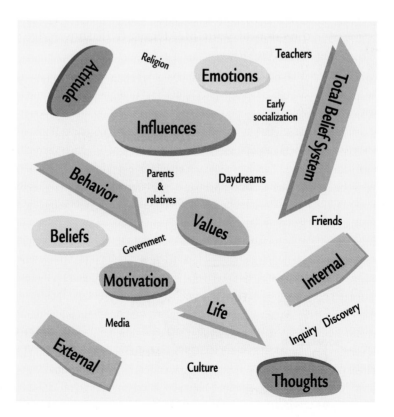

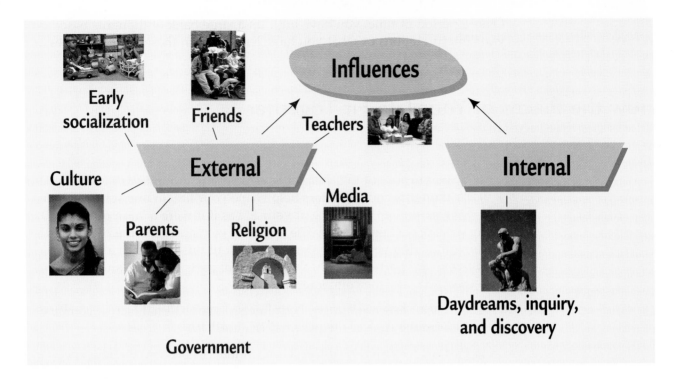

FIGURE 1.15
External and internal influences.

5. *Part five—your life.* External and internal influences form the basis of your total belief system. This system guides your thoughts, which contribute to your behavior. Behavior helps determine the direction of your life. Figure 1.19 shows the relationships of all these factors.

FIGURE 1.16

Influences as reference sources for total belief system.

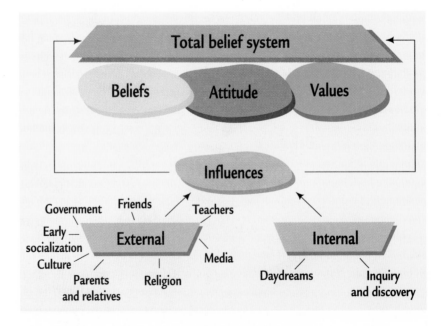

FIGURE 1.17
*Total belief system as
basis for thoughts.*

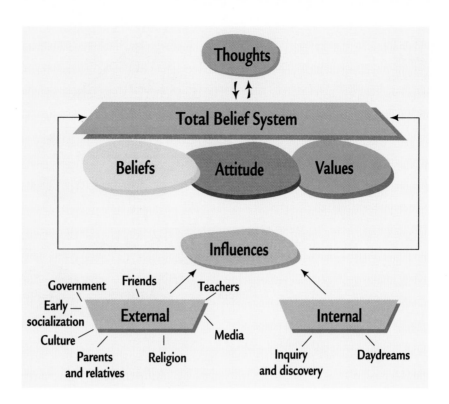

FIGURE 1.18
*Behavior affected by
thoughts, emotions,
and motivation, all
based in turn on total
belief system.*

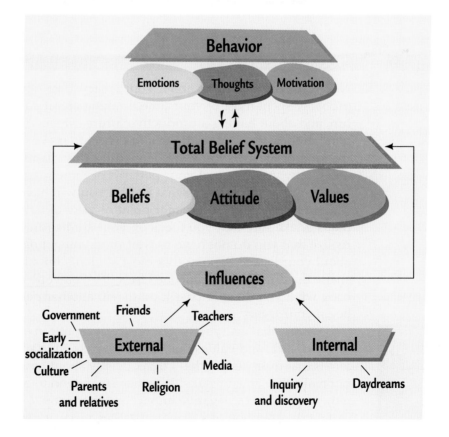

FIGURE 1.19

Relationships among influences, total belief system, and behavior, as impact on your life.

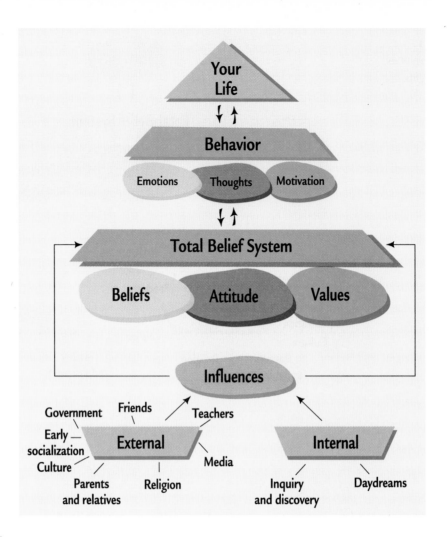

Now is the time to think about your legacy. Like other students, you have probably spent most of your time thinking about your studies, about having fun, and about having a productive future career. You might have visions of good grades, the contributions you expect to make to your chosen field, and the kind of lifestyle you want. Hopefully, this chapter helped you think about how you acquired your patterns of thoughts and behaviors. But have you given any thought to what impact you will have on society?

Consider adopting a broader point of view in terms of your interests and plans. Make sure that you focus on your studies and on your career, but realize that you do not have to wait until you get old before you think about your legacy. A point that most students miss is that each of you will shape the direction of someone else's life. Someone else will notice you, copy what you do, and pass it on to still another person. This process will begin your legacy.

Be aware that everybody demonstrates a pattern of behavior that reflects certain beliefs and values that they then pass on to someone else. The problem is that most people don't think deeply about how they affect others. Do not make the same mistake! Whether you intend to or not, you will have either a positive or negative impact on other people. You might have already caught the attention of a sister or brother, niece or nephew, neighbor or other acquaintance. You will influence other students, perhaps as a teammate, roommate, teaching assistant, or as a member of a campus organization. Later you will influence working associates, people in your community, and maybe even people throughout the world.

Since people are watching you, what do you want them to see and emulate? What kind of world would it be if thousands of people thought and behaved like you?

If you want to have a positive impact on the lives of others, you might need to change the direction of your life first. Chapter 2 will show you how. As you take on this daunting challenge, keep in mind the words of Walter Doyle Staples:

> *When you change your beliefs, you change your expectations; When you change your expectations, you change your attitude; When you change your attitude, you change your behavior; When you change your behavior; you change your performance; When you change your performance, YOU CHANGE YOUR LIFE!*[8]

NOTES

1. From *Think Like a Winner* by W.D. Staples, copyright © 1991 by Pelican Publishing Company, used by permission of the licenser, Pelican Publishers, Inc.

2. Excerpts and figure adapted from *Introduction to Psychology*, Tenth Edition by Rita L. Atkinson, Richard C. Atkinson, Edward E. Smith, and Daryl J. Bem, copyright © 1990, p. 402, by Harcourt Brace & Company, reprinted by permission of the publisher.

3. E. Deci: *Why We Do What We Do.* (New York: Penguin Books, 1995).

4. The Woodworth Model is described in R.S. Woodworth and H. Schlosberg: *Experimental Psychology* (New York: Holt, Rinehart and Winston, 1954), ch. 1.

5. Atkinson et al.: *Introduction to Psychology,* pp. 196–198.

6. Staples: *Think Like a Winner.*

7. M. Rokeach: "Attitudes" in D.L. Sills (ed.) *International Encyclopedia of the Social Sciences,* vol. 1 (New York: The Macmillan Co. and The Free Press, 1968), p. 450.

8. Staples: *Think Like a Winner.*

"Everyone thinks of changing the world, but no one thinks of changing himself."

Tolstoy

Personal Change: How You Can Improve Your Thinking and Behavior

MANY OF YOUR THOUGHT patterns have been carried over from childhood. A useful endeavor would be to ponder whether the way you think now is adequate to meet your present needs and future concerns. For example, how will your thought patterns affect your ability to learn, form productive relationships, and adapt in a rapidly changing society?

Most people have a mixture of thought patterns that range from productive to self-defeating. Productive thought patterns result from productive beliefs, attitudes, and values. Productive thought patterns lead to productive behaviors. Self-defeating thought patterns result from thinking errors and self-defeating values. Self-defeating thought patterns hinder people in their attempts to succeed in life.

Your continued success depends on your ability to maximize the use of productive thought patterns. This chapter will help you evaluate your thinking and make changes as needed. Specifically, you will learn how to

- Identify and correct self-defeating beliefs

- Identify and correct self-defeating values

overgeneralization

productive beliefs
   and values

productive thoughts

self-defeating beliefs
   and values

self-defeating thoughts

sound principles

thinking errors

unsound principles

········

Self-defeating thoughts: thoughts that hinder a person from achieving his short-term, intermediate, or long-term goals while at the same time meeting his responsibilities as a member of society.

Productive thoughts: thoughts that help a person achieve her short-term, intermediate, or long-term goals while at the same time meeting her responsibilities as a member of society.

Students often talk about the things that bother them. Here are some examples of situations that cause concerns and get in the way of real progress.

■ Reba spends a lot of time talking about various professors. She feels that the university should replace most of them. Also, she thinks that she can't get a good education unless the professors change how they teach.

■ Almost no one can meet Fred's expectations. His list of rules governs how he and everybody else *should* behave.

■ Charlene wants to be among the top performers in her major. She wants to get all As and mentally beats herself up when that doesn't happen.

These three situations reveal a pattern of self-defeating thoughts as the main source of the students' problems.

Figure 2.1 compares the impact of self-defeating versus productive thoughts on life outcomes. As you can see, self-defeating thoughts lead to self-defeating behavior, which leads to negative life outcomes. By contrast, productive thoughts lead to productive behavior, which leads to positive life outcomes. For example, compare Figure 2.2 and Figure 2.3, which show

FIGURE 2.1

Impact of thoughts on behavior and on life outcomes.

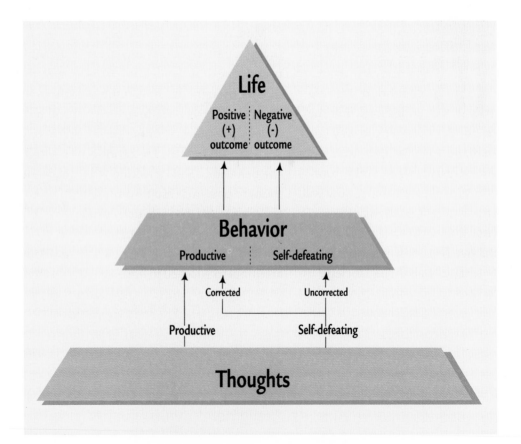

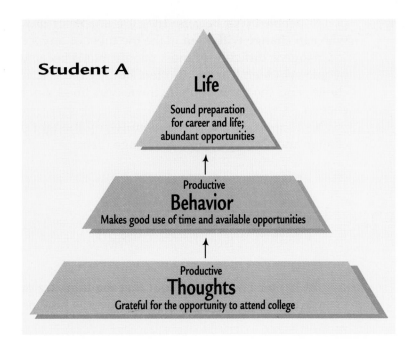

the situations of the fate of Student A and Student B, respectively. Both students have the same opportunities. The only difference between their situations is how they think about the opportunities afforded them. This difference in thought patterns has a profound impact on their life outcomes.

We can infer from Figure 2.2 and Figure 2.3 that Student B could enjoy the same outcome as Student A if Student B would correct his self-defeating thoughts. The main point of this discussion is that self-defeating thoughts often lead to behaviors that hinder rather than enhance a person's chances of success. Students with self-defeating thought patterns will face many problems unless they change these patterns. There is nothing odd about this claim. Much evidence exists to support it. Many of the bad things that hap-

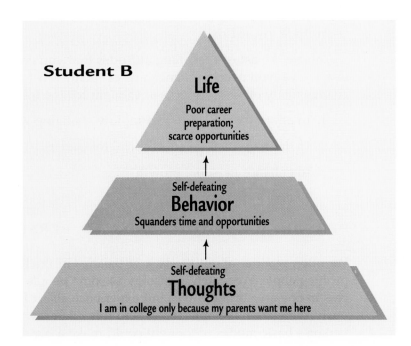

pen to people occur because they are unable or unwilling to change. People who can change will often make the most of any situation.

Change is difficult for most people, but it becomes even more difficult as people get older. Change is often, but not always, a matter of personal choice, and the older you get, the less inclined you may be to choose to change.

This chapter will help you identify any thought patterns you need to change and show you how to change them.

Why is Change Necessary?

In Chapter 1 we pointed out that the thinking process develops early during childhood. This process governs how people

- Study

- Learn new information

- Manage time

- Relate to other people

- Respond to circumstances

- Interact with parents, friends, and professors

Conditioned patterns of thoughts also govern

- Outlook

- Work habits

- Degree of flexibility

- Attitude toward risks

Review the list of prevailing attitudes that you created in Chapter 1, Exercise 1.1. Do you need to change any of them? Most people will need to change many of their patterns of thought for the following reasons:

1. To adapt more readily to a rapidly changing world

2. To improve their levels of social tolerance

3. To enhance personal growth

PERSONAL CHANGE LEADS TO PERSONAL GROWTH

We often wonder about the lack of balance in the lives of so many high-profile people. We watch in dismay as some people achieve spectacular success in one area of their lives but experience abject failure in others. Obviously, there are no simple answers to this dilemma. But a change in a person's basic modes of thought could make a big difference in the out-

Predicting the Importance of Personal Growth on Life Outcomes

Think about the following scenario: Assume that you received good grades in college and earned a degree in your major. But during that period, you paid no attention to your personal growth. Answer yes or no to the following questions based on this scenario.

1. Do you think you would qualify for a position that required high interpersonal skills? ___

2. Do you think that you would be a good role model? ___

3. Do you think you would be able to cope with the challenges of becoming a celebrity? ___

come. Many people work hard to achieve career success but invest little time or effort in becoming a better person. Exercise 2.1 addresses this issue.

If you want to achieve balance in your life, spend as much time working on yourself as on your career. Your thinking process is the appropriate place to start.

PERSONAL CHANGE LEADS TO IMPROVED ADAPTABILITY

The world is changing at an increasingly rapid rate, including the business world. This situation might have a profound impact on your life and career. For example, many corporations today reduce the size of their workforce and reorganize often. Most people can therefore no longer expect to join a firm,

(Source: SuperStock, Inc.)

advance through the ranks, and retire. Job security is a thing of the past, at least in this country. Yet many people do not have backup career plans.

You might not be able to retire—ever. So if you want a standard of living equal to or greater than that of your parents, you might have to think differently about your career plans. Many astute people now take a dual approach. They have a job or profession, but they also diversify their incomes through entrepreneurial ventures. If you pursue this approach, you will need to spend some time learning the skills required to be an entrepreneur.

Unfortunately, few people have updated their thinking to the level that they can adapt quickly to changing conditions. Many people rely mainly on what they learned in the past, only some of which might still be useful. Certain thought patterns carried over from the past might need to be discarded because of thinking errors that they contain.

Thinking errors occur because the mind is not always as efficient as we expect it to be; it makes mistakes. For example, we assume that people use reason—or logical, well-structured thought—to make conclusions, inferences, and judgments. However, some psychologists argue that this orderly process occurs only about 50 percent of the time. Dr. Donald Norman, in his book, *The Psychology of Everyday Things,* explains that the mind, "hops, skips, and jumps its way from idea to idea, tying together things that have no business being put together, forming new creative leaps, new insights and concepts."[1]

> **Thinking errors:** mistakes of the mind; for example, overgeneralizations and all-or-nothing thinking.

PROFILE FOR SUCCESS

Sam Fereidouni

When I was five years old, my parents and I moved from Iran, which is a predominantly Muslim country, to the United States, which is a "melting pot" of religions, although most media and outward signs point toward a predominantly Christian society. My parents are not particularly religious to begin with and are very moderate in their religious views. They really never forced me to accept any religion and instead let me find my own way. As a result, growing up I took an agnostic view. Later, as I matured, I slowly saw my views on religion changing and eventually lost my agnosticism.

This is one of the few—if not the only—beliefs or values that I can recall changing. Today I consider myself a Muslim. I could definitely be a better Muslim than I am, but I think in my current situation I am the best Muslim that I can be. I have

learned that many things are not so black and white, but rather, are very much gray. I believe there is not too much one can point to and say with absolute resolution that it is right or wrong, one way or another. For example, although I consider myself a Muslim, I go to a Christian church for Christmas and on Easter. I also have some beliefs that may be more closely aligned with Hindu or Buddhist faiths. My point is that I try to be flexible in my labels and focus on holding true to my values and beliefs, regardless of how they are labeled.

What prompted the change in my religious beliefs was becoming better educated as well as maturing to a point where I could resolve some of these complex issues. Specifically, before this change I used to think that humankind knows so much and has made so many advances that the existence of a god must be confirmed by science. Then, the more I became educated in the sciences, the more I realized how much humankind really doesn't know. I then still had not changed my agnostic viewpoint, but I was at least for the first time open to the idea of exploring various religions. After researching many religions to the best of my abilities, I realized how much various religions have in common, and I recognized that my belief system doesn't completely fit into any one particular religion more than another. I have since adopted pieces from each in changing from my original agnostic position.

....

Overgeneralization: making predictions about broad trends based on very few examples.

The lack of precise processing by the mind leads to many errors. These errors define how people interpret and respond to events. For example, one error is the tendency of the mind to overgeneralize. Overgeneralization about people leads to some of the most vexing problems in the world. This habit results in stereotyping and prejudiced thinking in regard to religion, race, gender, nationality, and sexual orientation. The next step after such prejudices are formed is often insults, fights, murders, and even wars.

The main point here is that people will act often on negative thoughts unless they work hard to change them.

Exercise 2.2 is the first step in identifying and correcting your thinking errors. For example, suppose you find that you tend to overgeneralize frequently. If you want to correct this thought pattern, you can use one of the change remedies described later in the chapter.

● ● ● ● ● ●EXERCISE 2.2

Recognizing Overgeneralizations

In the right column of the accompanying table, describe some overgeneralizations you might make about the items listed in the left column.

ITEM	OVERGENERALIZATION
Example: engineering students	*Example:* Engineering students are nerds.
Other countries	
College life	
Professors	
Administrations	
Senior citizens	

(continued)

Homosexuals	
Heterosexuals	
Native-Americans	
African-Americans	
Latin-Americans	
European-Americans	
Asian-Americans	
Arabs	
Jews	

PERSONAL CHANGE LEADS TO SOCIAL TOLERANCE

The current social climate in the United States is tense. Mean-spiritedness seems to pervade our society. For example, many people blame immigrants for many of our problems, and some want to close the door on new arrivals. Deep divisions exist over issues such as fairness and crime prevention. Racial strife is very high, and there is widespread intolerance of gays and lesbians.

These conditions might stem from two possibilities:

1. People unwilling to change

2. People changing, but in the wrong direction—that is, becoming less tolerant of others

More social tolerance will depend on more personal change, in the right direction.

Components of the Thinking Process

The main components of the thinking process are beliefs, attitudes, and values. The negative aspects of these components hinder people in their attempts to succeed in life. They are (1) self-defeating beliefs, (2) self-defeating attitudes, and (3) self-defeating values. Beliefs, atti-

FIGURE 2.4
Categories of thinking problems.

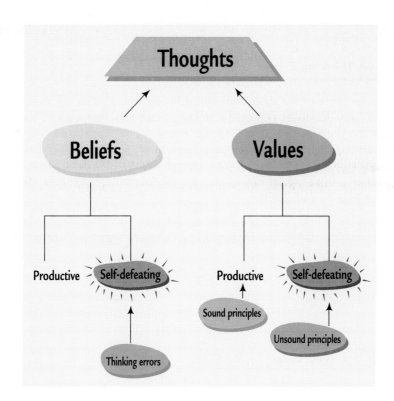

Self-defeating beliefs and values: lead to thoughts that hinder a person from achieving his short-term, intermediate, or long-term goals while at the same time meeting his responsibilities as a member of society.

Productive beliefs and values: lead to thoughts that help a person achieve her short-term, intermediate, or long-term goals while at the same time meeting her responsibilities as a member of society.

Sound principles: based on rules of human conduct that foster personal effectiveness and responsible behavior as a member of society.

Unsound principles: based on rules of human conduct that are incompatible with personal effectiveness and responsible behavior as a member of society.

tudes, and values are the three components of the *total belief system.* In this chapter and throughout the rest of this book, we will discuss how to change negative patterns in this belief system. For simplicity, however, we will focus on changing only beliefs and values. We assume that attitudes stem from beliefs and values. Thus, Figure 2.4 shows just two of the three components: beliefs and values.

Most people have a mixture of beliefs and values, ranging from productive to self-defeating. As Figure 2.4 shows, the productive beliefs lead to productive thoughts. The self-defeating beliefs, which result from thinking errors, lead to self-defeating thoughts. These thoughts determine behavior and life outcomes (Figures 2.2 and Figure 2.3).

As also shown in Figure 2.4, productive values, which stem from sound principles, lead to productive thoughts. Conversely, self-defeating values, which stem from unsound principles, lead to self-defeating thoughts. Again, thoughts lead to behavior and life outcomes (Figure 2.2 and Figure 2.3). We will discuss sound and unsound principles more fully later in this chapter.

THINKING ERRORS: SOURCES OF SELF-DEFEATING BELIEFS

As noted previously, self-defeating beliefs result from thinking errors. Recall that thinking errors occur when the mind does not process information correctly. The mind makes mistakes—a concept discussed earlier in this chapter. Exercise 2.3 deals with some common thinking errors.

Identifying Common Thinking Errors

The following list covers some of the most common thinking errors. After the description and example(s) of each thinking error, give your own example(s) in the spaces provided, using your own ideas or personal experiences.

1. **All-or-nothing thinking**—a tendency to see things in terms of black or white, win or lose, success or failure. For example, Rosalind set out to get straight As this semester. She considers herself a failure because she got four As and one B.

_____

_____

_____

_____

How often do you engage in all-or-nothing thinking?

    1   *2*   *3*   *4*   *5*

    Never   *Very often*

2. **Perfectionism**—an extreme form of all-or nothing thinking. The "do it right or not at all" syndrome. Jim had a paper to write for his economics class. Because he waited too late to start, it did not turn out the way he wanted. Jim thought the paper was unacceptable and refused to turn it in.

_____

_____

_____

_____

How often does your thinking tend toward perfectionism?

    1   *2*   *3*   *4*   *5*

    Never   *Very often*

3. **Overgeneralization**—the assumption that one or a few events apply to all situations. On three occasions, it rained after Rene washed her car. She concluded that it would always rain when she washes her car. This thinking error is also the basis for stereotyping. Ronette felt rejected when she tried to make friends with a Hispanic student. She concluded that all Hispanic people are unfriendly.

_____

_____

_____

_____

How often do you tend to overgeneralize?

   1   2   3   4   5

   Never   Very often

4. **Global labeling**—failure to distinguish between a specific behavior and the total person. Rayford brands people as totally bad if they have one characteristic he doesn't like. He labels his roommate as loud and boisterous. He refers to his girlfriend as a selfish person. He tells his friends: "Professor Smith is a jerk."

_____

_____

_____

How often do you engage in global labeling?

   1   2   3   4   5

   Never   Very often

5. **Magnification or minimization**—a tendency to either blow things out of proportion—to make a mountain out of a molehill—or to consider them less important than they really are. After being rejected when he asks a girl out, Gerhardt says to himself, "She wouldn't go out with me. Probably no one else will, either. I'll never get married and have a family." After he flunks his math midterm, he thinks, "I'll never get into medical school. My career is over!" In other situations, Gerhardt shrinks the importance of things inappropriately. "This paper is due at the end of the semester. I've got plenty of time before I need to begin working on it. I should be able to find all the books and articles I need in the library." In this case, Gerhardt does not realize that many if not all of the books he needs might be checked out when he starts working on his paper just one week before it is due.

_____

_____

_____

How often do you engage in magnification or minimization?

   1   2   3   4   5

   Never   Very often

6. **Comparative thinking**—a tendency to constantly compare yourself negatively to others. Liz assumes that the other students in her class are brighter, more talented, more personable, and more successful than she.

(continued)

_____

_____

_____

_____

How often do you engage in comparative thinking?

    1   2   3   4   5

    Never   Very often

7. **Uncritical acceptance of criticism**—failure to distinguish between valid and invalid criticism. Jesse lets people who know little about him define his self-worth. He frequently lets other students influence his goals, interests, or priorities.

_____

_____

_____

_____

How often do you engage in uncritical acceptance of criticism?

    1   2   3   4   5

    Never   Very often

8. **Selective editing**—a tendency to focus on the portions of an issue that support preconceived conclusions and leave out other portions. Five students congratulate Al on his article in the school newspaper, but he thinks only about the negative comment from the sixth student because he has already decided that he is a poor writer. Lena is a premed volunteer at a hospital. Many patients praise her bedside manner. She concludes from these comments that she will be a successful physician, ignoring her failing grades in chemistry and average grades in biology.

_____

_____

_____

_____

How often do you engage in selective editing?

    1   2   3   4   5

    Never   Very often

9. **Imperative thinking** (the "should" syndrome)—an attitude in which you make all the rules. You have a set of inflexible dictates and expectations about how you and other people should behave. You say to yourself, "I ought not to behave this way. . . . I should be ashamed of myself for what I did. . . .

You must not disturb me when I'm playing my stereo. . . . You should have been more grateful when I gave you a birthday gift."

When a person lets imperatives dominate his thinking, he frequently expects the world and universe to cater to his demands: "This is the worst holiday I have ever seen. . . . It ought not be so hot during the Christmas season."

A person who thinks in terms of imperatives believes that she is due certain entitlements. Anything that she wants strongly enough, she thinks that she should have. As a result, she demands that people cater to her desires, which frequently assume the status of needs.

_____

_____

_____

_____

How often do you use imperative thinking?

1   2   3   4   5

Never   Very often

10. **Personalization and blame**—blaming yourself when you aren't entirely responsible or blaming others when you are the responsible party. Listen to Afrika: "I would have gotten an A on my exam if you had not made me angry last night." In other situations, she might blame other people and overlook ways that she might have helped cause the problem. Afrika speaks again: "My roommate made me so angry I couldn't study for the final." Afrika blames her professor for her poor performance on the midterm. Blame is a major factor in conflicts between friends, relatives, married couples, tribes, and nations.

_____

_____

_____

11. **Jumping to conclusions**—takes one of two different forms: mind-reading and fortune-telling.

A. **Mind-reading**—thinking you know what other people are thinking. You might assume, for example, without evidence, that people are reacting negatively to you. Thelma sees two students by the window talking and periodically, looking at her. Thelma thinks, "Those students are criticizing me." In other situations, she might expect other people to know what she is thinking. Thelma complains, "He should have known that I was not interested in that movie."

B. **Fortune-telling**—arbitrarily predicting that things will turn out either badly or well. Hal thinks, "I will never pass English Lit." Or he may think, "I'm not going to spend much time studying for the next exam because I think it will be as easy as the last one."

(continued)

_____

_____

_____

_____

How often do you jump to conclusions?

    1   *2*   *3*   *4*   *5*

  Never   *Very often*

Journal Activity

From Exercise 2.3, you might have identified some of your own thinking errors. Record them below. You will learn how to correct these errors later in the chapter.

_____

_____

_____

_____

_____

_____

_____

SOUND AND UNSOUND PRINCIPLES: SOURCES OF VALUES

Productive values are those based on positive, or sound, principles. Principles are natural laws that govern human behavior[2] (Table 2.1). Sound principles have many positive characteristics.

Sound principles are:

1. Objective

2. Not trendy

3. Widely applicable codes of conduct for

- Individuals

- Families

- Cultures

- Religions

- Organizations

- Nations

4. Empower individuals to

- Achieve

- Interact effectively

- Contribute

They are not trendy; sound principles have endured for generations. These undeniable truths provide codes of conduct for individuals. They also apply to families, cultures, religions, organizations, and nations. Habits formed from these internalized principles empower individuals.

We often use the term *principle* to indicate positive rules of conduct. But principles can be not only sound (reflecting positive attributes) but also unsound (reflecting negative attributes). Table 2.2 shows that unsound principles are the opposite of sound principles. In this text, we will use the term *principles* or *sound principles* to describe those principles that fit the characteristics listed. The term *unsound principles* will refer to those principles that do not conform to the characteristics listed.

Recall from Chapter 1 that values reflect states of conduct such as courtesy or justice. This aspect of values overlaps with principles. But values also reflect states of being that people deem important. Some of these states of being overlap with principles while others do not. For example, courage is a principle that can also be a person's value if she thinks courage is a worthwhile state of being. On the other hand, a person can value fast cars, which have nothing to do with rules of human conduct (principles). Here are some examples of values that reflect principles and some values that do not.

Values that reflect principles:

- Honesty

- Justice

- Fairness

- Courage

- Integrity

- Initiative

- Sacrifice

- Generosity

- Gratitude

- Perseverance

	PRINCIPLE	DEFINITION
1	Abundance mentality®	Belief that there is plenty of opportunity and resources for everybody
2	Cooperation	Working with others; acting together
3	Courage	Mental or moral strength; ability to withstand danger, fear, or difficulty
4	Courtesy	Showing respect and consideration for others
5	Delayed gratification	Putting in effort now for results later
6	Discipline	Orderly pattern of behavior; self-restraint
7	Equity	Freedom from bias or favoritism
8	Excellence	Eminently good; of first-class quality
9	Fidelity	State of being faithful
10	Golden Rule	Do unto others as you would have them do unto you
11	Growth and change	Willingness to learn and adapt
12	Honesty	Freedom from fraud or corruption
13	Industry	Earnest, steady effort; working hard
14	Initiative	Willingness to take the first step
15	Integrity	Soundness; firm adherence to a code of moral or artistic values
16	Investing for the future	Self-explanatory; applies to material and mental resources
17	Justice	Impartiality; fairness
18	Loyalty	Faithfulness
19	Maturity	Full development
20	Modesty	Lack of conceit or vanity; propriety in dress/speech/conduct
21	Patience	Bearing pains or trials without complaint; delaying gratification
22	Perseverance	Persistence in spite of obstacles
23	Quality	Excellence
24	Reliability	Giving the same result on repeated trials
25	Resiliency	Ability to recover from or adjust easily to misfortune or change
26	Respect	Showing consideration or esteem for
27	Responsibility	Being accountable for one's behavior
28	Service	Contributing to the welfare of others
29	Tact	Finding ways to say or do something without offending
30	Temperance	Self-restraint; moderation
31	Thrift	Careful management of money and resources

TABLE 2.1

Definitions of Principles That Govern Personal and Social Behavior (Abundance Mentality is a registered trademark of Franklin Covey Co. and is used with permission. All rights reserved. (800) 654-1776.)

TABLE 2.2

*Sound and Unsound
Principles*

SOUND	UNSOUND
Abundance mentality	Scarcity mentality
Cooperation	Individualism
Courage	Timidity
Courtesy	Rudeness
Delayed gratification	Immediate return
Discipline	Disorganization
Equity	Partiality; favoritism
Excellence	Mediocrity
Fidelity	Unfaithfulness
Do unto others. . . .	Do it to others . . .
Growth and change	Apathy; complacency
Honesty	Dishonesty
Industry	Slothfulness
Initiative	Passivity
Integrity	Morally corrupt
Investing for future needs	Present-oriented
Justice	Injustice
Loyalty	Disloyalty
Maturity	Immaturity
Modesty	Vanity; arrogance
Patience	Impatience
Perseverance	Reluctance; wavering
Quality	Flimsy; thin and weak
Reliability	Unaccountability
Resiliency	Inflexibility
Respect	Contempt; arrogance
Responsibility	Irresponsibility
Service	Contributing only to self
Tact	Lack of diplomacy
Temperance	Extremism
Thrift	Wastefulness

Values not reflective of principles:

- Fast cars
- Luxurious homes
- Warm climates
- Quiet surrounding
- Art
- Music
- Security
- Money
- Holiday seasons
- Beauty

How to Improve the Quality of Your Thinking

ny person can improve her thinking quality by identifying and correcting the appropriate thinking errors. This section explains the tools for carrying out this process.

BENEFITS OF USING COGNITIVE TECHNIQUES

Hundreds of books, audiocassettes, and video programs focus on how to change thoughts and behaviors. Many of these programs approach change from the standpoint of *positive thinking*. This means they encourage people to think positive thoughts and make positive statements to themselves. There is anecdotal but no scientific evidence to support the effectiveness of this approach.

A cognitive approach seems more suitable for students. *Cognition* refers to thoughts or perceptions (Chapter 1). The basic premise for this approach is as follows:

1. Certain basic assumptions govern emotions and behavior.

2. Basic assumptions, which surface as automatic thoughts, often turn out to be incorrect because of thinking errors.

3. People can use cognitive techniques to change these assumptions and thus solve many of their problems.

The main benefits of the cognitive approach are its

- Simplicity
- Proven effectiveness
- Counteraction of negative thinking

(Source: Goldberg/Monkmeyer Press.)

- Strengthening effect on critical thinking skills

- Fortification of problem-solving ability

- Applicability to academic, personal, and career concerns

Many government and private studies confirm the effectiveness of cognitive approaches. This type of approach does not focus on positive thinking per se; instead, it helps people avoid, or work around, negative and self-defeating thinking. Self-defeating thinking is often the major factor that holds people back from succeeding in life and hinders change.

Cognitive approaches rely on your ability to think rationally and solve problems. These are natural skills that you already have. Professors expect you to use these skills routinely as you prepare for classes and exams. They expect you to think critically about what you observe and hear. Usually, the students who make the best use of their cognitive skills get the best grades.

Furthermore, cognitive skills will help you in your career. Although many people complain about fewer job opportunities in the new, global economy, it is mostly jobs requiring manual skills that are disappearing. The growing trend is to hire workers with strong mental skills. The people most seriously hurt in the new economy are those who refuse to change and adapt. Don't let this happen to you. Prepare yourself for continual change and adaptation. When you refine your cognitive skills, you become more competitive for jobs and promotions.

In summary, cognitive techniques provide a unique tool for growth and change, with which you can address academic, personal, and career concerns.

USE THIS GENERAL STRATEGY FOR CHANGE

You can use cognitive techniques to broaden your knowledge about a subject or to correct errors in thinking. The *Change Formula* in Figure 2.5 covers both conditions. Figures 2.6–2.10 show how beliefs influence thoughts and behaviors. For example, you experience an event that causes you to make statements to yourself (thoughts). The beliefs stored in your mind influence the quality of your automatic self-statements. Productive beliefs lead to productive automatic self-statements. In contrast, self-defeating beliefs lead to self-defeating automatic self-statements. And, as shown earlier, productive thoughts lead to productive behaviors, whereas self-defeating thoughts lead to self-defeating behaviors. We will give examples and assign exercises to illustrate these processes in the following sections and chapters.

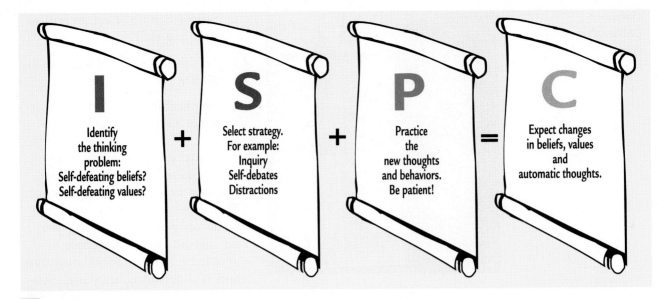

HOW TO CORRECT SELF-DEFEATING BELIEFS

Figure 2.11 shows some common techniques (remedies) for correcting error thinking problems that lead to self-defeating beliefs.[3] An explanation of each of these remedies follows:

1. *Inquiry*—asking questions to expand your knowledge.

2. *Distractions*—shifting your attention from the negative thought to another subject.

3. *Self-debates*—arguing with yourself. Using this approach, you challenge your groundless beliefs and convince yourself that they just don't make sense. You can apply this technique to a large number of situations.

4. *Semantic methods*—replacing imperative language with language indicating choices, preferences, and desires.

FIGURE 2.6
The effect of beliefs on thoughts.

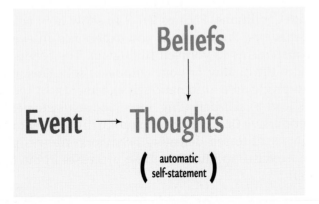

FIGURE 2.7
The effect of productive beliefs on thoughts.

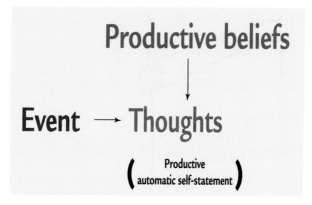

FIGURE 2.8
The effect of self-defeating beliefs on thoughts.

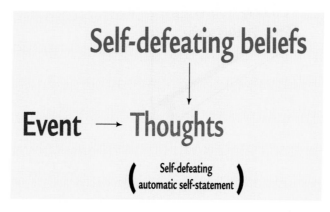

FIGURE 2.9
The effect of productive beliefs and thoughts on behaviors.

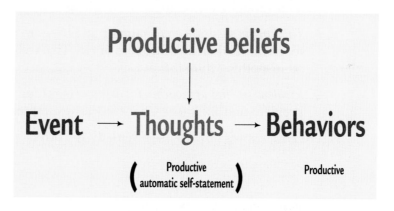

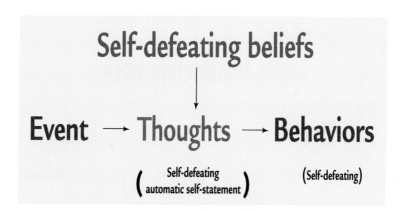

FIGURE 2.11
Remedies for correcting thinking problems.

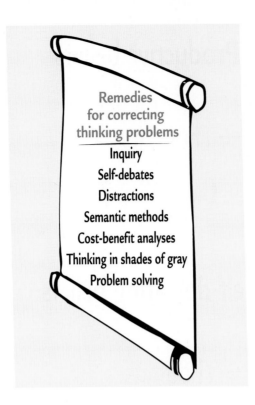

5. *Cost-benefit analysis*—attempting to determine if the advantages of a negative thought outweigh its disadvantages.

6. *Thinking in shades of gray*—attempting to see matters on a scale from one to ten rather than as either zero or ten. This technique is the opposite of all-or-nothing thinking.

7. *Problem-solving approach*—focusing on solutions. Here you identify the problem and fix it (see Chapter 3 for examples).

Figure 2.12. shows how to use a remedy to correct a self-defeating belief.

FIGURE 2.12
Use of a remedy to correct a self-defeating belief.

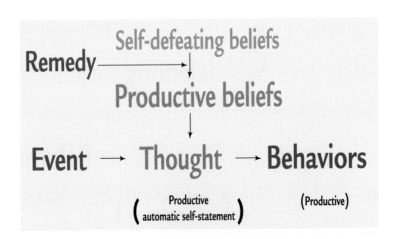

The examples that follow (Examples 2.1–2.3) illustrate the use of cognitive techniques to correct thinking errors. You will find more examples in successive chapters. Exercise 2.4 gives you an opportunity to apply a remedy in an hypothetical situation involving yourself. Exercise 2.5 will give you further practice in applying rememdies to events.

EXAMPLE 2.1

Event

Disappointment—Rae flunked her mid-term in Music Theory 102.

Rae's Self-Statement

I'm a failure. I might as well give up on being a music major.

(I) Identify the Thinking Problem

Magnification

(S) Select a Remedy

One of the simplest techniques for Rae to use in this instance is that of "distractions." Rae can get very creative with this technique. She might stomp on the floor, slap herself on the face, or pull a red flag out of her purse. After interrupting her habitual thought, she can shift her attention to a more pleasant subject. This is not the time to focus on her major. Instead, she might think about her upcoming date on Saturday night (assuming that it will be pleasant). The point is to quickly replace her negative thoughts with positive thoughts. By distracting herself, she will postpone thoughts about the test. She will probably think more constructively following a period of reflection.

(C) Productive Belief

Setbacks are a part of the growth process.

Productive Self-Statement

One failed test does not mean that I will fail the next one. I will find out what I can do to overcome this setback.

(P) Practice

Rehearse the remedy and the productive self-statement.

EXAMPLE 2.2

Event

Rico is running for student body president. He is anxious about the upcoming election results.

Rico's Self-Statement

I must win the election for student body president. It would be a personal disaster if I did not win.

(I) Thinking Problems

1. Imperative thinking ("must" is an imperative)
2. Magnification

(S) Select a Remedy

1. Semantic methods: Replace imperative language. Change "must" to "prefer to" or "would like to."
2. Self-debate:

   Q. What makes me feel that I must win?
   A. I want to, very badly.
   Q. In what ways would it be catastrophic if I did not win?
   A. I would question whether I'm a good leader.
   Q. What is the worst thing that could happen to me if I did not win?
   A. I would feel very sad. Some of my friends would be disappointed.
   Q. What good things could happen to me if I did not win?
   A. I might have more time to study. I might learn more about how to bounce back from defeat.

(C) Productive Beliefs

Needs become preferences or desires.

Setbacks are disappointing, not catastrophic.

Productive Self-Statement

I really don't need to win this election, but I would like to. I would be disappointed if I did not win, but not devastated.

(P) Practice

Rehearse the remedy and the productive self-statement.

EXAMPLE 2.3

Event

Fred has a habit of making assumptions about himself, other people, and the universe.

Fred's Self-Statements

I ought to be ashamed of myself for behaving like a child.

I should have known better than to spend so much time doing committee work.

If you loved me, you would pay more attention to special occasions such as holidays and my birthday.

People should be more courteous to each other when they are driving in traffic.

You must not disturb me when I'm talking on the phone.

It should not rain during spring break.

(I) Thinking Problems

This is a bagful of imperatives—*Fred's* list of rules, for himself and everybody else.

(S) Select a Remedy

1. Semantic methods: Replace "ought" and "should" statements with "I prefer" or "I would like to" statements.
2. Cost-benefit analysis: Fred could view this list as a pattern of negative thinking and challenge it with a cost-benefit analysis. Fred needs to know how much he would be hurt compared with how much he would gain from continuing this negative pattern of thought. If the disadvantages outweigh the advantages, he is more likely to wage a vigorous debate with himself to challenge his thinking.

ADVANTAGES	DISADVANTAGES
Avoidance of personal responsibility	Anger
High expectations	Hostility
	Frustration
	Depression
	guilt (for self and others)
	Blame (on self and others)
	Unrealistic expectations
	Interpersonal conflicts
	Alienation

(C) Productive Beliefs

Needs become preferences; "ought to" becomes "would like to."

Productive Self-Statement

Clearly, the disadvantages of using imperatives outweigh the advantages.

(P) Practice

Rehearse the remedy and the productive self-statement.

Using the Change Formula to Correct a Thinking Problem

Assume the following event and fill in the appropriate responses to it.

Event

Someone cut you off while driving on a busy highway (assume a negative reaction on your part).

Automatic Self-Statement

_____

(I) Identify the Thinking Problem

_____

(S) Select a Remedy

_____

_____

_____

_____

_____

_____

_____

_____

_____

_____

(C) Productive Belief

_____

Productive Self-Statement

_____

_____

(P) Practice
Rehearse the remedy and the productive self-statement.

Identifying and Correcting Hypothetical Thinking Errors

The table contains some common thinking errors. In the space provided, create a hypothetical event for each of the errors listed. Then generate an automatic self-statement, select a remedy, and generate a productive self-statement for the specific error and event.

Event	Identify the Thinking Problem (I)	Automatic Self-Statement	Select a Remedy (S)	Productive Self-Statement
Example: I could not answer a question the professor asked me in class.	Global labeling	The professor will think of me as a dummy.	Self-debate	I am not a dummy. I was not prepared for class that day. In the future I will prepare for my classes and stay alert so that the professor will know that I am a serious student.
	All-or-nothing thinking			
	Perfectionism			
	Overgeneralization			
	Magnification or minimization			
	Comparative thinking			
	Uncritical acceptance of criticism			
	Selective editing			
	Imperative thinking			
	Personalization and blame			
	Jumping to conclusions			

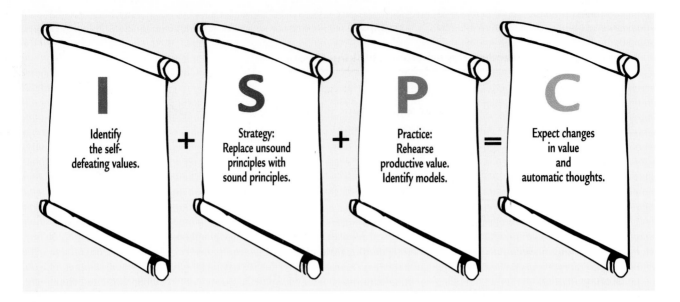

FIGURE 2.13
Change formula for correcting self-defeating values.

You can correct self-defeating values in a manner similar to how you correct other thinking problems: you use the Change Formula, as shown in Figure 2.13. The remedy for self-defeating values is replacement with productive values. Note that under "Practice" in the figure, we ask you to identify models. This process involves finding and modeling individuals who live by the principles you are trying to adopt. You may find these models among people you know—parents, relatives, college staff people, other students. Or you may use community leaders or national or international figures as your models. Scan books and articles about people that have the values you want to acquire. You may even choose a historical figure as a model.

Example 2.4 and Exercise 2.6 illustrate how to identify and correct self-defeating values.

EXAMPLE 2.4

Event

Reba ponders her future plans.

Reba's Self-Statement

I want to control the lives of 500,000 people.

(I) Identify the Thinking Problem

Possible self-defeating value based on unsound principles (see analysis under following item, "Select a Remedy")

EXAMPLE 2.4 *(continued)*

(S) Select a Remedy

Reba analyzes her reasons. She asks why she wants to control these people? Is it for power or to serve? If for power, her value reflects unsound principles: contempt, selfishness, moral corruption, and injustice. She can replace these unsound principles with sound principles: respect, generosity, integrity, and justice.

Productive Value

Service to others

Reba's Productive Self-Statement

I want to help 500,000 people improve the quality of their lives.

(P) Practice

Rehearse the productive value and the productive self-statement.

Now that you have completed this exercise, you should be able to identify self-defeating values associated with a wide variety of situations that you might encounter. In your journal, note some of these self-defeating values. We will see how values affect performance in Chapter 4.

●●●●●●EXERCISE 2.6

Correcting Self-Defeating Values Associated with Hypothetical Events

Below are some examples of self-defeating values. In the space provided, create a hypothetical event for each of the values. Then generate an automatic self-statement, show a replacement value, and generate a productive self-statement for the specific self-defeating value and event.

EVENT	SELF-STATEMENT	SELF-DEFEATING VALUE	PRODUCTIVE VALUE	PRODUCTIVE SELF-STATEMENT
Example: Tim damaged several pages of a library book and refused to report the damage.	They will never know the difference.	Irresponsibility	Responsibility	I take responsibility for material in my possession.

(continued)

		Immediate return		
		Immaturity		
		Complacency		
		Arrogance		
		Irresponsibility		
		Lack of diplomacy		
		Impatience		
		Mediocrity		

CHAPTER SUMMARY

You now have the tools that will help you identify and correct any self-defeating beliefs and values that might hinder your success. In the next chapters, you will learn how proactive and reactive students differ in terms of six major traits. These traits often dictate how students respond to various challenges. You will see that you can solve your problems using cognitive techniques and become more proactive in a number of areas: academic, personal, social, or career-related. The only requirement is that you be willing to change. You might not always find it possible or necessary to find the right technique for a given problem. The important point is to override your negative thoughts. Exploit your natural ability to think critically. Then, *do something!*

NOTES

1. D. A. Norman: *The Psychology of Everyday Things* (New York: Basic Books, 1988).

2. Stephen Covey stresses the importance of principles for successful living in his book, *The Seven Habits of Highly Effective People* (New York: Simon and Schuster, 1989), © 1989 Stephen R. Covey. Used with permission. All rights reserved.

3. The remedies for identifying and correcting thinking errors used in this book are based on techniques used by many cognitive therapists. For examples, see D. Burns: *The Feeling Good Handbook: Using the New Mood Therapy in Everyday Life* (New York: William Morrow, 1989); and A. Freeman and R. DeWolf: *Woulda, Coulda, Shoulda* (New York: Harper Perennial, 1989).

PRE-CHAPTER SELF-ASSESSMENT

Read each statement and circle the number that best reflects your response.

NEVER   ALWAYS

1   2   3   4   5   6   7   8   9   10

1. When I encounter adverse circumstances, I assume that it is within my power to overcome them.

   1   2   3   4   5   6   7   8   9   10

2. When I make mistakes, I acknowledge, correct, and learn from them

   1   2   3   4   5   6   7   8   9   10

3. When faced with risky situations, I assess the worst and best possible consequences and my ability to cope with these alternatives, and then I make a decision.

   1   2   3   4   5   6   7   8   9   10

4. I choose constructive options to help me relieve stress.

   1   2   3   4   5   6   7   8   9   10

5. When I encounter a stressful event, my automatic thoughts are usually positive.

   1   2   3   4   5   6   7   8   9   10

6. When I encounter adverse events, I see them as temporary.

   1   2   3   4   5   6   7   8   9   10

7. I take responsibility for my behavior.

   1   2   3   4   5   6   7   8   9   10

8. I speak in terms that suggest that I have the power to overcome circumstances.

   1   2   3   4   5   6   7   8   9   10

9. When I experience complex events, I focus on issues that I can do something about.

   1   2   3   4   5   6   7   8   9   10

10. I take a step-by-step problem-solving approach to complex situations that I encounter.

    1   2   3   4   5   6   7   8   9   10

11. I read ahead for my classes, stay alert during lectures, and review notes after class.

    1   2   3   4   5   6   7   8   9   10

12. I spend time with people whose actions reveal their passion for what they believe.

    1   2   3   4   5   6   7   8   9   10

13. I make time in my schedule to maintain strong ties with family members.

    1   2   3   4   5   6   7   8   9   10

14. I take steps to cultivate my network of friends and supporters.

    1   2   3   4   5   6   7   8   9   10

15. I welcome opportunities to share ideas with people of different backgrounds such as those of a different age, race, culture, religion, or sexual orientation.

    1   2   3   4   5   6   7   8   9   10

16. I look for opportunities to help other people.

    1   2   3   4   5   6   7   8   9   10

17. I set aside time to relax and have fun.

    1   2   3   4   5   6   7   8   9   10

18. I seek out opportunities to learn and to broaden my perspective and add to my life experiences.

    1   2   3   4   5   6   7   8   9   10

19. I seek to balance my life by tending to my mental, physical, social, and spiritual needs.

    1   2   3   4   5   6   7   8   9   10

20. I can identify and fix the self-defeating thought patterns that lead to pessimism.

    1   2   3   4   5   6   7   8   9   10

Determine your relative degree of proactivity for this trait by using the following formula:

Percent Proactivity = Sum of Circled Numbers ÷ 200 × 100

(Note that 200 is the maximum sum possible. It would result in a score of 100 percent.)

Percent Proactivity = _____

For example, if you checked 5 for each question, your score would be

Percent Proactivity for Outlook = 100/200 × 100 = 50

"We can improve our moods by such simple acts as taking a brisk walk; we can improve our health by acting the way healthy people act; and we can become more optimistic by being cheerful."

Alan Loy McGinnis, psychologist[1]

Outlook: Proactive Students Choose Optimism over Pessimism

OPTIMISM IS THE normal mental state of high achievers. Optimists differ from pessimists in their thinking styles. When they face bad circumstances, optimists see options for response. Pessimists quickly lose hope and become victims of circumstances. This chapter highlights some of the major differences between optimists and pessimists and describes some of the benefits of optimism, such as better health,

more wealth, and a higher quality of life than that of pessimists.

Proactive students tend to be optimists; reactive students tend to be pessimists. The pessimism of reactive students is due to their self-defeating thinking styles. This chapter will help you learn the thinking styles of optimists and apply them to your own outlook as needed. You will learn how to

■ Resist helplessness and depression

■ Focus on issues under your personal control

■ Take a problem-solving approach to complex circumstances

■ Bounce back from setbacks

■ Maintain high levels of enthusiasm

■ Connect with people

■ Take rational risks

■ Value opportunities to grow and refresh yourself

optimism   outlook   pessimism   worst-case scenario approach

Outlook: the attitude that reflects your overall view of how you see events and the world around you.

Optimism: the tendency to see setbacks as opportunities and defeat as temporary, to focus on issues under personal control rather than on external influences; a proactive trait.

Pessimism: a tendency to see setbacks and defeats as pervasive and final, to focus on external influences rather than issues under personal control; a reactive trait.

Outlook is an attitude—your overall view of how you see events and the world around you. Few students realize how much this trait affects how well they do in school and in life. Your outlook has a strong impact on how you behave and hence on the level of success you attain in life. For example, it governs how you respond to circumstances and also determines how you manage risks and bounce back from defeat.

In terms of outlook, you can be a pessimist or an optimist. Proactive students are more likely to be optimists; reactive students are more likely to be pessimists.

(Source: Mieke Maas/ The Image Bank.)

Why Some People Are Pessimists While Others Are Optimists

The stress cycle (Figure 3.1) is a variation on the ABC model for thinking first shown in Chapter 1 (Figure 1.8). The process works in the following way:

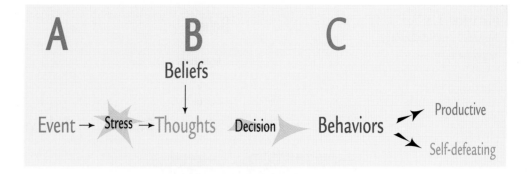

A: You encounter a provocative event or thought.

B: The resulting stress triggers thoughts in your mind that come from the beliefs and values stored in your unconscious mind.

C: You make a decision (automatic) about how to respond to the stress.

Note that a person can choose either positive (productive) or negative (self-defeating thoughts) to relieve the stress caused by the event. Positive responses might include problem solving (looking for answers, as indicated in Figure 3.2), debates, listening to music, journal writing, reading poetry, exercising, or other recreation. Negative responses might include anger (as indicated in Figure 3.3), frustration, rage, fighting, or name calling. When the response to stress takes the form of self-defeating behaviors (Figure 3.4), even more stress is triggered, forming an almost endless cycle.

Why is the response to stress so often negative? Recall that you acquired your system of beliefs through input from many sources: parents, relatives, teachers, mass media, culture, and religious faith. Your personal belief system governs the way you think about yourself as well as about others and the world around you. If you acquired a mostly productive belief system early in life, you will have mostly productive thought patterns. You will then respond to circumstances in ways that are mostly productive. Most people, however, have a mixture of thought patterns that range from productive to self-defeating, and many psychologists contend that the self-defeating patterns often produce stronger responses than the productive patterns.

A repeated pattern of negative responses gives rise to a pessimistic outlook. By contrast, a repeated pattern of positive responses leads to an optimistic outlook. Let's look at each of these outlooks.

FIGURE 3.2

Positive (productive) response to stress.

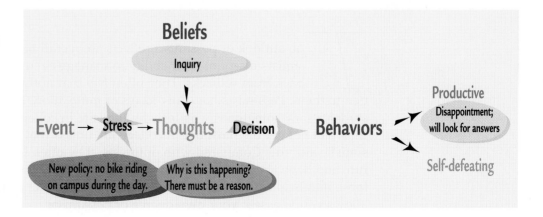

FIGURE 3.3
*Negative (self-defeating)
response to stress.*

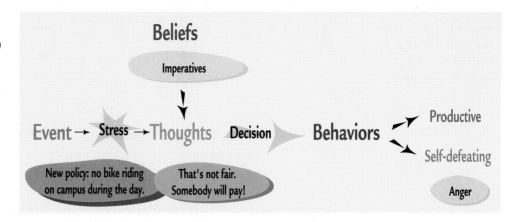

FIGURE 3.4
*Cycle of negative
responses to stress, cre-
ating more stress.*

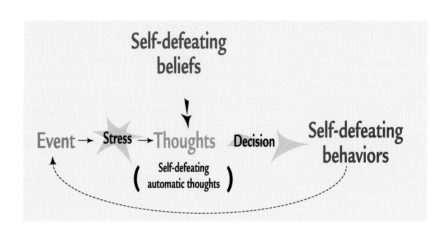

Pessimists and the Consequsences of Pessimism

The outlook of pessimists reflects an overall negative tone. Pessimists discount their ability to manage circumstances or bounce back from setbacks. They often feel that nothing good will happen to them. Pessimists have low levels of motivation. Pessimistic college students may sometimes wonder why they are in college at all. Certainly they will not get the most out of college life unless they change their pessimistic attitude. Compared with optimists, they often learn less, have less fun, and have fewer career options. The sad fact is that pessimists often lapse into helplessness or depression—very serious conditions. Exercise 3.1 allows you to assess your own degree of pessimism.

Assess Your Level of Pessimism

Based on the preceding description of pessimism, assess your present degree of pessimism.

Low   *High*

   1   2   3   4   5   6   7   8   9   10

   Sometimes close friends will influence the outlook of each other. For example, if most of your friends are optimists, you might find it difficult to be a pessimist. If most of your friends are pessimists, you might find it difficult to be optimistic.

HELPLESSNESS

Helplessness is an extreme form of pessimism. This trait is a carryover of the thought patterns developed during childhood and adolescence and tends to get more rigid as time goes by. Individuals who feel helpless believe that nothing they do will make a difference. This is an attitude that causes them to give up easily. They are less likely to vote or involve themselves in social issues. Helpless people often see themselves as victims.

Comparing Your Level of Pessimism with That of Your Closest Friends

How does your degree of pessimism compare with that of your closest friends?

Name of friend	*Low*									*High*
_____	1	2	3	4	5	6	7	8	9	10
_____	1	2	3	4	5	6	7	8	9	10
_____	1	2	3	4	5	6	7	8	9	10
_____	1	2	3	4	5	6	7	8	9	10
_____	1	2	3	4	5	6	7	8	9	10
_____	1	2	3	4	5	6	7	8	9	10

From this activity, you might be able to predict which of your friends has the greatest impact on your own outlook. You can then make some decisions about one way in which you might improve your outlook. For example, if you tend to be pessimistic and want to change your outlook, you might spend more time with your optimistic friends.

DEPRESSION

Depression is the most serious consequence of pessimism and seems more widespread in the United States than at any point in our recent history. Dr. Martin Seligman, an authority on depression, stresses this point in his book, *Learned Optimism:*

> *We are in the middle of an epidemic of depression, one with consequences that, through suicide, takes as many lives as the AIDS epidemic and is more widespread. Severe depression is ten times more prevalent today than it was fifty years ago. It assaults women twice as often as men, and it now strikes a full decade earlier in life on average than it did a generation ago.[2]*

The most disturbing finding is the number of adolescents affected by this ailment. A survey showed that about one third of all youth between the ages of ten and eighteen suffer from some form of depression.

Depressed people have a poor quality of life, which results from the kinds of problems shown here.

- Low confidence levels

- Lethargy

- Poor concentration

- Diminished ability to think

- Sadness

- Feelings of worthlessness and guilt

- Insomnia

(Source: Shackman/ Monkmeyer Press.)

Assessing Signs of Pessimism

I have had the following problems during the last three months (circle the appropriate numbers):

1. Low confidence levels

2. Lethargy

3. Insomnia

4. Inertia

5. Sadness

6. Feelings of worthlessness and guilt

7. Poor concentration

8. Diminished ability to think

9. Loss of appetite

If you checked any of the problems on this list, see if you can recall whether they were fleeting or persisted over a period of days or weeks. If you find that these problems occur often or linger, you might discuss the situation with your counselor.

■ Inertia

■ Loss of appetite

Exercise 3.3 will help you determine whether or not you have experienced effects of pessimism during the past three months.

Optimists and the Benefits of Optimism

Optimists have a different way of thinking about the world and events than pessimists. For example, when they face adverse circumstances, they view them as fleeting. Optimists believe that although certain circumstances are beyond their power to correct, they can control their response to these events.

Most optimists lead happier lives than pessimists do. Optimists often have better health, better family lives, and better social relationships. They often make more money. Optimists are more likely to inspire other people and become strong leaders. Optimism is the prevailing attitude among high achievers.

Contrary to what some people believe, optimists do not always think positive thoughts or assume that things will always turn out all right. True optimists do not ignore negative reality. But they tend to focus on the things they can control and on the positive aspects of a given situation. Actually, they often fail at tasks—but they bounce back. They understand that life is not always fair and that people are not always good. They know that bad things occasionally happen to good people. What they do differently from pessimists is that they deal with issues in a rational, businesslike manner instead of giving in to feelings of helplessness and depression.

The sections that follow expand on the general points made thus far and highlight many more characteristics of optimists. You will notice that we cover some topics in more detail than others, particularly those that closely match the themes of this book. For a broader coverage of outlook, you may wish to read books by psychologists McGinnis and Seligman.[3]

OPTIMISTS RESIST HELPLESSNESS AND DEPRESSION

Life does not always present us with good news. Every person will experience bad events at some point in their lives. Bad events take the form of setbacks, failures, and disappointments. When faced with bad events, some people give up while others persist. The difference lies in how they explain the events to themselves. Table 3.1 illustrates this point. Exercise 3.4 will test your ability to distinguish optimists from pessimists by the language they use to explain events.

By now you should be able to detect the language associated with a particular outlook. Over the next few weeks, record the statements that you make to yourself as you encounter various events. The results might further reveal whether you have an optimistic or pessimistic outlook.

OPTIMISTS FOCUS ON ISSUES UNDER PERSONAL CONTROL

Rachael cannot focus on her classes because of her other problems. One area of concern is what is happening to her on campus (such as money problems and class issues). In addition, her imagination is running wild. She seems to have taken on the world (Figure 3.5).

TABLE 3.1
How Optimists and Pessimists Explain Events to Themselves

PESSIMISTS	OPTIMISTS
*See failure as final	*See failure as temporary
*Think that one failure applies to all situations	*Think that a single failure applies only to a specific situation
*Believe that bad events will always exert control over their lives	*Believe that they have the power to react to bad events in a way that gives them control over their lives
*Blame themselves for the bad things that happen to them, even when they had nothing to do with the cause of the event	*Take responsibility for their own actions but do not blame themselves when they had nothing to do with the cause of a bad event

Optimist or Pessimist?

Place an X in the space to indicate whether the statement reflects the views of an optimist or pessimist. Then use the key to determine how well you can distinguish optimism from pessimism.

STATEMENT	OPTIMIST	PESSIMIST
1. I failed the final; I will never have a career.		
2. I failed the final; I will find a way to overcome this setback.		
3. Some textbooks are better than others.		
4. Textbooks are a waste of money.		
5. Professors lecture too fast.		
6. Professor Chu is a fast but good lecturer.		
7. I lost the election for student body president because my opponent had more support from student groups than I did.		
8. I lost the election for student body president because I'm not good enough for the position.		
9. Professor Garcia seemed unfriendly when I went to his office. I'm not a good enough student for him to spend time with me.		
10. Professor Garcia seemed unfriendly when I went to his office. He was probably just preoccupied with his work during the time I was there.		

Key
O = Optimist; P = Pessimist
1,P; 2,O; 3,O; 4,P; 5,P; 6,O; 7,O; 8,P; 9,P; 10,O

FIGURE 3.5
Student feeling frustrated over a complex set of circumstances.

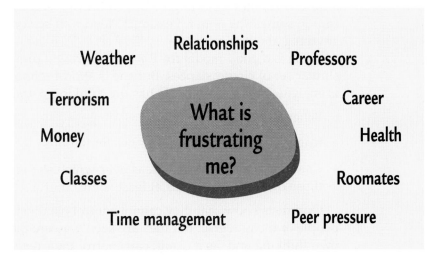

Journal Activity

What would you do in Rachael's situation?

_____

_____

_____

_____

_____

_____

Rachael can see no options and appears to be totally overwhelmed. She is aware that there are counselors on campus, but she believes that they can offer little help to someone in her condition. At this point, Rachael is about ready to quit school altogether. She wishes that she could just drop out of society. Rachael's outlook keeps her from performing well in school, and she also stands a greater chance of getting sick.

Rachael thinks and behaves like most pessimists. They passively accept circumstances and often see themselves as victims. They will often focus on the wrong issues. For example, they often

- Complain about the weather

- Get bogged down because of other peoples' attitudes and behaviors

- Dwell on war, terrorism, and crime in the streets

To say that these are "wrong" issues to focus on does not mean that they are unimportant. The problem is that an individual can do little or nothing about them directly. And when people don't readily see how they can make a difference, they tend to give up. Optimists tend to focus on things they can do something about. Pessimists tend to focus on things they cannot do anything about.

Paula is a good model for Rachael. During a previous year, Paula faced a similar set of circumstances. But she is still in school, an honor student, and is enjoying college life. Paula has the thinking pattern of an optimist. She

- Believes that she has choices

- Knows her options as well as her limitations

- Can distinguish between areas over which she has no control versus those over which she has at least some control.

Optimists know that they cannot control circumstances created by other people or the universe. But they are keenly aware that they can manage their own thinking and, as a result, can control their response to circumstances.

OPTIMISTS TAKE A PROBLEM-SOLVING APPROACH TO CIRCUMSTANCES

When Paula faced a complex situation, she took a problem-solving approach. She saw herself not as a victim but rather as a person with options. She knew that she had the choice to dwell on either productive or self-defeating thoughts (Figures 3.2 and 3.3). First she did a preliminary analysis of the issues. Then she devised and acted on a detailed plan.

Paula learned from her analysis that there are two major groups of issues (Figure 3.6):

A (Issues beyond personal control): This group contains global issues and those involving people and circumstances that the individual cannot directly influence.

B (Issues under personal control): This group contains issues that the individual can directly influence.

Paula made three lists. The first two lists contained issues that were beyond her personal control. The first list pertained to global issues.

- Weather

- Terrorism

- Prejudice

- The world

FIGURE 3.6

Analysis of a complex set of issues.

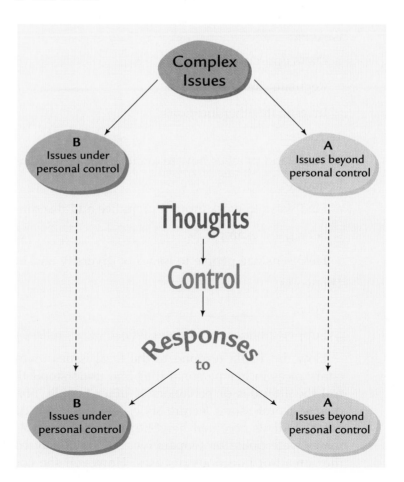

The second pertained to people and circumstances in her personal life (local issues).

- Family
- Professors
- Peer pressure
- Roommates
- Illness and disease

The third list was of issues under her personal control.

- Money
- Classes
- Assignments
- Time management

Next, Paula thought about how she could respond to these issues. Even in the situations that were beyond her control, she could see that she was not helpless. She could adjust to the weather. She could learn how to minimize her exposure to terrorism. She could help curtail injustices resulting from prejudice. Rather than take on the whole world as a concern, she could support U.S. political candidates who supported her views. She could also seek out opportunities, starting locally, where she could use her time and talents to contribute to a better world. Here are Paula's responses to the global issues.

Weather:

- Dress appropriately.
- Regulate climate controls.
- Investigate other locations.

Terrorism:

- Learn and practice how to avoid hazardous situations.

Prejudice:

- Find ways to work around prejudice and discrimination.
- Set a good example.
- Help sensitize people to issues of diversity and tolerance.

The world:

- Vote.
- Support political candidates whose views reflect your own.

How did Paula respond to the local issues involving people and circumstances in her personal life? She understood that she could not control the attitudes or behaviors of other people. For example, she could not dictate a professor's lecture style. She could not directly control whether other students accepted her. She could not control whether her roommates were polite or cooperative. She obviously could not directly halt the spread of infectious diseases. However, she could adapt herself to the professor's lecture style. She could be friendly to other students. She could set a good example for her roommates. She could practice good sanitation. The following list shows Paula's responses to the local issues (people and circumstances in her personal life).

People:

- Choose how to react to the attitudes and behaviors of other people.

- Choose friends selectively.

- Seek win-win situations with roommates (see Chapter 7).

- Make strong efforts to resist peer pressure.

Circumstances:

- Focus on disease prevention.

Paula did not ignore the Group A issues, but she spent most of her time of Group B issues, the ones that she could directly influence. Yet even Group B issues seemed complex. Paula used her problem-solving skills to help her avoid decision-making paralysis. On Group B issues, she chose to establish priorities, set goals, take action, and then follow through (Figure 3.7).

Paula made a list of specific tasks, priorities, and goals. (We will cover goal setting in Chapter 4.)

Tasks:

- Solve money problems.

- Improve time-management skills.

- Complete assignments.

- Select classes.

FIGURE 3.7
Steps in the identification and completion of tasks.

Priorities:

1. Complete assignments.

2. Solve money problems.

3. Select classes for next semester.

4. Improve Time-management skills.

Goals:

- Solve Priority 1 by February 15.

- Solve Priority 2 by May 30.

- Solve Priority 3 by April 1.

- Solve Priority 4 by September 1.

First, Paula spent most of her time on Priority 1, completing her school assignments.

Action:

- Identify all assignments and due dates.

- Estimate time required for each assignment.

- Set priorities based on due dates.

Follow-Through:

- Turn in assignments.

- Summarize lessons learned.

- Make plans to avoid getting behind again.

Next she chose to address her money problems, Priority 2. These money problems arose because of increases in fees, book prices, rent, and car repairs. After planning her budget for the year, Paula found that she had a $2,000 deficit.

Action:

- Make analysis of how to overcome deficit spending.

- Make evaluation of how each option affects various goals.

- Hold discussion with counselor.

- Make decision.

Follow-Through:

- Register with student employment office.

- Check ads in newspapers.

- Respond to ads.

- Show up for interviews when called.

- Accept a job.

Paula weighed various options for making up the deficit. Her list of options included the following: part-time work, alternate transportation, buying used books, gifts from parents, cutbacks on food, cutbacks on entertainment and recreation, and new loans. Paula also weighed how each option would affect her various goals—academic, personal, and social. Then she assessed the long-term financial impact of each option. Finally, she assessed the probable impact of each decision on her overall state of health.

Paula's next step was to discuss her plans with a counselor. She decided that she would seek part-time work. She followed through with her plans and was successful in getting a job.

After handling Priority 2, Paula took on Priority 3, selecting her classes for the next semester. One of the major items in this category was to assess the progress toward her degree. This step would help her avoid any unpleasant surprises. Another action item was to check with her professors about each course. This was an important first step in getting to know her professors. Also, a discussion with her professors would guide her in how to focus her time and energy for each course.

Another important follow-through step was to find out what assignments each course would require. Would there be term papers due and when? Did the course require problem sets? Were sections optional or required? She was careful to avoid taking too many difficult courses at the same time.

Action:

- Get copy of catalog.
- Make a degree check.
- Consult with academic advisor.
- Consult with professors to discuss their expectations.
- Balance courses with respect to levels of difficulty.
- Register for classes.

Follow-Through:

- Purchase books and syllabi.
- Attend classes.
- Preview assignments.

Paula's fourth priority was to improve her time-management skills. Her most important task here was to determine how she was spending her time. How much time was she devoting to academic matters? How much time was she devoting to social life and recreation? After this analysis she explored options for making better use of her time. These options included reading certain books, attending certain seminars, and viewing and listening to certain videotapes and audiotapes. She also searched for good role models among the faculty and staff. She decided that she would attend a workshop offered in the Student Learning Center.

Action:

- Conduct self-analysis.
- Explore possible solutions.

Follow-Through:

- Register for workshop.

- Attend workshop.

- Practice lessons learned.

We can predict that Rachael's outlook and performance would improve if she, like Paula, applied a problem-solving approach to her situation.

Paula is also a good role model for Blaine. Blaine's situation is like that of many ethnic minority students. He is a sophomore and majors in economics. He likes his classes but thinks that the campus is hostile to him. Blaine never participates in class or visits his professors. He studies alone and thinks teaching-assistant (TA) sections are a waste of time. He often thinks that people are watching him. He is not a member of any club or organization because he feels that he would not be accepted. Blaine's grades are average. He would like to improve but does not know how to do so. He is aware of academic support programs on campus, but he avoids these services because he does not want people to think that he is academically inferior. Blaine feels very lonely and isolated; he plans to transfer to another school that he feels is more receptive to students like him.

● ● ● ● ● ● EXERCISE 3.5

Applying a Problem-Solving Approach

1. List the issues involved in Blaine's situation. Place an X in the space to indicate whether each issue is under personal control or beyond personal control.

ISSUE	UNDER PERSONAL CONTROL	BEYOND PERSONAL CONTROL

2. List and assign a priority for each task that will help Blaine overcome or work around his concerns.

TASK	PRIORITY

3. Describe the action and follow-through steps associated with the tasks.

ACTION	FOLLOW THROUGH

Blaine's situation lends itself to a problem-solving approach. For Exercise 3.5, assume that you are Blaine's counselor and your task is to help him devise a plan to deal with his concerns.

In summary, these examples highlight a major difference in the way people think about events. Pessimists give up when they cannot readily see how they can affect the event; optimists always see options. Optimists take direct action on issues that they can control. They choose productive responses to issues beyond their control.

OPTIMISTS BOUNCE BACK FROM SETBACKS

Consider this situation. Rae flunked her Music Theory midterm and is very upset over the potential consequences. Rae fears that this might be the end of her career. Maybe she's right, but what if she's wrong? Is she really a failure? Is there anything unusual about Rae's case?

Like Rae, many students encounter setbacks as they pursue their goals. Setbacks show up as mistakes, failures, or miscalculations. When setbacks happen, many students wallow in self-pity or self-recriminations. Perhaps you have heard the following expressions many times: "If only I had studied harder for the midterm. . . . I should have known better than to wait until the last minute to study for the final. . . . How stupid of me, why did I join the sorority when I had such a heavy course-load?"

If you have difficulty in bouncing back from setbacks, you might find it helpful to complete Exercise 3.6.

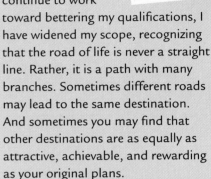

Juliette Zelada

As I come from a business-oriented family of accountants and office administrators, my choice of a career in medicine was an oddity. My dream was to become a primary-care physician and practice in developing countries or underserved areas. I had obtained a bachelor's degree in biology, participated in research, and was involved in numerous extracurricular activities. In my mind, I was ready for medical school. But the many rejection letters from medical schools that followed dampened my dream. I was turned away from every medical school to which I had applied.

This is where a positive outlook came into play. Recognizing the need for options, I reevaluated my goals and made modifications. I realized that in order to gain admittance into a medical school, I needed to improve my qualifications. My approach was simple: I would use the rejections to my benefit. By identifying what went wrong, I knew how to make the needed corrections. I viewed these rejections as a transient setback that could be altered.

I now am in a post-baccalaureate program that has been instrumental in reshaping my candidacy. My course grades and medical school admissions test scores have improved. Although I continue to work toward bettering my qualifications, I have widened my scope, recognizing that the road of life is never a straight line. Rather, it is a path with many branches. Sometimes different roads may lead to the same destination. And sometimes you may find that other destinations are as equally as attractive, achievable, and rewarding as your original plans.

Maintaining a positive outlook enables me to work through challenges. Instead of blaming others for my mishaps, I identify my weaknesses and focus on my strengths. In this way, I am able to maintain the motivation and perseverance to carry me through the defeats and into victory. Giving myself credit and feeling good about the incremental improvements I am making has provided me with a greater enthusiasm to tackle the more challenging decisions I need to make.

OPTIMISTS MAINTAIN A HIGH LEVEL OF ENTHUSIASM

Before you read further, complete Exercise 3.7.

You might wonder how you could increase your enthusiasm from its present level. Most of the research on this subject points to two approaches:

1. *Act enthusiastic.* In this case, your behavior might need to precede your thinking. In other words, you might need to act more enthusiastic than you are feeling. For example, you can become a more enthusiastic student by doing the following:

   ■ Spend more time preparing for lectures.

   ■ Ask more questions.

How Much Do You Worry?

Estimate the amount of time you devote to worrying about each type of issue listed here.

TYPES OF ISSUES	PERCENTAGE OF TIME PER WEEK SPENT WORRYING ABOUT THIS ISSUE
Things that were likely never to happen	
Past decisions that could not be changed	
Criticism from others that didn't matter anyway	
Personal health issues (that you were already doing your best to protect against)	
Legitimate causes for worry	

Compare your results with those of a chronic worrier as shown next.

TYPES OF ISSUES	PERCENTAGE OF TIME SPENT WORRYING ABOUT THIS ISSUE
Things that were likely never to happen	40%
Past decisions that could not be changed	30%
Criticism from others that didn't matter anyway	12%
Personal health issues (which he was already doing his best to protect against)	10%
Legitimate causes for worry	8%

Source: From *The Power of Optimism* by Alan Loy McGinnis. Copyright © 1990 by Alan Loy McGinnis. Reprinted by permission of Harper Collins Publishers, Inc.

The chronic worrier found that there was no firm basis for 92 percent of the issues that he was worrying about. How do your results compare? Perhaps optimists can bounce back so quickly because they know where to devote their time and energy.

- Be more thorough in your review of the material.

- Attend TA sessions and the professor's office hours on a frequent basis.

2. *Connect with enthusiastic people.* Spend more time with people who act in ways that reflect their passion for what they believe.

This advice might seem strange unless you recall how the mind works. Remember that the mind stores both positive and negative habits. If you act enthusiastic long enough, you mind will cause you to act in concert with the new habit. When you spend time with enthusiastic people, you may become more like them. You can catch enthusiasm as easily as you can catch a cold.

(Source: Mark Scott/FPG International.)

Which Type of Person Would You Choose?

The following questions ask you to choose between two different types of individuals based on the characteristics indicated. Circle a or b to indicate your choice for each question.

1. Which student would you prefer to have in your study group?

   a. Shows little interest in learning; does not seem to get much out of her courses or college life in general

   b. Shows strong interest in her courses and seems excited about student life and her prospects for the future

2. Which professor would capture your interest and be the better role model for you?

   a. Lectures in a dry, monotone voice; gives the impression of wanting to be somewhere else; relies on outdated information; has a poor sense of humor; discourages questions; shows little interest in students in or out of the classroom

   b. Delivers lectures with vigor; stays current in his field; mixes serious content with occasional humor; draws parallels between academic and real-life situations; gives the impression that he enjoys doing what he's doing when he is doing it; shows obvious signs of a keen interest in student growth and development

3. Which academic administrator (e.g., vice-president, dean, provost, etc.) would more likely gain your attention and respect?

   a. Makes no efforts to interact with students outside of her office; is more fixed on her role as a manager than as an educator; shows little awareness of the complexities of the campus and student life

   b. Occasionally chats with students on campus; displays broad knowledge of campus issues and their impact on students; enjoys her work; is concerned about her role in helping students make the most of their lives

4. Which politician would you more likely support?

   a. Demonstrates a mundane approach to the position; has a superficial knowledge of the issues; avoids interaction with the public

   b. Communicates a bold vision for the future; has a broad knowledge of the issues; is passionate about his beliefs; thrives on interaction with the public

5. Which singer would you find more appealing?

   a. Has good technical skills but gives a listless performance

   b. Has good technical skills and gives vibrant performance

If you circled b in each case, you respond well to people who show enthusiasm. You are not alone! Many people would respond to this exercise in the way that you did. Enthusiasm is about excitement, energy, zest, and passion for what one does and believes. People with high levels of enthusiasm often create a wake that extends far beyond their own interests or concerns. This exercise makes it easy to see why optimists make good leaders. Optimists exude enthusiasm; enthusiasm inspires people and holds their attention.

Journal Activity

Devise a personal plan for how you will increase your level of enthusiasm.

_____

_____

_____

_____

_____

_____

OPTIMISTS CONNECT WITH PEOPLE

Optimists embrace opportunities that help them form strong networks of social support. They maintain firm ties with their families and value the time they spend with their friends. Optimists view relationships both in terms of what they can gain and what they can give.

■ PERSONAL GAIN

Support networks help a person grow and adjust to the challenges of life. When a person knows that others care about him, he gains confidence in his abilities, has higher self-esteem, and is more likely to perform at his best.

Many studies confirm the health benefits of social support networks.[4] For example, people who undergo stressful events such as anxiety, death of loved ones, job loss, or frequent changes tend to be more susceptible to disease. During times of stress, people who use their social networks suffer fewer ill effects than those who withdraw and spend most of their time alone.

■ GIVING TO OTHERS

Many optimists tend to benefit more from what they give to others than from the support that they receive. The feeling that they can help improve the lives of others heightens their own self-esteem and motivation. During her first year of college, Sonya chose to tutor four struggling students at an inner-city school. She continued to help the students on weekends until she finished college. The results four years later were as follows:

■ Each of the four students received an offer from the college of his or her choice.

(Source: Bob Daemrich/The Image Works.)

- One of the students finished at the top of his class.

- All four students gave Sonya the credit for having the strongest impact on their academic development.

During her own college career, Sonya always performed at her best because she knew that her four tutees were counting on her. She wanted to be a good role model for them. Whenever she had her own tough times, Sonya had more of an incentive to persist because she wanted to be a good role model for her students. Sonya now believes that what she did for the four high school students made more of a difference in her own success than any other factor.

OPTIMISTS TAKE RATIONAL RISKS

All students face some risky situations while they are in college. Their responses can have a strong impact on their success and well being. For example, Rory is struggling in his economics course but he is afraid to visit with the professor. He feels intimidated by someone who he thinks knows more than he does. In addition, a visit with the professor might expose some of his weaknesses, making him feel even less confident about his abilities. The bottom line is that Rory sees visiting with professors as a risk that he should avoid; he does not go.

Any significant accomplishment in life involves taking risks. Optimists and pessimists differ in their response to risks. Pessimists either take risks indiscriminately or try to avoid them altogether. Optimists evaluate risks in terms of the costs versus the benefits.

Professor James Adams, author of *Conceptual Blockbusting,* advises readers to use a worst-case scenario approach to assessing risks.[5] Here are the steps:

1. Write down the positive and negative consequences of a particular course of action.

2. Through mental rehearsal, imagine the worst thing that could possibly happen. After this exercise, ask yourself, "Could I cope with this worst case if it happened? If so, how would I cope?"

3. If you decide that you can live with the worst possible outcome, then proceed with confidence as if no risk existed.

4. On the other hand, if the most negative outcome is too severe, then eliminate that particular course of action from consideration.

On one occasion, Peter had the same problem as Rory. But Peter, an optimist, used a cost-benefit analysis (similar to Professor Adam's worst-case scenario approach) to sort out his options. He made two columns: In one he wrote down what it would cost him if he visited the instructor. In the other he listed what benefits he might receive if he went. Peter looked at the costs and did not see anything life-threatening. On the other hand, he saw many potential benefits in the other column. He chose to visit his instructor.

Use Exercise 3.8 to describe your own feelings about visiting instructors during office hours. Now do another such cost-benefit analysis in Exercise 3.9.

● ● ● ● ● ●●EXERCISE 3.8

Visiting Your Instructors: The Costs and the Benefits

In the columns provided, write down what you believe would be the costs versus the benefits of going to visit an instructor.

COSTS	BENEFITS

Cost vs. Benefit Analysis

During one quarter you and Lan took the same course in American History. The major assignment was to read and turn in a written report on seven books. The report was due before the end of the quarter. Two days before the deadline, Lan approached you in a state of panic. She had procrastinated throughout the quarter and had not done the assignment. Lan wanted to borrow your report for some ideas and would give you $100 for this favor.

What would you do and why? Would you see the risk in this case as rational or irrational? Write down the costs versus the benefits of the risks involved.

COSTS	BENEFITS

Lan's behavior in Exercise 3.9 raises serious issues relative to honesty and integrity. But another issue relevant to the present topic is *procrastination*. Perhaps all people have to deal with this problem to some extent. For example, most students delay doing their assignments and put off studying for exams until the last minute. The key to handling procrastination is to treat it as a risk. Then you can subject the risk to a cost-benefit analysis and determine whether or not it is a rational risk. Exercise 3.9 will help you grasp this point.

Another student who had to determine whether an activity would be a rational risk is Pam. Pam is a premed student who has taken most of the required courses but has not yet done any volunteer work. For one project she decided to help out in a homeless shelter on weekends and during the summer. She thought of three benefits of this plan. For example, working in a homeless shelter would

1. Demonstrate how much she cares about people

2. Help resolve a major social problem

3. Strengthen her application to medical school

Pam met with the premed advisor to discuss her plans. During the interview the advisor told her the bad news, or the costs. The incidence of tuberculosis (TB) is high among the homeless; therefore, Pam would be at high

Procrastination: What Are the Costs and the Benefits?

Compare the costs with the benefits of procrastination. For example, what impact will this habit have on your academic performance, health, and relationships?

COSTS	BENEFITS

risk for infection. Pam wanted to know more about this disease so that she could make an informed decision. Her advisor pointed out several sources on campus that helped her get more information. The following list highlights what she found:

- TB is a major worldwide health problem.
- About one third of the world's population is infected with TB.
- There are about 8 million new cases of TB each year.
- About 3 million people die each year from this disease.
- TB has reemerged as a major problem in western societies.
- The rate of TB is high among the poor, malnourished, and homeless, as well as among people who have weak immune systems.
- Long-term exposure increases the risk for TB.
- A cure for TB requires taking drugs for several months to over a year.
- Many strains of the bacterium are now resistant to the drugs used to kill them.

Pam paid close attention to one point. Long-term exposure does increase the risk for infection. But infection is not the same as the disease, and only 3 percent to 5 percent of infected people ever get the disease.

Journal Activity

Put yourself in Pam's situation. How would you decide what to do? What would you do?

_____

_____

_____

_____

_____

_____

OPTIMISTS VALUE OPPORTUNITIES TO GROW AND REFRESH THEMSELVES

You will not learn everything you need to know in college. In addition, much of what you learn will be obsolete within a few months or years. Optimists are self-learners who seek to extend their knowledge beyond the concepts covered in their classes. Lifelong learning is second nature to optimists. They also learn broadly, on the assumption that they never know for sure what they will need in life, either for themselves or to help others. Also, optimistic students are more likely to interact with and learn from students with diverse backgrounds.

All work and no play leads to a very dull life and often causes early burnout. Optimists sense and routinely address this point in two major ways. First, they look for ways to build fun into their work. They assume that there is more than one way to accomplish a task, so that they will look for the way that provides the greatest stimulation for them. Second, optimists set aside time to relax and have fun—sometimes by themselves and at other times with friends. Optimists find ways to enrich their lives, such as through music or the other arts, frequent contacts with nature, or other recreational activities. In addition, optimists are more likely to live by sound values, tend to their spiritual needs, and maintain good health practices.

In other words, optimists try to arrange a well-balanced life for themselves, with opportunities to grow and to refresh themselves. Exercise 3.11 will help you rate yourself on how well you are maintaining balance in your life as you attend college. Remember, there is no real conflict between preparing for a career and having a satisfying life.

Checklist for Balancing Your Life

Place an X in the boxes that indicate your responses to the questions asked.

HOW OFTEN DO YOU:	NEVER	RARELY	SOMETIMES	OFTEN
Exercise?				
Go to a movie?				
Attend a play?				
Attend a place of worship?				
Visit a park?				
Meditate or set aside some quiet time to think and reflect?				
Attend a lecture outside your field of interest?				
Read an unassigned book?				

Journal Activity

Keep a record of major lessons learned each day from various sources.

Date	Source	Lessons Learned
	Classes	
	Contacts with people	
	Books	
	Communications media	
	Other source:	
	Other source:	

Keep in mind the point that you can learn *something* from every experience that you have.

How to Move from Pessimism to Optimism

*P*essimists have many thinking problems that cause them to react in the manner that they do. These problems may result from self-defeating values or thinking errors (see Chapter 2 for descriptions and examples).

Examples of the relevant self-defeating values are

- *Immediate return:* unwillingness to put in the work in advance and wait for the results over the long term

- *Complacency, apathy:* unwillingness to change and grow

- *Passivity:* lack of initiative

- *Impatience:* hastiness; unwillingness to wait

Examples of the relevant thinking errors involved are

- *All-or-nothing thinking:* thinking in black-or-white, win-or-lose terms

- *Magnification or minimization:* making a mountain out of a molehill

- *Overgeneralization:* applying one or a few events to all situations

- *Jumping to conclusions:* attempting mind reading; trying to predict the future

- *Imperative thinking:* making demands or inflexible dictates

Remember, your outlook is an attitude, and attitudes stem from clusters of beliefs. Therefore, changing your beliefs will change your attitude. For example, changing self-defeating beliefs to productive beliefs will change a pessimistic attitude to a productive attitude such as optimism (compare Figures 3.8 and 3.9).

If you want to improve your attitude, you can use the Change Formula presented in Chapter 2 (Figure 2.5), a condensed version of which appears in Figure 3.10.

FIGURE 3.8
Origin of optimism and its effect on thoughts and behaviors.

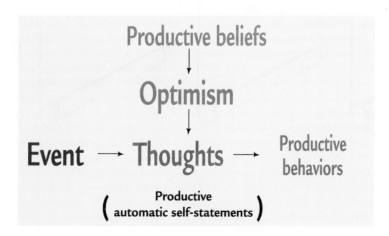

FIGURE 3.9

*Origin of pessimism and
its effect on thoughts
and behaviors.*

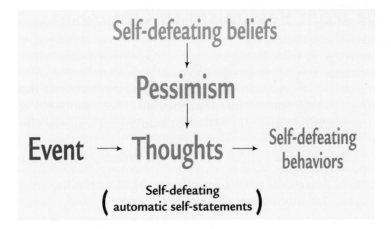

In this process, you select a remedy (S) to change the self-defeating beliefs or values to productive beliefs or values that result in an optimistic attitude and thereby productive thoughts and behaviors. A condensed version of the remedies given in Chapter 2 appears in Figure 3.11.

Figure 3.12 shows how the process works for self-defeating beliefs. You can use the same process for self-defeating values. Figure 3.13 gives an example of a possible effect on life outcomes from changing one's attitude from pessimistic to optimistic.

When you apply the Change Formula consistently to your own concerns, you will gain more confidence in your ability to

1. Resist helplessness and depression

2. Focus on issues under your personal control

3. Take a problem-solving approach to complex circumstances

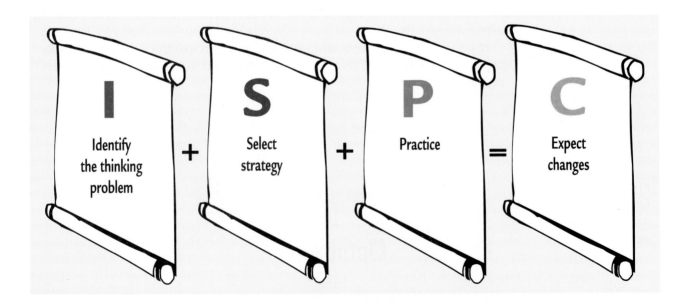

FIGURE 3.10

*Condensed version of
Change Formula.*

FIGURE 3.11

Remedies for correcting thinking problems.

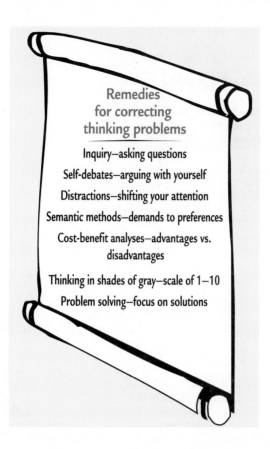

Remedies
for correcting
thinking problems

Inquiry—asking questions

Self-debates—arguing with yourself

Distractions—shifting your attention

Semantic methods—demands to preferences

Cost-benefit analyses—advantages vs.
disadvantages

Thinking in shades of gray—scale of 1–10

Problem solving—focus on solutions

4. Bounce back from setbacks

5. Maintain high levels of enthusiasm

6. Connect with people

7. Take rational risks

8. Value opportunities to grow and refresh yourself

Example 3.1 shows the approach one student took to change the thought pattern that led her toward helplessness. Use this example as a guide in working through Exercises 3.11 and 3.12.

FIGURE 3.12

Changing self-defeating to productive beliefs leads to optimism and productive thoughts and behaviors.

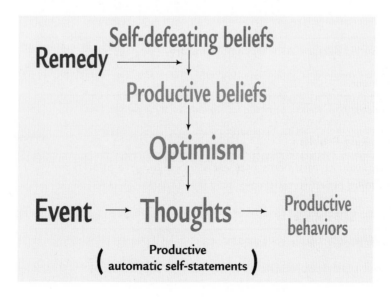

Remedy → Self-defeating beliefs ↓

Productive beliefs
↓
Optimism
↓
Event → Thoughts → Productive behaviors

(Productive automatic self-statements)

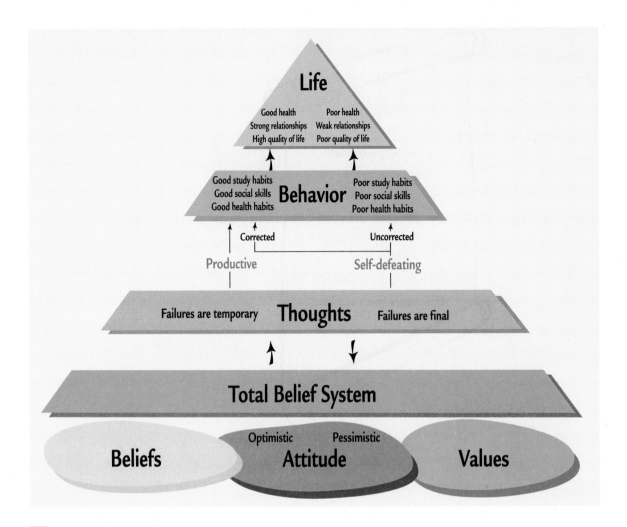

FIGURE 3.13

Possible effect on life outcomes by changing attitudes.

EXAMPLE 3.1

Event

Derek is anxious over his performance on the final exam

Derek's Self-Statement

I should have known better than to wait until the last minute to study for the final.

(I) Identify the Thinking Problem

Self-defeating values: valuing mediocrity over excellence; failing to appreciate the value of overcoming procrastination

(S) Select a Remedy—Self-debate

Q. Why did I wait until the last minute, anyway?

A. No particular reason. I just procrastinated.

EXAMPLE 3.1 *(continued)*

Q. Is there a law that says that I have to procrastinate?

A. No. There is no such law.

Q. Is there something in my genes that make me procrastinate?

A. No. There is no evidence that procrastination is inherited.

Q. Is there anything that I can do about procrastination?

A. Yes. One approach is to weigh the cost of procrastination against the benefits of getting the task done. Another approach is to choose to stay current. I can review notes after each class and at prescribed periods during the semester. I can make up and take practice exams.

Q. What have I learned from this experience?

A. I do not have to procrastinate. It is a choice.

(C) Productive Values

Excellence over mediocrity; understands the pitfalls of procrastination

Productive Self-Statement

I value academic excellence. I will make it a priority to stay current in my classes throughout the semester.

(P) Practice

Rehearse the remedy and the productive self-statement.

● ● ● ● ● ●EXERCISE 3.12

Applying the Change Formula to Habits of Thought

Fill in the blanks with the missing information, using Example 3.9 a a guide.

Event

Tyrone is thinking about one of his decisions

Tyrone's Self-Statement

How stupid of me. Why did I join the fraternity when I had such a heavy coarse-load?

(I) Identify the Thinking Problem

_____

(S) Select a Remedy

_____

_____

_____

(continued)

_____

_____

_____

_____

_____

_____

(C) Production Beliefs/Values

_____

_____

Tyrone's Productive Self-Statement

_____

_____

(P) Practice

Rehearse the remedy and the productive self-statement.

● ● ● ● ● ●EXERCISE 3.13

Applying the Change Formula to a Pessimistic Outlook

Fill in the blanks with the missing information, using Example 3.9 as a guide.

Event

Doreen is worried about her future.

Doreen's Self-Statement

I want to be a writer, but my career is falling apart. I'm having trouble with English Composition classes. It seems to me that there are too many writers and too few opportunities.

(I) Identify the Thinking Problem

_____

_____

(S) Select a Remedy

_____

_____

_____

_____

_____

_____

_____

_____

_____

_____

_____

_____

_____

_____

(C) Productive Beliefs/Values

_____

_____

Doreen's Productive Self-Statement

_____

_____

(P) Practice

Rehearse the remedy and the productive self-statement.

Journal Activity

Based on your self-assessment for outlook, identify and correct the thinking problems responsible for any degree of pessimism in your outlook.

_____

_____

_____

_____

_____

_____

CHAPTER SUMMARY

How do you respond to the circumstances you face in life? Are you a pessimist or an optimist? Do you see yourself as a victim or as one who has choices? Pessimists tend to see themselves as victims. Optimists focus on issues that they can do something about and work around the rest. Optimism is the hallmark of proactivity. If you want to increase your degree of proactivity, find ways to be more optimistic. Use the examples in this book as your guide.

NOTES

1. Excerpts from *The Power of Optimism* by Alan Loy McGinnis. Copyright © 1990 by Alan Loy McGinnis. Reprinted by permission of Harper Collins Publishers, Inc.

2. From *Learned Optimism* by Martin E.P. Seligman. Copyright © 1991 by Martin E.P. Seligman. Reprinted by permission of Alfred A. Knopf Inc.

3. McGinnis: *The Power of Optimism.*

4. J. G. Rabkin and E. L. Struening: "Life Events, Stress, and Illness," *Science* 194 (1976): 1013–1020, and I. G. Sarason, and B. R. Sarason: "Life Change, Social Support, Coping, and Health," in R. M. Kaplan and M. H. Criqui (eds.): *Behavioral Epidemiology and Disease Prevention* (New York: Plenum Press, 1983), pp. 219–236.

5. Adapted from J.L. Adams, *Conceptual Blockbusting*, pp. 43–45. Copyright © 1986 by James L. Adams. Reprinted by permission of Addison Wesley Longman.

PRE-CHAPTER SELF-ASSESSMENT

Read each statement and circle the number that best reflects your response.

NEVER								ALWAYS	
1	*2*	*3*	*4*	*5*	*6*	*7*	*8*	*9*	*10*

1. I feel that I have a high degree of control over my life.

   1   2   3   4   5   6   7   8   9   10

2. I feel that I am good at completing tasks.

   1   2   3   4   5   6   7   8   9   10

3. I have people in my life whom I love and care about.

   1   2   3   4   5   6   7   8   9   10

4. I have people in my life who love and care about me.

   1   2   3   4   5   6   7   8   9   10

5. I feel that I have a clear sense of what I think is important in my life.

   1   2   3   4   5   6   7   8   9   10

6. I feel that I know what I stand for and what I will fight for.

   1   2   3   4   5   6   7   8   9   10

7. I feel that the world will be a better place because of my contributions.

   1   2   3   4   5   6   7   8   9   10

8. I have a list of things that I intend to achieve by a certain date.

   1   2   3   4   5   6   7   8   9   10

9. I feel that I have a high level of enthusiasm for learning.

   1   2   3   4   5   6   7   8   9   10

10. I form mental pictures of what I want to do and achieve in life.

    1   2   3   4   5   6   7   8   9   10

11. I make sacrifices so that I can achieve my goals.

    1   2   3   4   5   6   7   8   9   10

12. My values—the things I think are important—do not conflict with my goals—what I want to achieve in life.

    1   2   3   4   5   6   7   8   9   10

13. I bounce back quickly when I don't achieve my goals.

    1   2   3   4   5   6   7   8   9   10

14. I can identify and correct thinking problems that hinder my performance.

    1   2   3   4   5   6   7   8   9   10

Determine your relative degree of proactivity for this trait by using the following formula:

Percent Proactivity = Sum of Circled Numbers ÷ 140 × 100

(Note that 140 is the maximum sum possible. It would result in a score of 100 percent.)

Percent Proactivity = _____

For example, if you checked 5 for each question, your score would be

Percent proactivity for Performance = 70/140 × 100 = 50

"The differences between peak performers and their less productive co-workers are much smaller than most people think—extraordinary achievers are ordinary people who have found ways to make a major impact."

Charles Garfield[1]

Performance: How to Make the Most of Your Abilities

THIS CHAPTER PROPOSES a model for high performance. The central theme is that high performance stems from self-motivation. Thus, students achieve more when they take responsibility for their own motivation. Self-motivation occurs only when a person find ways to (1) be in control of his life, (2) be effective, and (3) feel connected to others. An individual fulfills these requirements when she does the following: (1) defines her values, (2) decides on a mission, and (3) sets goals.

This chapter can provide you with the skills to motivate yourself. You will learn how to

- Define your values

- Formulate a mission statement

- Set and follow through on goals

- Identify and correct any thinking problems that hinder high performance

competence   goals   mission   self-motivation
connectedness   high performance   self-determination

Jan and Earl want to do well in school, but they put forth little effort. They lack purpose and direction in their lives. Jan and Earl have poor study habits, lack focus, procrastinate, and make excuses. They would rather have a good time with their friends than study for exams.

Ray and Dee take three classes with Jan and Earl, but they have little else in common with them. Ray and Dee act as if they know

- Where they are going
- Why they want to go there
- How they are going to get there
- When they are going to get there
- What they are going to do after they get there

Self-motivation: finding ways to satisfy one's own needs of the mind rather than relying on external influences.

High performance: making the most of one's talents and abilities in the pursuit of task opportunities; putting forth one's best efforts.

Ray and Dee are among the leaders in their classes. What accounts for the differences between these two pairs of students? Ray's and Dee's success results from having high levels of self-motivation. Self-motivation is a key factor in high performance, or making the most of one's talents and abilities. All students can achieve more when they take steps to motivate themselves. This chapter dissects the components of self-motivation to show how you can magnify this vital trait in yourself.

A Model for High Performance

Mission: that which defines a person's highest aspirations; a personal creed or constitution.

Goals: the practical means for working toward and achieving a mission.

The high-performance model shown in Figure 4.1 illustrates how values, mission, and goals affect self-motivation and thus high performance. Students achieve more when they motivate themselves and take responsibility for their own actions. Self-motivation occurs when a person finds ways to take control of her actions and choices, feels that she can accomplish meaningful tasks, and is able to maintain solid connections with other people.

Values, mission, and goals are the foundation for high performance. As discussed in Chapters 1 and 2, each person has certain values. Values form the basis for a person's mission, which defines his highest aspirations. In the process of fulfilling his mission, a person needs to set goals. Goals, then, become the practical means for working toward and achieving the mission. To clarify these terms, let's look at an example of a list of values written by a student:

- *I want to fully develop and apply my natural skills, talents, and abilities.*
- *Recognizing the worth and potential of every human being is important to me.*

FIGURE 4.1
A model for high performance.

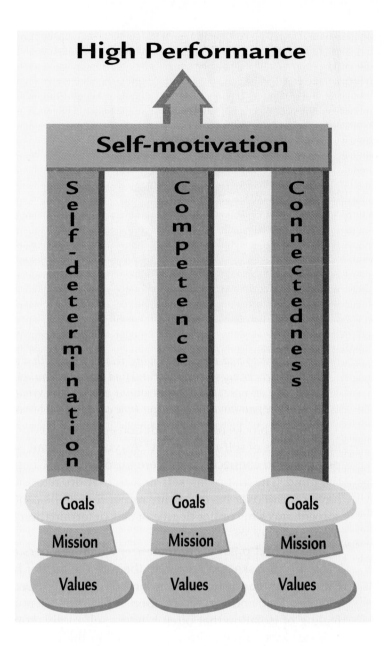

- *Working hard and working smart are important to me because they are essential for success in life.*
- *Making the world a better place to live is important to me.*
- *I want to constantly mature in the spiritual, emotional, and intellectual aspects of my life.*

This student's mission statement, based on her values is as follows:

My mission is to help make the world a better place by improving the lives of people. To fulfill my mission, I will

- *Fully develop my skills, talents, and abilities*
- *Maintain balance in my life by attending to my spiritual, emotional, and intellectual needs*
- *Use my talents and abilities to help people help themselves*

Her goals to propel her toward her mission are as follows:

- *Complete my college degree within five years*
- *Form and maintain friendships with others who challenge me to be a better person*

- *Develop and nurture a loving relationship with a single partner*
- *Discover my spiritual self and find a practical outlet for this side of my life*
- *Pay off my student loans within five years of graduation*
- *Give four hours of volunteer time every month to a cause in my community*

All three blocks of the foundation—values, mission, and goals—contribute to the pillars of self-motivation.[2] As you may recall, self-determination, competence, and connectedness were introduced in Chapter 1 as three needs of the mind. The first pillar, **self-determination,** refers to a person's need to have control over his or her life rather than to be controlled by others. A person enhances his or her degree of self-determination through sound judgment and choices.

The second pillar is **competence,** which is a person's ability to take on meaningful tasks and complete them to the best of his or her ability. The third pillar, **connectedness,** refers to a person's need to relate to other people with love and caring. Relationships with others help a person avoid the feeling of isolation that often hinders self-motivation. The sections that follow describe in detail how each block of the foundation supports the pillars of self-motivation.

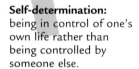

Self-determination:
being in control of one's
own life rather than
being controlled by
someone else.

Competence: the ability
to take on tasks and
complete them to the
best of one's ability.

Connectedness: relating
to other people with
love and caring.

HOW VALUES CONTRIBUTE TO PILLARS OF SELF-MOTIVATION

Values contribute to the pillars of self-motivation by doing the following:

1. Fostering the sound choices and behaviors that determine the degree of one's self-determination

2. Providing the enthusiasm that causes a person to do a better job and gain competence

3. Fostering the sound choices and behaviors that determine how one connects with others

Table 4.1 illustrates these points for a student who has productive values.

VALUES	Self-Determination (control over one's life)	Competence (ability to do a job well)	Connectedness (relating to others with love and caring)
Working hard and working smart	Chooses to stay current in course-work to avoid the stress caused by procrastination; chooses studying for an exam over going to a movie with a friend	Has enthusiasm for initiating and completing tasks	Spends some time studying with and enjoying the company of others
Excellence	Chooses to live by high standards and seek constant improvement	Works enthusiastically to accomplish tasks	Chooses to spend time with people who have high standards
Service to others	Seeks opportunities to volunteer time and effort in helping others	Shows enthusiasm for working with others	Shows kindness, respect, empathy, and generosity in working with others

TABLE 4.1

Example of How Values Contribute to Pillars of Self-Motivation

HOW MISSION CONTRIBUTES TO PILLARS OF SELF-MOTIVATION

A mission contributes to the pillars of self-motivation by doing the following:

1. Fostering the sound choices and behaviors that determine the degree of one's self-determination

2. Generating the passion and commitment needed to do a good job in carrying out tasks

3. Determining how a person connects with others.

Table 4.2 illustrates these points for a student who has a mission.

HOW GOALS CONTRIBUTE TO PILLARS OF SELF-MOTIVATION

As mentioned earlier, goals provide the practical steps for achieving the mission. Goals contribute to the pillars of self-motivation by doing the following:

1. Giving structure to thoughts and behaviors that determine the degree of one's self-determination and how one connects with others

2. Providing the action plans that helps one accomplish tasks.

	THOUGHTS AND BEHAVIORS WITH RESPECT TO:		
MISSION	**Self-Determination** (control over one's life)	**Competence** (ability to do a job well)	**Connectedness** (relating to others with love and caring)
To help make the world a better place to live by using my skills, talents, and abilities to help people help themselves	Works to develop to full potential Commits to lifelong learning	Has a passion for and commitment to helping people help themselves	Spends time with people to identify their needs and concerns

TABLE 4.2

Example of How Mission Contributes to Pillars of Self-Motivation

Table 4.3 illustrates these points for a student who has goals designed to fulfill his mission.

In summary, values, mission, and goals are the foundation of high performance. This foundation supports the pillars of self-determination, competence, and connectedness, traits that lead to self-motivation. High performance is the outcome, or the result, of self-motivation. Just as a

	THOUGHTS AND BEHAVIORS WITH RESPECT TO:		
GOALS	**Self-Determination** (control over one's life)	**Competence** (ability to do a job well)	**Connectedness** (relating to others with love and caring)
Complete college degree within five years	Attend classes and make strong efforts to stay alert	Plan and follow through on class choices, study time, and assignments	Study with and spend time with other students
During college career, form and maintain friendships with others who inspire growth and change	Take the lead in meeting people	Follow through on plans to improve interpersonal skills	Fine-tune interpersonal skills by applying lessons learned to real-life situations
Pay off student loans within five years of graduation	Develop discipline in managing financial affairs	Plan and stick to a budget; make regular loan payments	Spend time with people who make responsible choices in handling financial affairs

TABLE 4.3

Example of How Goals Contribute to Pillars of Self-Motivation

building will collapse if its structure is not in place, so must each of these factors—values, mission, goals, self-determination, competence, connectedness, and self-motivation—be in place for a person to achieve high performance. They are the building blocks of high performance.

The remaining sections of this chapter will focus in detail on the foundation concepts of values, mission, and goals. When you master these concepts, you are more likely to be self-motivated and thereby achieve consistently high levels of performance.

Role of Values in High Performance

Chapters 1 and 2 dealt with basic concepts of values. For example, Chapter 1 defined values, and Chapter 2 discussed the link between values and principles. Chapter 2 stressed the difference between productive versus self-defeating values and sound versus unsound principles.

HOW VALUES HELP YOU SET GOALS

Some students contend that goal setting does not work for them. The reason for this claim might be as follows: Parents and teachers urge young people to set goals early in their lives. At that point, the student's values largely reflect those of his parents. Thus, the student might start setting goals before he defines his own values. A person will be more prone to follow through on a goal that is related to something he really cares about.

Values give you a basic sense of direction and help you make decisions. Values form the basis for meaningful goals. Motivator and author Anthony Robbins writes:

> All decision making comes down to values clarification. If you've ever found yourself in a situation where you had a tough time making a decision about something, the reason is that you weren't clear about what you value most within that situation. When you know what's most important to you, making a decision is quite simple. Most people are unclear about what's most important in their lives, and thus decision making becomes a form of internal torture.[3]

IDENTIFYING YOUR VALUES

Exercise 4.1 will help you identify your value system. Exercise 4.2 will help you fine-tune your understanding of your value system.

SOUND PRINCIPLES: THE FOUNDATION FOR PRODUCTIVE VALUES

The fact that someone has values doesn't tell you much about the person. Everybody can recite a list of things they care about. Hitler had values. Drug dealers and gang leaders have values. But are these the kind of people

Identifying Your Values[4]

Assume that you will devote 100 months of your life to achieving or obtaining the things on the list of 35 items below. You might expect that by choosing to spend more time on some items, you have a greater chance of achieving them. You decide how much time you want to spend on each of the items. You do not have to select all of the items, but you must use up the entire 100 months. For example, suppose you select only three items. You might spend 50 months on the first item, 25 on the second and 25 on the third. Or you might select only one item and spend the entire 100 months on that item. You decide.

Each of the items on the list corresponds to a value. After you finish checking off the items and noting how many months you will spend on each, consult the key at the end of the table to determine the values that are important to you based on this exercise. Write those values in the right-hand column.

ITEM TO ACHIEVE OR OBTAIN	MONTHS I WOULD DEVOTE	VALUE REPRESENTED
1. A chance to rid the world of prejudice		
2. A chance to serve the sick and needy		
3. A guarantee to become a famous figure (movie star, baseball hero, astronaut, etc.)		
4. A proposal that will triple my company's earnings		
5. Enough money for a daily massage and the world's finest cuisine from the world's best chef		
6. Perfect insight into the meaning of life		
7. A vaccine that makes all persons incapable of graft or lying		
8. An opportunity to set my own working conditions		
9. Enough money to be one of the richest persons in the world		
10. Election as president of the United States		
11. The experience of a perfect love affair		
12. A house overlooking the most beautiful view in the world and containing my favorite works of art		
13. The experience of being one of the most attractive people in the world		
14. Living to 100 with no illness		
15. Free psychoanalysis with a highly acclaimed analyst		
16. The most complete library of great books for my own private use		
17. Harmony with God; doing God's work		
18. Knowledge of a way to rid the world of unfairness		

19.	The resources to donate 1 million ounces of gold to my favorite charity		
20.	The experience of being voted Outstanding Person of the Year and praised by every newspaper in the world		
21.	The ability to master the profession of my choice		
22.	Time with nothing to do but enjoy myself, with all needs and desires automatically met		
23.	The experience of being one of the wisest people in the world		
24.	A chance to sneak "authenticity serum" into every water supply in the world		
25.	Freedom to do my own thing without being hassled.		
26.	Possession of a large room full of silver dollars		
27.	The opportunity to control the destinies of 5,000,000 people.		
28.	The love and admiration of the whole world		
29.	Unlimited travel opportunities and tickets to attend any concert, play, opera, or ballet		
30.	A total makeover; new hairstyle, whole new wardrobe from the designer of my choice, and two weeks at a beauty spa		
31.	Membership in a great health club		
32.	Anti-hang-up pill		
33.	My own omniscient computer, for any and all facts I might need		
34.	Unlimited time to spend with the greatest religious figure of my faith, past or present		
35.	The ability to design a completely pollution-free automobile		

Key

1 and 18—Justice

2 and 19—Humanitarianism

3 and 20—Recognition

4 and 21—Achievement

5 and 22—Pleasure

6 and 23—Wisdom

7 and 24—Honesty

8 and 25—Autonomy

9 and 26—Economics

10 and 27—Power

11 and 28—Love

12 and 29—Aesthetics

13 and 30—Physical Attractiveness

14, 31, 35—Health

15 and 32—Emotional Well-being

16 and 33—Knowledge

17 and 34—Religious Faith

Ranking and Analyzing Your Values

After completing Exercise 4.1, list your top five values, ranking them in order from 1 to 5.

Value Rank

1.

2.

3.

4.

5.

Briefly answer the following questions based on the values you identified in this exercise:

Is your approach to college consistent with your values?

_____

_____

_____

Are your values consistent with the kind of person you want to be?

_____

_____

_____

Are there any changes that you would like to make in your value system?

_____

_____

_____

As you complete this exercise, you might find some conflicts. For example, suppose you want to be a teacher, but knowledge and service are not among your top values. You have three choices: work at making knowledge and service high-priority values, concede that you will be an ineffective and unhappy teacher, or give up on the idea of being a teacher and do something that more closely matches your values.

who would be good role models for you? It is not enough to just have values. Here are some questions that you will want to answer about your values:

- Will your values help or hinder you over time?

- How will your values affect your academic performance?

- How will your values affect your career goals?

- How will your values affect your quality of life?

- How will your values affect your relationships?

- How will your values affect your contributions to society?

One objective test of your value system is to ask the following question about each value: how well does this value reflect sound principles of personal and social behavior? In Chapter 2 we referred to values that pass this test as "productive values."

You can expect values to be a key issue when you apply for a job or to a graduate or professional school. The person who makes the best showing in terms of productive values will often win out over someone with better grades, test scores, or job skills. The reason for this practice might be the following: Productive values reflect sound principles. Review committees find principles a more objective measure of a person than values. Why? Because while people vary widely on their concept of values, there is broad agreement on what constitutes sound principles.

Exercise 4.3 will help you begin to evaluate your values in terms of how they can help you improve your degree of self-motivation. As your self-motivation improves, so will your performance.

● ● ● ● ● ● EXERCISE 4.3

Relationships between Your Values and the Components of Self-Motivation

List your top five values in the left column. In the other columns, briefly describe how your values will affect your choices and actions leading to self-determination, competence, and connectedness. Refer back to Table 4.1 for examples.

VALUE	SELF-MANAGEMENT (CONTROL OVER ONE'S LIFE)	COMPETENCE (ABILITY TO DO A JOB WELL)	CONNECTEDNESS (RELATING TO OTHERS WITH LOVE AND CARING)
1.			
2.			
3.			
4.			
5.			

Role of Mission in High Performance

WHAT IS A MISSION?

A mission is an extension of a person's highest values.[5] You can think of it as your personal creed or constitution. This document describes the criteria by which you will live your life. For example, your mission statement defines the following:

- What you stand for

- What you will fight for

- How the world will be a better place because of your contributions.

A mission is the highest source of self-motivation. With a mission, you know where you are going over the long term. A mission provides a sound basis for self-evaluation. For example, when you face a challenge, you can ask yourself the following question: "Will this thought, behavior, or decision enhance or impede the fulfillment of my mission?"

HOW TO DEFINE YOUR MISSION

Assume that you have only one semester (or quarter) to live. Also assume that you will stay in school during this period and be a good student. How would you spend your last days on earth? Would you adopt values that

(Source: Tom McCarthy/PhotoEdit.)

you had never thought of before? Would you be more likely to write your parents to tell them how much you love and appreciate them? Would you seek to reconcile with an estranged brother or sister? Would you attempt to resurrect a strained relationship with a friend? Would you be more or less likely to engage in bad-mouthing, bad-thinking, put-downs, and accusations?

Before you begin to define your own mission, consider the plan that Dr. Stephen Covey uses to help students define their mission.[6] It involves four major steps:

1. Identify your top two or three values.

2. Visualize three or more major results you want to achieve that reflect those values.

3. Write down the most important thoughts and feelings that arise during the visualization step.

4. Take action. Do something that will start you on your mission.

Step 2, the visualization step, helps you see beyond your present abilities and circumstances and grasp the big picture. You identify what the needs around you are and how you might contribute to meeting them. Use these four steps to begin your mission statement in Exercise 4.4.

Dr. Covey found that most students changed their value system significantly after they thought deeply about a mission. They thought about principles more than they had before. (Incidentally, love was high on the value list of most of these students.) Covey found that these exercises put students more in touch with their values. He concludes:

When people seriously undertake to identify what really matters most to them in their lives, what they really want to be and to do, they become very reverent. They start to think in larger terms than today and tomorrow.[7]

● ● ● ● ●EXERCISE 4.4

Beginning a Mission Statement

1. Review your top five values and narrow them down to three top values.

_____

_____

_____

_____

_____

_____

(continued)

2. Visualize three or more major results you want to achieve that reflect those values.

_____

_____

_____

_____

3. Write down the most important thoughts and feelings that arose during the visualization step.

_____

_____

_____

_____

_____

_____

4. What action can you take that will start you on your mission?

_____

_____

_____

_____

Your mission statement should reflect your highest goals and aspirations. You might spend months or years working on a mission statement before you complete the task. Meanwhile, do not wait! Start with a draft, and fine-tune it as you live your life.

The more you define your mission, the less you will rely on external forms of motivation such as grades and exams. The latter sources of motivation are short-lived and often lead to poor results. A mission helps you achieve more and avoid self-defeating behaviors.

Parvathi Aarthi Myer

My mission is two-pronged, involving both personal and professional components. To find peace, fulfillment, and value in living, my personal mission is to live a life centered upon spiritual faith. I also strive to build quality relationships, to continually learn from others, and to empower myself by working hard, practicing regular self-improvement and evaluation, and achieving financial independence. My professional mission is to mobilize underserved populations to achieve access to health care, because I believe that health care should be a universal right, not a privilege.

My academic and professional experiences as well as a mental kinship I have always had for less fortunate individuals have shaped my career goals in the field of public health. I have always wanted to know why certain segments of the population have access to health care and why others do not. Based on my experiences, I view the health care system as a chain embedded within a cultural, political, and economic context that should meet the needs of the people.

Globally, the links in the chain are often very brittle because of overpopulation, lack of resources, corruption, and bureaucracy.

I want to use science as a tool to bring underserved populations the resource of effective health care. Over the past five years, my academic background and professional experiences have focused on merging the scientific and social perspectives to improve indigent populations' access to health care. My goals include developing scientific solutions and health policies that are culturally appropriate to the served community. I am also motivated to go beyond putting Band-Aids on health problems at the curative level. I plan to accomplish this by working with populations to change harmful health beliefs and behaviors in a manner that is culturally accepted, understood, and practiced so that it will eventually improve peoples' overall quality of health. I have the desire, stamina, and optimism to weld some of the brittle links in the chain.

Role of Goals in High Performance

WHY IS IT IMPORTANT TO SET GOALS?

Many authors use the story about the Yale class of 1953 to stress the importance of goals. In the year prior to graduation, the class mix was as follows: 3 percent of the class had an extensive goal-setting workshop; 10 percent had a modest, incomplete workshop; and 87 percent had no program. Researchers looked at the class members 20 years later and found the following: The 3 percent group was happier, had better family lives, were more successful in their careers, and had more wealth than the other 10 and 87 percent combined.

We infer from these studies that the goal-setting skills that the 3 percent had learned helped them become high performers. Because they set goals, they were able to reach the top of the high-performance model in many aspects of their lives. But how does goal setting lead to high performance? The answer lies in what goals do for the mind. Psychologist Mihaly Csikszentmihalyi explains:

> *Contrary to what we tend to assume, the normal state of the mind is chaos. Without training, and without an object in the external world that demands attention, people are unable to focus their thoughts for more than a few minutes at a time. It is relatively easy to concentrate when attention is structured by outside stimuli, such as when a movie is playing on the screen, or when while driving [and] heavy traffic is encountered on the road.*
>
> *But with no demands on attention, the basic disorder of the mind reveals itself. With nothing to do, it begins to follow random patterns, usually stopping to consider something painful or disturbing. Unless a person knows how to give order to his or her thoughts, attention will be attracted to whatever is most problematic at the moment: it will focus on some real or imaginary pain, on recent grudges or long-term frustration.[8]*

Csikszentmihalyi calls this plight *entropy*, or psychic disorder. He claims that people try to correct this state by watching television. Will this tactic help or hinder? The choice of programs is the key. Some programs help block out negative mental images. Other programs bolster negative thoughts.

A simple way to structure the mind is through daydreaming.[9] In this text, we will use the term *dreams* in this context of daydreaming. Some small children form mental pictures, or dream, with ease. They see themselves as doctors, lawyers, nurses, chefs, policemen, firefighters, and pilots. Some even see themselves as the president of the United States! Children also dream of imaginary lifestyles, living in palaces with servants, riding in chauffeur-driven limousines, traveling around the world.

Other children never learn to dream.[10] As a result, they don't develop cognitively as well as their peers. Many inner-city youths are in this class. They live in the midst of dire conditions. They find it hard to dream and expect a better life while in these settings. These youths focus most of their thoughts on survival. Lacking hope or aspirations, many of them turn to joining gangs, dealing drugs, or other destructive pursuits.

As Figure 4.2 shows, dreams have many uses. And dreams are not just for children. People from all walks of life use dreams to motivate themselves. Sometimes they raise these dreams to a higher level and make them "goals." The real value of goals is how they affect the mind. Goals put you in control of your life. When this happens, external sources, such as television programs, will have less impact. Csikszentmihalyi sums up this point as follows:

> *The pursuit of a goal brings order in awareness because a person must concentrate attention on the task at hand and momentarily forget everything else.[11]*

To summarize, dreams lead to goals, and setting goals is important, because goals bring structure to the natural chaos of the mind. By setting goals, you are better able to achieve high performance and reach your potential.

FIGURE 4.2
Uses of dreams.

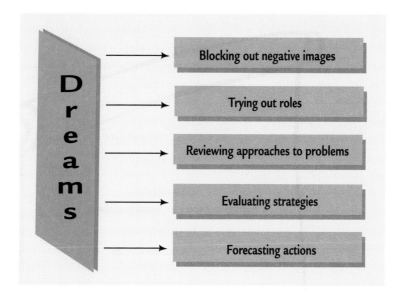

CHARACTERISTICS OF A GOAL

Figure 4.3 shows the five characteristics that define a goal and distinguish it from a dream. The most basic characteristic required of a goal is that it be *credible*; it must be something you can do. The second characteristic required of a goal is that it be *challenging*. A challenging goal causes you to stretch. For example, "I want to save some money" is not a challenging goal. To make it challenging, you can restate the goal as, "I intend to pay off my student loans within five years of graduation." This is a challenging goal because it will require hard work, discipline, and sacrifices.

Journal Activity

Describe how you use dreams, using Figure 4.2 as a guide.

_____

_____

_____

_____

_____

_____

_____

FIGURE 4.3

Characteristics of a goal.

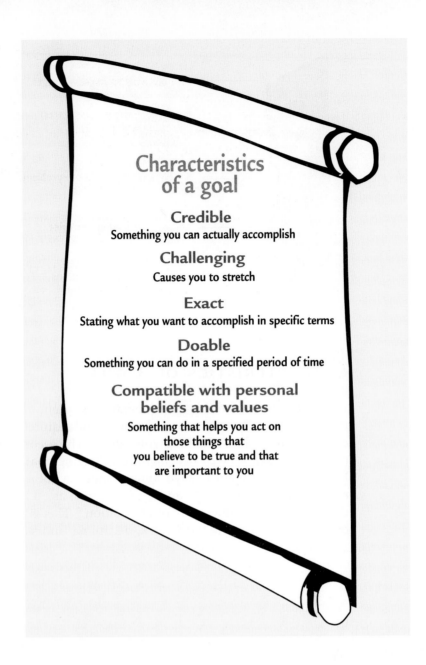

Characteristics
of a goal

Credible
Something you can actually accomplish

Challenging
Causes you to stretch

Exact
Stating what you want to accomplish in specific terms

Doable
Something you can do in a specified period of time

Compatible with personal beliefs and values
Something that helps you act on
those things that
you believe to be true and that
are important to you

The third characteristic required of a goal is that it be *exact*, meaning that it must be stated in specific terms. You should specify how you are going to accomplish the goal. For example, "I will do better in my classes this semester" is too general. "I will complete my assignments, stay current in my reading, and receive a B or better in all my classes" is specific. Our previous example about saving money also shows how a goal can be made specific, or exact. Instead of saying "some money," you need to specify how much and by what time.

The fourth characteristic required of a goal is that it be *doable*. The difference between being credible and being doable has to do with time. To meet the doable characteristic, you put a timeline on the goal. You might say that a goal is a dream with a deadline.

Break the goal down into pieces small enough to complete by a specific date. Break long-term goals into several short-term goals. Meet each short-term goal, one by one. For example, "I will get a good letter of recommendation from my instructor" is a dream. Revising this dream to say, "I will develop a list of questions and visit each of my instructors at least three times in the quarter" makes the dream a goal. Setting specific times for visiting each instructor makes the goal doable.

Finally, a goal must be compatible with your personal beliefs and values. When a goal is compatible with your beliefs and values, you are more likely to follow through on it. Imagine the frustration you would encounter if you wanted to be a professor but did not value lifelong learning. And how could you expect to be a manager of people in an organization if you valued long stretches of solitude?

Now let's look at an example of how each of these five characteristics applies to a single goal. Samantha wants to set a goal for paying off her school loan. To set this goal, she needs to identify and state each of the five elements in the model in Figure 4.3. Here is how she does it:

Goal: I will pay off my school loan.

Credible: Is this goal credible? That is, is it something I can accomplish?

Yes. I can pay off my school loan after I have obtained a job and am earning a paycheck.

Challenging: Is this goal challenging?

Yes! I have to discipline myself to make regular payments.

Exact: Is my goal stated in specific terms about how I'm going to accomplish it?

No. I need to modify it as follows:

Modified goal: I will set up a payment schedule, make regular payments, and if possible, gradually increase the monthly payment to pay off my school loan.

Doable: Does my goal have a deadline?

No. I need to add to it as follows:

Further modified goal: I will set up a payment schedule, make regular payments, and if possible, gradually increase the monthly payment to pay off my school loan by six years from the date I graduate.

Compatible with personal beliefs and values: Is my goal compatible with what I believe and value?

Yes, it is. I value financial security and responsibility, and I believe it is important to pay off my debts as soon as I can.

Now that we have broken Samantha's goal down into the five characteristics, it's your turn to break down the two goals in Exercise 4.5. This exercise will help you analyze goals and understand the differences among the five characteristics of a goal.

• • • • • •EXERCISE 4.5

Goals Analysis

1. **Mike's goal:** Like most people, Mike gets nervous speaking in front of large groups. His goal is to become a better public speaker. Help him analyze his goal so that he can be sure it is something he can achieve.

Credible. Is this goal credible? That is, is it something Mike can accomplish?

_____

_____

_____

Challenging. Is this goal challenging?

_____

_____

_____

Exact. Is Mike's goal stated in specific terms about how he is going to accomplish it?

_____

_____

_____

Doable. Does Mike's goal have a deadline?

_____

_____

_____

Compatible with personal beliefs and values. You don't know Mike's personal beliefs and values, but what beliefs and values should he have in order to accomplish this goal?

_____

_____

_____

2. **Jennifer's goal:** Jennifer is a sophomore who wants to save money for a car. She has not decided whether the car will be a new or used car. All she knows is that she could get to her part-time job much faster if she had her own set of wheels.

Credible. Is this goal credible? That is, is it something Jennifer can accomplish? What information do you need to determine this?

_____

_____

_____

Challenging. Is this goal challenging?

_____

_____

_____

Exact. Is Jennifer's goal stated in specific terms about how she is going to accomplish it?

_____

_____

_____

Doable. Does Jennifer's goal have a deadline?

_____

_____

_____

(continued)

Compatible with personal beliefs and values. You don't know Jennifer's personal beliefs and values, but what beliefs and values should she have in order to accomplish this goal?

_____

_____

_____

FOUR-STEP GOAL-SETTING PLAN

Now let's look at a four-step goal-setting plan.[12] The steps are as follows:

1. Set goals.

2. Develop a plan.

3. Identify and address the challenges.

4. Take action and follow through.

■ STEP ONE: SET GOALS

The first step is to identify your goals. You can have specific goals in various areas of your life:

■ *Career goals*—choice of job or profession; level of desired achievements and income

■ *Personal-relationship goals*—how you interact with your partner, relatives, friends, and others

■ *Recreation and entertainment goals*—fun, relaxation, adventure (e.g., movies, shows, plays, concerts, reading, travel)

■ *Material-possessions goals*—the things you want to have (e.g., houses, cars, boats, furniture, stereo equipment)

■ *Self-improvement goals*—the kind of person you want to be (e.g., scholarly, caring, optimistic)

■ *Charity goals*—what you want to do for others (e.g., donation of money and time to a place or worship, a service organization, or a community event)

■ *Spiritual goals*—your relationship to a higher power (e.g., participation in activities at a place of worship; personal rituals of prayer, meditation, or chants)

Recall that two required characteristics of goals are that they be credible and compatible with one's beliefs and values. In this step, you'll want to check to be sure the goals you set meet both of these criteria.

Exercise 4.6 gives you an opportunity to list each of these categories of goals.

Fine-tuning Your Goals

1. Write down what you want to accomplish in each category of goals. Don't evaluate your goals at this point; just write them down. (Be sure you leave a little space next to each goal for the second instruction in this exercise.)

My Career Goals:

_____

_____

_____

_____

_____

_____

My Personal-Relationship Goals:

_____

_____

_____

_____

_____

_____

My Recreation and Entertainment Goals:

_____

_____

_____

_____

_____

_____

(continued)

My Material-Possessions Goals:

_____
_____
_____
_____
_____

My Self-Improvement Goals:

_____
_____
_____
_____
_____

My Charity Goals:

_____
_____
_____
_____
_____

My Spiritual Goals:

_____
_____
_____
_____
_____

2. Establish a timeline. Decide when you want to accomplish each of the goals. Then write this down next to each of the goals.

3. From the goals you have listed, choose your most important goal to achieve in the next year from each category. Write a paragraph that contains strong reasons why you will commit yourself to achieving these goals within the year.

_____

_____

_____

_____

_____

_____

_____

_____

_____

_____

_____

_____

_____

_____

_____

_____

_____

_____

_____

_____

_____

_____

The result of this exercise is that you will have seven "major" exciting goals that will motivate you.

Grace Jang

When those around me tell me that something is "impossible" or "cannot be done" or—my favorite—"should not be done," it fuels my fire. Recently I was told that I should not strive for a Ph.D. because I am female; I should raise a family and leave the Ph.D.s to be earned by others, namely, men. This comment angered me—not simply because one individual had directed it at me, but because I knew that the assertion is indicative of a sentiment more widely held.

It is this type of comment that hinders many women, especially women of color, from striving to achieve their potential. Hence, because there are naysayers, I strive even harder—to prove them wrong. However, I have discovered that revenge and spitefulness make for weak ammunition in achieving goals. Although it is important and healthy to strengthen your position against counter-movement, defeat of opposition should be the means, not the end. So, in an ironic way, it is precisely because others have told me "you shouldn't" that I do—and, in the end, accomplish even more than I thought I was capable of achieving.

I think there is always a higher level to which to aspire. Because I hate to sit still, twiddling my thumbs, before I reach a goal, I am already planning my next one. Also, I am not content with simply doing something; I am almost obsessed with the determination to make significant everything I do. When I start a task, there absolutely must be a justifiable reason to it—and money or fame is never an enriching or satisfying end, because such things are so ephemeral and addictive.

My parents raised me to never compare myself with others, because others' achievements make for poor and inaccurate rulers. Each person is equipped with her own tool belt, and how she uses those tools differs from the next person. When I look to those next to me as markers for my growth and achievement, I stay at the same plane and grow horizontally. However, when I compare myself and my achievements to none other than myself and my best performance, I am not sidelined; hence, I reach the next plateau and grow vertically—I move up. Therefore, I think it's imperative never to settle into complacency, for success is a journey and not a destination.

■ STEP TWO: DEVELOP A PLAN

The next step in the goal-setting process is to map out a plan. At this stage, you make a task list that contains all the things you need to do to achieve your goal. You also note a deadline for each item on the task list. As you complete each item, check it off. The unchecked items will signal how much more you have to do. Revise your plan as needed.

For example, Sara's career goal is to be a foreign service officer, which is a person who represents her home country in a governmental capacity in a foreign country. She developed the following task list for her goal:

Application procedures for internships, Year: 4 ____

Appointments to meet with key advisers and contacts,
Year 3.5 ____

Background preparation, Year 3: ____

Plans to visit some foreign countries, Year 2: ____

As discussed earlier, two characteristics required of goals are that they be exact and doable. This step helps you ensure that your goals meet these requirements. Exercise 4.7 allows you to make task lists the way Sara did.

● ● ● ● ●EXERCISE 4.7

Task Lists for Achieving Goals

Take the most important goal from each of the seven categories and make a task list for each. Note a deadline for each task.

My Career Goal:

_____

_____

_____

_____

My Personal-Relationship Goal:

_____

_____

_____

_____

My Recreation and Entertainment Goal:

_____

_____

_____

_____

(continued)

My Material-Possessions Goal:

_____

_____

_____

_____

My Self-Improvement Goal:

_____

_____

_____

_____

My Charity Goal:

_____

_____

_____

_____

My Spiritual Goal:

_____

_____

_____

_____

■ STEP THREE: IDENTIFY AND ADDRESS THE CHALLENGES

Before you can achieve a goal, you often need to address any possible problems that might hinder your success. This step helps you identify how your goals are challenging, how they require you to stretch and grow. Here are some questions that might help you prepare for the challenges your goals will bring:

■ *What new skills will you need to acquire?* For example, to be a foreign service officer, Sara might need to learn new languages. She also might need to improve her negotiation skills.

■ *What thoughts, attitudes, and behaviors will you need to change?* For example, if Sara tends to stereotype people, she will want to correct this habit.

■ *What sacrifices do you need to make?* For example, as a foreign service officer, Sara will sacrifice time spent with friends and family in her home country.

■ *How will you respond to setbacks and defeats?* For example, what will Sara do if she fails the language course? What if one of her key professors leaves town before she can ask for a letter of recommendation? What if she misses an important deadline in the application process? What if she has a fight with her roommate on the night before a key exam?

Exercise 4.8 allows you to identify challenges for each of your most important goals.

This step highlights the hidden benefit of setting goals—each goal will help you learn a new skill, change a habit, or have a better attitude. Noted author Anthony Robbins speaks to this issue in *Awaken the Giant Within:*

> *Achieving goals by themselves will never make us happy in the long term; it's who you become as you overcome the obstacles necessary to achieve your goals that can give you the deepest and most long-lasting sense of fulfillment.*[13]

● ● ● ● ●**EXERCISE 4.8**

Identifying and Addressing the Challenges Connected with Setting Goals

For each of your major goals, identify the challenges you will have. Then describe how you will address each challenge.

My Career Goal:

_____

_____

_____

_____

_____

_____

My Personal-Relationship Goal:

_____

_____

_____

_____

_____

_____

(continued)

My Recreation and Entertainment Goal:

_____

_____

_____

_____

_____

My Material-Possessions Goal:

_____

_____

_____

_____

_____

My Self-Improvement Goal:

_____

_____

_____

_____

_____

My Charity Goal:

_____

_____

_____

_____

_____

My Spiritual Goal:

_____

_____

_____

_____

_____

_____

■ STEP FOUR: TAKE ACTION AND FOLLOW THROUGH

Many people believe that the goal-setting process does not work. The same people claim that New Year's resolutions don't work and that affirmations don't work. Indeed, none of these techniques will work unless you *do* something with them. Firm up your plan with action! To prepare for a career as a foreign service officer, Sara decides to enroll in a language course. She also plans to attend a seminar on how to negotiate and to send for internship applications. She might want to visit a country in her area of interest. She even could make contact with an experienced diplomat.

To monitor your progress toward your goals, keep a journal of your activities. Check off each event as it occurs. Monitor your progress to keep track of what you have achieved and what still needs to be done.

Always set a new goal before you reach a current goal. If you follow this advice, you will avoid the empty feelings that many people have after they

Journal Activity

What actions can you take to move toward the goals you have identified in this chapter?

_____

_____

_____

_____

_____

_____

_____

(Source: Loren Santow/
Tony Stone Images.)

achieve a goal. For example, some students graduate from college and are
not sure what to do next. For several years, their only goal was to make it
through school and graduate. They did not stop to think about what they
wanted to do after school. You can avoid this mistake by setting several
goals and continually revising them, as shown in the four-step goal-setting
process summarized in Figure 4.4. Note how the goals overlap and continue
indefinitely.

The four-step goal-setting process can tie in with the high-performance
model presented at the beginning of this chapter. Recall that self-determination, competence, and connectedness are the traits that lead to self-motivation and high performance. The actions you plan to take to move toward
your goals should address how you can build these traits.

For example, suppose your career goal is to own your own marketing
business within ten years of graduation. Developing your leadership abilities would be one way to build self-determination. You could accomplish
this by serving as an officer in a campus organization. To develop competence, you could sign up for an internship in the marketing department of a
local company. Internships are a great way to build competence because
they allow you to work on a specific task, and in the process of striving for
excellence in that endeavor, feel competent and energized.

Finally, to develop connectedness, you could focus on developing the attitudes and behaviors you need to interact with people outside your campus
life. For example, if you worked as an intern in a marketing department,
you would have an opportunity to interact with people in a business setting. You also would learn protocol for an office environment and, assuming
you did a good job, make some connections for your future career.

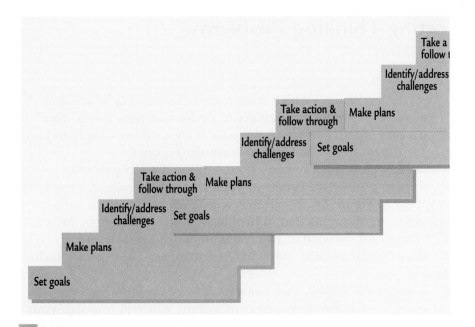

FIGURE 4.4

Four-step goal-setting plan as an ongoing process.

These examples illustrate how a career goal of owning your own company can be broken down into actions that would develop the three pillars of self-determination, competence, and connectedness. Remember, these are the three traits that move you toward self-motivation and hence high performance. You can apply this example to all the goals you established earlier in this chapter, not just career goals.

Journal Activity

Describe how the actions you plan to take toward your goals (described in the previous journal activity) will develop your self-determination, competence, and connectedness.

_____

_____

_____

_____

_____

_____

Identifying and Correcting Thinking Problems

*T*hinking problems—which stem from self-defeating beliefs and values—can hinder your ability to perform at high levels. Your task is to identify which of these thinking problems apply to you and then correct them using the Change Formula (Figure 4.5).

In this process, you select a remedy (S) to change the self-defeating beliefs or values to productive beliefs or values. Some remedies for thinking problems appear in Figure 4.6. Recall that self-defeating beliefs or values lead to self-defeating thoughts that in turn lead to self-defeating behaviors (Figure 4.7). Figure 4.8 shows that you can correct these self-defeating beliefs or values by using one or more of the remedies. The result is productive behaviors.

Figure 4.9 shows the impact that values can have on life outcomes. When you apply the Change Formula consistently, you will improve your ability to establish and maintain effective relationships and achieve success in all areas of your life. Example 4.1 and Exercise 4.9 will help you achieve this goal.

Many of the problems that people have in achieving high performance and success result from self-defeating values. Exercise 4.9 will help you see how values can affect behavior and life outcomes.

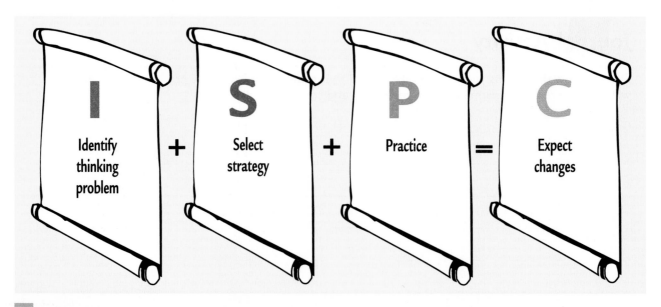

I Identify thinking problem **+** **S** Select strategy **+** **P** Practice **=** **C** Expect changes

FIGURE 4.5

Change formula to apply to thinking problems.

FIGURE 4.6
*Remedies for thinking
problems.*

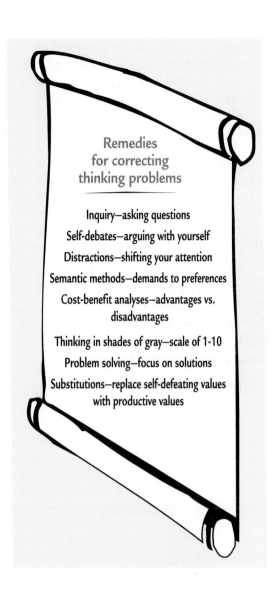

FIGURE 4.7
*How self-defeating
beliefs or values lead to
self-defeating behaviors.*

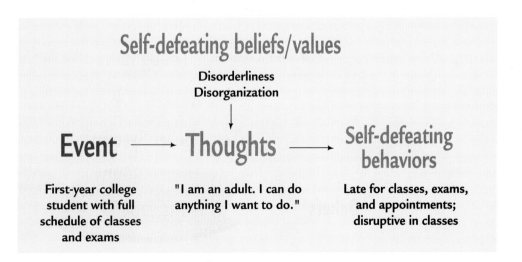

FIGURE 4.8
How corrected self-defeating beliefs or values lead to productive behaviors.

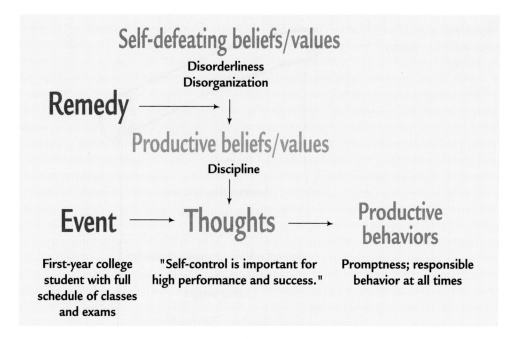

FIGURE 4.9

Impact of beliefs on life outcomes.

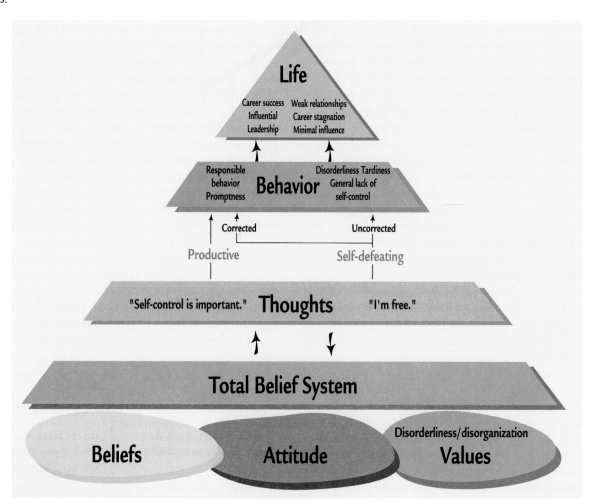

EXAMPLE 4.1

Event
Ervin blames others for his lack of motivation.

Ervin's Self-Statement
This campus has the most boring professors. I could get a lot more interested in my courses if they would give better lectures.

(I) Identify the Thinking Problem
Personalization and blame

(S) Select a Remedy: self-debate
Q. How do I know that the professors are the most boring professors?
A. I don't know for sure. Well, let's just say that they are really boring.
Q. I see, then tell me, if I applied for a job, would they expect me to have the right academic background?
A. Yes, they would.
Q. So, does having boring professors give me an excuse not to learn?
A. No, it does not.
Q. Are there other ways to get motivated other than rely on the professor?
A. Yes, I can motivate myself.

(C) Productive Belief/Value
Self-motivation

Productive Self-Statement
Motivation to learn is my responsibility. Professors can help, but the buck stops with me.

(P) Practice
Practice the productive beliefs and the self-statements.

Journal Activity

How can you use the Change Formula to identify and correct thinking problems that hinder your performance?

_____

_____

_____

_____

_____

How Values Affect Thoughts, Behaviors, and Life Outcomes

Supply some examples of thoughts, behaviors, and life outcomes that might result from the self-defeating values listed here. In the last column write the productive value that should replace each self-defeating value.

VALUE	THOUGHTS	BEHAVIORS	POTENTIAL LIFE OUTCOMES	REPLACEMENT VALUE
Immediate Gratification				
Mediocrity				
Complacency				
Dishonesty				
Irresponsibility				
Perseverance				
Immaturity				
Selfishness				
Passivity				
Slothfulness				

CHAPTER SUMMARY

The high-performance model helps explain why some people achieve more than others. If you are highly proactive, your pattern of thinking and behavior probably conform to this model. Keep doing what you are doing. If you are reactive, you have some changes to make. Don't waste time envying your proactive peers. Use the strategies in this chapter to improve. Forget about comparisons. If the grades you receive are not as high as those of other students, do not give up. Compete only with yourself. Let the high-performance model help you be best that you can be.

There is some irony in this advice. Many people break the rules and still succeed. Some students cheat and get As. Many affluent people in our society have self-defeating values. Many successful people do not set goals. Why, then, should you follow the high-performance model when it is possible you could succeed without it? The answer depends on what kind of person you want to be. Do you want to fit into Group A or Group B? Group A people are successful in only one way—they have plenty of money and material goods. But in terms of morality, spirituality, and relationships with other people, they are lacking. Some might have made their money by exploiting others. Some might have succeeded by helping other people succumb to weaknesses—drug habits, gambling, prostitution. Are these your models of success?

In contrast, Group B individuals are successful in ways that involve more than money. They have a clear sense of purpose. They set goals and follow through. They are productive, prosperous, and at the same time live by wholesome principles and values. They seek to be the best that they can be. Over the long term, they are the happiest and most important contributors to our society.

The choices you make determine the direction of your life. We suggest that you choose to follow the guidelines in this chapter. This decision will put you on track for high performance, high self-esteem, and a well-balanced life.

NOTES

1. From *Peak Performance* by Charles Garfield. Copyright © 1986 by Charles Garfield. By permission of William Morrow and Co., Inc.

2. Based on the self-motivation model in E. Deci: *Why We Do What We Do* (New York: Penguin Books, 1995).

3. Adapted and modified with permission from A. Robbins: *Awaken the Giant Within* (New York: Summit, 1991).

4. This exercise is based on a similar one by L. Swell: *Success: You Can Make It Happen* (New York: Jove/HBJ, 1976), © 1989 Stephen R. Covey. Used with permission. All rights reserved.

5. The discussion on mission was adapted and modified from Stephen R. Covey: *The Seven Habits of Highly Effective People* (New York: Simon and Schuster, 1989), © 1989 Stephen R. Covey. Used with permission. All rights reserved.

6. Ibid.

7. Ibid.

8. M. Csikszentmihalyi: *Flow: The Psychology of Optimal Experience* (New York: Harper and Row, copyright © 1990), pp. 6, 116. Used with permission of Harper Collins Publishers.

9. Ibid.

10. Concepts based on the work of Yale psychologist Jerome Singer: *Daydreaming: An Introduction to the Experimental Study of Inner Experiences* (New York: Random House, 1966). Used with permission of the author.

11. Csikszentmihalyi: *Flow*.

12. Robbins: *Awaken the Giant Within*.

13. Ibid.

CHAPTER 5

PRE-CHAPTER SELF-ASSESSMENT

Read each statement and circle the number that best reflects your response.

	NEVER							ALWAYS		
	1	2	3	4	5	6	7	8	9	10

1. I feel in charge of my education.

   1 2 3 4 5 6 7 8 9 10

2. I am able to focus on how I can use what I know and learn.

   1 2 3 4 5 6 7 8 9 10

3. The source of my motivation for learning is internal rather than from external sources such as grades and test scores.

   1 2 3 4 5 6 7 8 9 10

4. I use role models to help me learn and grow.

   1 2 3 4 5 6 7 8 9 10

5. I use a set of criteria for choosing the right role models for me.

   1 2 3 4 5 6 7 8 9 10

6. My behavior in the classroom promotes effective learning and shows respect for my professors and classmates.

   1 2 3 4 5 6 7 8 9 10

7. In addition to my private efforts, I spend some time studying with other students.

   1 2 3 4 5 6 7 8 9 10

8. I use my analytical, creative, and practical abilities when I study for courses and manage my personal affairs.

   1 2 3 4 5 6 7 8 9 10

9. I use mental rehearsal when I prepare for events such as taking exams and making speeches.

   1 2 3 4 5 6 7 8 9 10

10. I use study materials to strengthen my memory, and I also use higher thinking skills, such as comprehension, synthesis, and judgment.

    1 2 3 4 5 6 7 8 9 10

11. I have a notetaking system that lets me both recall facts and grasp concepts.

    1 2 3 4 5 6 7 8 9 10

12. When I read, I first preview the material, propose questions, and then read for answers to the questions.

    1 2 3 4 5 6 7 8 9 10

13. I have a task-organization system that involves breaking big tasks into smaller segments, setting priorities, and checking off items on To Do Lists.

    1 2 3 4 5 6 7 8 9 10

14. When I write a paper, I first identify the questions I want to answer.

    1 2 3 4 5 6 7 8 9 10

15. I solve academic and nonacademic problems using ordered rather than random procedures.

    1 2 3 4 5 6 7 8 9 10

16. During problem-solving exercises, I read the problem many times in the process of finding a solution.

    1 2 3 4 5 6 7 8 9 10

17. I view exam preparation as an ongoing process rather than as periodic all-night events.

    1 2 3 4 5 6 7 8 9 10

18. I am able to identify and correct problems in thinking that hinder learning.

    1 2 3 4 5 6 7 8 9 10

Determine your relative degree of proactivity for this trait by using the following formula:

Percent Proactivity = Sum of Circled Numbers ÷ 180 × 100

(Note that 180 is the maximum sum possible. It would result in a score of 100 percent.)

Percent Proactivity = _____

For example, if you checked 5 for each question, your score would be

Percent Proactivity for Learning = 90/180 × 100 = 50

"Anyone who stops learning is old, whether at twenty or eighty. Anyone who keeps learning stays young. The greatest thing in life is to keep your mind young."

Henry Ford

Learning Strategies: You Are Responsible for Your Education

PROACTIVE AND REACTIVE students differ in their attitudes and habits as learners. For example, many reactive students often blame professors and other sources for their poor performance. They often feel bored during lectures and rely solely on exams and grades as a source of motivation. In contrast, proactive students take full responsibility for their education. They learn as much as they can from professors. But they also put forth the effort to identify other people and resources that can help them learn and grow. They are motivated by more than just exams and grades. They also want to learn for the sake of learning. Thus, the source of their motivation for learning is internal rather than external.

This chapter describes a set of tools, techniques, and strategies that will help you be more proactive as a learner. In this chapter, you will learn how to

- Benefit from the success of others by using role models.

- Achieve excellence and buffer the potential ill effects of competition by focusing on how to be the best that you can be.

- Multiply your own study efforts by spending some time studying with other students

- Use a wider range of your mental resources than those called for in most classroom situations.

- Master systems that help you take better notes, read with greater focus, and write better papers.

- Use a task-organization system that will help you be more effective and save time.

- Improve your ability to solve academic and nonacademic problems

- Treat exam preparation as an ongoing process rather than as periodic all-night efforts.

- Identify and correct the thinking problems that hinder your ability to learn.

comparison grid	focus words	mental rehearsal/	spaced repetition
concept questions	inert intelligence	mental imagery	synergy
focus questions	knowledge	modeling	To Do List
focus word links	Master Task Worksheet	mosaic role model	

The best source of information about students is the students themselves. This point is obvious to some but not to others. Some professors tend to rely too heavily on reports, studies, and other second-hand sources for information about students. The result is that they often operate under assumptions that might be only partly if at all true. For example:

■ A quiet classroom does not indicate that students are paying attention to the lecture.

■ "A" students do not always make the best candidates for jobs or post-graduate programs. (Because professors focus on "A" students, they often overlook the hidden potential of many "C" students.)

■ The fact that the professor covers a certain amount of material does not mean that the students learn that material.

■ The fact that the professor conveys state-of-the art knowledge does not mean that students have acquired the skills to keep up to date with new information on their own in the future.

The following comments from one group of students paint a dim view of how much real learning might take place on our campuses:

■ Students say that they may or may not take notes. If they do take notes, they may not look at them. If they do look at them, they probably do so the day before the exam.

■ Many students say they pay little attention to lectures. They sleep, balance checkbooks, play games, or communicate with each other.

■ Students say that they study only just before test time. In other words, they study for deadlines. And they study in a haphazard way, with little real discipline involved.

Most of the students in this group had focused so much on grades and their grade point average that they had failed to give attention to actually learning anything. They could get As on the tests yet comprehend very little of the course content. Some students were even graduating with honors and still felt they had not learned much.

Few of these graduating seniors said they were comfortable with what they knew or with their learning skills. Few felt that they could connect what they had studied in class to broader issues of society. Indeed, most had failed to carry over much information from one class to another. In this group of interviewed students, only a small proportion believed that their work habits demonstrated discipline, drive, and high enthusiasm for learning.

Some students blame professors for their plight. They see many professors as aloof, boring, and unable to motivate students to high performance. Probably some professors do contribute to the problems that plague higher

Journal Activity

Do your observations confirm the views of this group of students? If so, what do you think are the reasons for this situation? What are the solutions?

_____

_____

_____

_____

_____

_____

education. But what good does it do to blame someone else when your education is at risk? It would be nice if professors did more to improve their overall effectiveness, but if that does not happen, what are *you*, the student, going to do?

Remember, *you* are responsible for *your* education. Professors can help, but *you* must take the lead. Focus on issues that you can control, and acquire the skills that will help you learn for the rest of your life. For example, you have the power to do the following:

1. Motivate yourself.

2. Develop the kinds of attitudes and habits that foster learning.

3. Identify individuals (Chapter 7) and resources that can help you achieve your goals.

4. Expand the use of your mental resources

5. Identify and utilize strategies that enhance your ability to learn.

6. Identify and correct thinking problems that hinder your ability to learn.

Empowering Attitudes and Behaviors

TAKE CHARGE OF YOUR EDUCATION

Maude, an education student, attempted to enroll in a learning theory course. There were two such classes offered that quarter. Class A, taught by the most popular professor, was full. There were plenty of vacancies in

Class B, taught by a professor who lacked strong rapport with students. He was more demanding than the other professors were, and he was somewhat hostile to students. Maude had the option of taking Class B now, or waiting until the next quarter for Class A. She enrolled in Class B even though she knew she would have to work much harder. Maude's reason for her choice was impressive. She remarked, "If I can perform well in that professor's class, I can do well in anyone's."

Maude's attitude differs from that of many students; she was willing to work around issues that might hinder her success. Many students fail because they fret over issues that are ultimately less important than the course content—issues such as the textbook, the teaching assistant (TA), or the professor's personality.

Proactive students focus on areas within their span of control. For example, they might do the following:

- Make notes about what they would do differently if they were the professor. When and if the time comes to give feedback, they have something to contribute.

- Realize that it is not always in their best interest to choose the easiest professor or the one with the best personality.

- Find ways to adapt to the professor once they decide to take her class.

- Speak to the department chair or dean if a professor fails to conform to appropriate standards.

- Give the professor feedback on the performance of the TAs.

- Go beyond the textbook material by consulting other references as needed.

- Study with other serious students.

Your *attitude* will dictate whether or not you reach your full potential as a learner. Adopt the attitude of proactive learners. They routinely ask themselves, "How can I make the most of this learning situation?"

MOTIVATE YOURSELF

In Chapter 4, we stressed the point that self-motivated students often learn more and perform better than students who rely on external sources of motivation. Stan's approach to his classes shows a pattern that would help any student get more out his college experience. For example, Stan did not take a course just to satisfy his major requirements. Biology pointed him toward the nature and control of disease. Psychology helped him better understand himself and how to relate to others. Sociology and anthropology courses caused him to reflect on the state of world society and how he could make a contribution.

Like many proactive students, Stan's secret was that he would always find a way to connect what he learned to a bigger process. Exams, lectures, and assignments were all part of a larger project that would prepare him for a career and help him fulfill his mission.

Proactive students like Stan are aware of the reasons for learning each subject they study—that is, how it might benefit them or society. They

Lawrence Crane

I was a typical student my freshman and sophomore years in college. I went to most of my classes, took fair notes, and received fair grades. At the time, I thought I studied quite a bit, but I never really seemed to "get it." I had no focus, no plan. Today, seven years—and a bachelor's degree in science, a master's degree in public health, and two years of medical school—later, when you ask me about learning strategies, I have plenty to say. Have I learned "shortcuts" or "tricks" to get good grades? Not by a long shot. By becoming an active participant in my education, I have learned to study more effectively.

The first step in learning is to listen to the experts by attending all lectures. This sounds obvious, but there are many students who feel that attending class is a waste of time. I disagree. I may be able to memorize more facts by sitting with a textbook, but learning is about much more than acquiring facts. Lecture is a time to see how the professor weaves the multitude of facts into a story and places that story into a historical context. It is a time to see what a professional in the field feels is important enough to present when time is limited. I learned the way to get the most out of lecture is to take copious notes. I write down every word the professor says because I know it is impossible to try to distill out what is "important" and what is "fluff"—and I thrive upon the information that many students think is fluff. It's easier to remember facts and complex theories when I have written down all of the anecdotes, analogies, and examples given in lecture. I view lecture as the building of an apprentice-mentor relationship.

The next step in learning is to thoroughly review my lecture notes. I do this by considering the lecture material as the "answers" and thinking it is my job to figure out what "questions" the professor is asking. I actually write down the questions in the margins of my notes (I use wide-margin paper). I do this lecture review before the next lecture, while the last lecture is still fresh in my mind. Since adopting this technique, I rarely have been surprised by a test question because I have already written and answered most of them.

My final step is to analyze and synthesize these notes into a form from which it is easier to learn. For instance, after a pharmacology class, I will make a chart comparing each of the drugs I learned that day. Instead of memorizing ten flashcards that are all very similar, I will make one chart that compares each drug in terms of its mechanism of action, uses, side effects, contraindications, and pharmacokinetic properties. These charts allow me to learn one specific medication in the context of other related drugs. By mentally comparing and contrasting each of the items on the chart, I get a much more comprehensive view of the subject.

Does my method take time? Yes. Does my method work? I am proud to say that after I became an active leaner and adopted these techniques, I improved my undergraduate grades. More importantly, I have built a foundation upon which I can grow throughout my career.

The key to learning is to be an active participant and ask critical questions. The ability to ask important questions is what separates the naive from the professionals.

derive their motivation for studying from a cause, dream, or goal based on their values. The result is that there is no room for boredom.

Reactive students, on the other hand, often speak of being bored. They have tunnel vision, failing to see the relevance of what they learn to larger issues. They often ask, "Why should I take these classes when I will never need them in my career?" Reactive students seldom do much active learning on their own. Instead, they merely respond to the deadlines set by the professor by "cramming" for tests. Between tests, they do little or nothing to increase their knowledge or understanding. After graduating, they take their place with co-workers who choose to learn little unless required to do so by their employers.

Clearly, proactive students stand out from most students. They use their time in college to fine-tune skills that help them challenge the known, acquire the new, and solve problems. They focus on learning fundamentals so that they can grow continuously throughout their lifetimes.

Your degree of self-motivation will improve as you link your desire for higher education to specific issues that extend beyond the requirements of your classes. Exercise 5.1 provides an opportunity for you to think about how your current studies relate to society in general. Exercise 5.2 provides the same opportunity in regard to your specific career goals.

• • • • • •EXERCISE 5.1

Relating Your Current Studies to Societal Contributions

Give five examples of how what you are learning now will help you understand and contribute to society.

1. _____

_____

2. _____

_____

3. _____

_____

4. _____

_____

5. _____

_____

Journal Activity

As you begin or continue your studies, some courses will appeal to you more than others. Explain how you will motivate yourself to do well in courses that you don't like but have to take anyway.

_____

_____

_____

_____

Relationships of College Courses to Career or Mission

If you have already chosen your career or your life's mission, show how each of your current courses might relate to it.

Name of Course _____

_____

_____

Name of Course _____

_____

_____

Name of Course _____

_____

_____

Name of Course _____

_____

_____

USE ROLE MODELS TO ENHANCE LEARNING

Modeling: the process of adapting the attitudes and or habits of other people for your use.

Some students like to figure everything out for themselves. They shun help from professors or other students because they feel that this help would curb their creativity. Perhaps these students never know how much time they waste because of this attitude. Modeling, which represents the opposite attitude, is a much more efficient approach to learning, because it allows you to benefit from the lessons others have learned from their successes and failures. You use systems that other people have developed, tested, and proved. Modeling actually allows more time for creativity. You can take the time you would use to "reinvent the wheel" and use it for other purposes. For example, you can improve on existing knowledge or use it as a launching pad to create something entirely new. Scholars use a similar process as they conduct their research. After they propose a hypothesis, they check to find out what other scholars have already published on the subject. They then use their mental powers to build on the known as well as to venture into the unknown. Most successful people have or have had models at some point during their career.

In most cases, people urge you to seek out adult models such as your parents, teachers, administrators, or members of your college staff. You might also find people in your community that set the kind of example that inspires you to be like them. But many students overlook one of the best sources of models—other students. Studies have shown that successful student learners can make good role models. Through practice, you can acquire the attitudes and habits of peer models that help you improve. Two types of role models are possible: individual role models and mosaic roles models. We will look at each.

▪ INDIVIDUAL ROLE MODELS

People you know well, such as close friends, co-workers, or family members, might serve as individual role models. Other individual role models might be people you've never met but have read about, such as historical

(Source: Loren Santow/Tony Stone Images.)

If you have different or additional criteria for what makes a good role model, write them down here.

_____

_____

_____

_____

_____

_____

figures or television personalities. Good individual role models should show strength in one or more of the following areas:

1. Personal philosophy

2. Moral and ethical values

3. Intellectual skills

4. Interpersonal skills

If you can find a person who is strong in all of these four areas, you might try to establish a relationship either with that person or with someone who resembles that person in the ways that you admire. However, often it is not possible or even necessary for you to personally know your role model, because you can model that person's behaviors, attitudes, and habits simply by observing or reading about him or her. Think of five such people for Exercise 5.3.

■ MOSAIC ROLE MODELS

People often face setbacks when their role model disappoints them. For example, a person might be a strong role model for career success but weak in the area of personal integrity. You can avoid this disappointment by choosing more than one person—each competent in a specific area—to make up a mosaic role model.

Mosaic role model: a role model made of many people, with each person serving as an example for a specific area of strength.

In Exercise 5.3, you might have discovered that none of your role models is strong in all four areas listed. If this is true, you might want to complete Exercise 5.4.

You might even serve as a role model for someone else. See the boxed features on setting an example for good classroom behavior and on being the best that you can be.

Individual Role Models

Identify five individuals who fit your basic qualifications for a role model. Indicate in the table below their relative strengths or weaknesses in the four areas listed, plus any other area that is appropriate in the last column.

NAME	PERSONAL PHILOSOPHY AND OUTLOOK	INTELLECTUAL SKILLS	MORAL AND ETHICAL VALUES	INTERPERSONAL SKILLS	OTHER

Identifying a Mosaic Role Model

In this table, name individuals who might contribute to your concept of a mosaic role model.

NAME	AREA OF STRENGTH

Set the Example for Good Classroom Behavior

Some students do not know what kind of behavior professors expect from them in the classroom. If your professors have guidelines, such as in their syllabi, use them as much as possible. Otherwise you might want to follow these general guidelines:

1. *Arrive on time.* If this is your first class of the day, get up early; walk briskly; don't stop to talk to friends. If you are leaving a class that frequently runs overtime, meet with the professor. Respectfully remind her that you have another class to go to across campus and would appreciate her ending on time.

2. *Sit as close to the front as possible.* Arrive early so that you can sit near the front of the room. Studies show that students in front are more involved, get bored less often, experience fewer distractions, and get better grades. If the room has auditorium-like seating, with seats higher in the back than in the front, sit so that you are at least at eye level with the professor.

3. *Avoid distracting behavior.* Most people have trouble learning in an atmosphere of confusion. Limit the talk to your neighbor while class is in session. Make a note of anything you want to talk about and discuss it after class. Do not shuffle papers and books or pack up until class is dismissed.

4. *Stay alert.* Sometimes you might find it difficult to stay attentive during a lecture. Your mind will wander less if you prepare for the class and participate in it by asking questions. If participation is not appropriate, you can always ask yourself questions about each of the concepts covered, such as, "How can I use this information?" "What is this topic related to?"

5. *Turn off your beeper/cell phone.* Unless you are a doctor and expect emergency calls, you probably will not receive any important calls during an hour or hour-and-a-half lecture.

6. *Do not leave until the class is over.* Instructors will often make some of their most important points and may assign homework during the last few minutes of the class. You will want to be present to hear the closing remarks and announcements.

Remember this point: When you follow these guidelines of expected behavior, you not only enhance the learning atmosphere for yourself and your fellow students, you might also enhance your chances of success. You never know whom you might need to help you advance to the next stage of your career. Will your instructors be able to write a strong, positive letter of support, or will they say, "He got a passing grade in my class, but he also came in late, sat in the back, was disruptive, and left early."

Be the Best That You Can Be

In college, students compete for grades. After college, they compete for jobs. Our culture in the United States promotes this behavior. It has its advantages, but a disadvantage is that some people suffer ill effects from competition, namely, low self-esteem and high anxiety.

If you have trouble dealing with competition, use the following guidelines to be the best that you can be. The end result should be healthier outlook and a well-balanced life.

1. *Avoid excuses.* No one cares about your excuses; they only care about your results. If you have problems, find ways to fix them using problem-solving strategies such as those in Chapter 3.

2. *Reject boredom.* Focus your attention. Go to each lecture with a list of questions you expect the lecture to answer. Pay close attention to see if the professor answers your questions. Make a note of other questions that he might raise during the lecture.

3. *Sit on the front row or at eye level with the professor.* This helps you stay mentally involved in the class.

4. *Visit your professor during office hours and attend TA sessions.* These are opportunities for you to get questions answered, meet other students, and develop rapport with the professor and TA.

5. *Join or form a study group.* Choose people near your skill level. The section in this chapter on individual and group study covers this issue in more detail.

6. *Review notes for scheduled courses every day.* This process will reduce the need for cramming before exams.

7. *Stay Healthy.* Poor health could hinder your performance. Do what you can to maintain good health. Eat well, exercise, and learn how to manage stress (see Chapter 6).

8. *Take a long-term view.* Go to each lecture or seminar looking for at least one piece of information that you might use in the future. Keep notes; what you don't use now, you might discover to be useful later.

9. *Choose friends wisely.* Chapter 7, on relationships, points out the impact that friends can have on your performance.

10. *Look for relevance.* Find ways to link the subject matter of your studies with real-life situations.

11. *Choose optimism over pessimism.* Always remember that you are not a victim of the learning process or a passive participant in it. You can make a difference in what and how you learn through your own efforts.

12. *Assemble your team of personal advisors.* Find a few key people who can give you feedback on your ideas and activities and help you know if you are on the right track or headed in the wrong direction. Your group might consist of students, staff members, instructors, and people outside the campus.

Although there is no guarantee that any of these strategies will help you get straight As, they will help you be the best that you can be.

Reactive students tend to study alone most of the time. Proactive students study alone, but they also spend some time studying in groups. Students who study in groups often learn more, accomplish more, and have more fun. Group study might be formal, informal, or both.

Many campuses today have formal group-study programs. For example, in a program started by Dr. Uri Treisman at the University of California at Berkeley, students taking math and science courses study in groups of 15 to 20 for four to six hours per week. Prior to the workshop sessions, students work on their homework assignments individually. During the workshop, students may do the following:

- Collaborate with other students to work on problems encountered during individual study.

- Participate in group discussions about points made during lectures that need clarification.

- Work problems that were not assigned.

- Participate in reading and discussions about upcoming material.

- Prepare and take mock exams.

Each meeting has a workshop leader present who might be a staff person, a graduate student, or an undergraduate student. The workshop leader may do the following:

- Plan ways to help students avoid misunderstandings and difficulties, including conducting mini-lectures and assigning extra problem sets.

- Observe students to see if they are spending time on nonproductive approaches and advise them of more efficient approaches.

(Source: Phil Schofield/ Tony Stone Images.)

- Encourage equal participation by students to avoid domination by a few.

- Challenge students to stretch themselves.

- Help generate an atmosphere of cooperation rather than one of competition.

The key to successful workshop meetings is having students prepare individually before they come to the workshop. Without such preparation, they will have little to contribute to or gain from the sessions.

Informal groups consist of students who meet with other students they know to compare notes and share ideas. A student might join such a group or form one herself by seeking out friends, classmates, or members of social clubs. Many informal groups get started during a professor's office hours or during TA sessions. Group study works best when each member takes responsibility for his share of the total effort. See the boxed feature for some guidelines on starting a group study.

Synergy: a combining of efforts to produce a result greater than the sum of the individual efforts.

Students learn more through group study because of synergy. Each student might view a given issue from a different perspective. The result of sharing these perspectives with one another is often better than the combined efforts of each student working on her own. Thus, some people describe synergy as a process in which the whole is greater than the sum of its parts, or one plus one equals more than two.

In addition to gaining a better understanding of course material, students who study in groups learn skills that will help them later in their careers. For example, they will be familiar with one of the most prevailing strategies in the workplace, people working in teams.

Guidelines for Group Study

1. Call the students on your list to set a time, place, and agenda for your meeting.

2. Select a place where you can all sit around a table and talk, such as a reading room in the library or a quiet dorm room.

3. Come prepared. Bring all necessary books and notes.

4. Schedule activities such as the following for the meeting:

- Comparing/completing notes

- Preparing focus questions*

- Comparing concept questions*

- Creating practice exams

- Creating/comparing comparison grids*

- Creating/comparing focus word links*

- Quizzing each other on facts, vocabulary, etc.

- Generating questions for Socratic writing exercises*

- Generating questions from reading material

*These subjects are addressed later in this chapter.

Make the Most of Your Mental Resources

Most students use a narrow range of learning strategies. They derive most of their knowledge from what they read in books and notes or what they see and hear during lectures. These students lend support to the widely held view that most people use only about 10 percent or less of their mental resources.

Scientists are working to expand our knowledge about the brain and how it works. But you do not have to wait for the results of these studies. There are at least two steps that you can take now to increase your ability to learn: (1) use more than one kind of intelligence, and (2) exploit the power of your imagination.

USE MORE THAN ONE KIND OF INTELLIGENCE

Inert intelligence: mental skills that can be measured by standardized intelligence tests.

A person's thinking style can enhance or hinder her success. For example, some students have high academic intelligence, or inert intelligence, a trait that helps them excel in certain courses. But these same students might do poorly in courses that require more creative or practical forms of

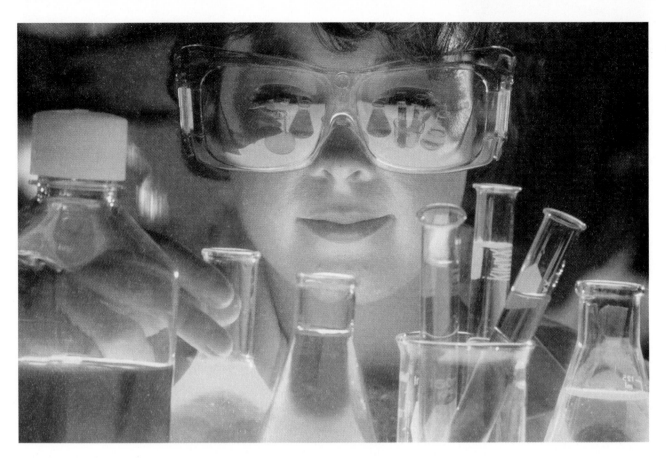

(Source: SuperStock, Inc.)

intelligence. In addition, these students might have problems in careers that require skills in areas other than their strengths. The converse is true for students with the opposite skills. The point is that problems arise when a person uses only one style of thinking and neglects all others. Noted educator Ronald Gross explains:

> Most of us become entrenched in only one or at most two kinds of thinking (rational versus emotional, for example). We grind away in our accustomed ways, with less and less return on the energy expended. If we merely changed to an alternative mode of thinking, we'd regain our energy and enthusiasm. Learning is most effective when we use the full range of our powers, not just the ones we use most.[1]

Often factors beyond a person's control contribute to her patterns of thinking. For example, sometimes children show talent for sports or one of the performing arts at an early age. When this happens, parents and teachers might urge them to pursue these subjects at the expense of math and science courses. In similar manner, parents and teachers might encourage children to favor math and science but neglect other subjects. Schools also play a strong role in influencing what students focus on by favoring those who perform well on standardized tests. The result of these influences is that people form certain habits of thought that might lock them into using just one type of intelligence.

Your success will depend on your efforts to use as much of your abilities as possible, and that includes using more than one kind of thinking. The next two sections cover the how and why of this issue.

TAP MORE OF YOUR MENTAL RESOURCES

You can use a narrow range of your mental resources and still do well in school. Then why should you use more of your abilities? You should use more of your abilities because you want to attain success not only in school but in all other segments of your life. Following are advantages of broadening your base of skills:

1. *You will be more likely to achieve your goals.* Granted, you can achieve much through the use of only inert intelligence. But imagine how much more effective you might become if you also master the skills associated with other aspects of your intelligence: concepts, synthesis, intuition, hunches, imagery, and cooperation.

2. *You will be more adaptable in a rapidly changing society.* The rate of change in world society is more rapid than at any time in recent history. You can expect to face issues of far greater complexity than people had to face in the past. The people who survive and thrive will be those who can tap the full range of their mental resources.

3. *You will have a broader base for career options and contributions.* People often find themselves in jobs or situations that require different skills from those that match their strengths. For example, someone who excels in mathematical logic might have to resolve a complex personnel issue that involves psychological insight and human relations skills. The point is that you increase your flexibility and employability when you can function well in more than one dimension. Also, your main contributions might even come from forays outside your areas of strength. The basic idea for Einstein's theory of relativity came to him through a dream, not through the subject he was studying at the time. Michelangelo produced some of his best works by switching back and forth between art and science.

4. *You will improve your ability to solve problems.* Schools stress the analytical side of problem solving and often slight the other aspects. The best solution to complex problems often requires the use of analytical, creative, and practical mental skills. We will expand on this concept in the discussion of problem solving later in this chapter under "Effective Tools and Strategies for Learning." Exercise 5.5 asks you to consider some other ways in which you might need more than inert intelligence.

• • • • • •EXERCISE 5.5

Potential Benefits of Using More Than One Type of Intelligence

List several additional reasons why you could benefit from using more than one kind of intelligence:

_____

_____

_____

_____

In Chapter 1 through 4, we covered how you think, how thinking relates to behavior, and the importance of self-motivation. The present section is about how to use more of your mental capacity.

"When people are admitted to competitive programs because of their test scores, it often turns out that the only thing the tests predict for them are similar scores on more of the same kinds of tests," says psychologist Robert J. Sternberg.[2] Presumably, your college accepted you because of your grades and test scores. This set of skills has helped you get to where you are and will help you succeed in college if you continue the same pattern. But before you get excited about your prospects for the future, consider whether the skills you have now will do the following:

- Help you learn as much as possible from your courses?

- Help you make the most of your abilities?

- Ensure your career success?

- Ensure your personal success?

- Help you develop the level of proactivity needed for success in all areas of your life?

- Help you develop the skills that lead to good relationships and teamwork?

If you answered no to most of these questions, you need to expand your skill base. The guidelines in this book will help you make the necessary changes to give you a higher probability of success than most of your peers have.

A major problem in our society is that we assume too much about the potential of individuals from their test scores. We place strong emphasis on standardized tests such as the SAT and GRE, which suffer from two major flaws: (1) they fail to measure how well you can think, and (2) they fail to measure the commonsense mental skills needed to be successful in life. Psychologist Robert Sternberg refers to standardized test skills as "inert" intelligence because they fail to predict how well a person can function in a nonacademic world.

Many experts have revised their thinking and now favor views on intelligence that take the following into consideration:

1. Learning from experience

2. Adapting to a different environment

3. Understanding and controlling one's own thinking

4. Recognizing cultural differences

The fourth point deserves a few more comments. Many studies show that cultures differ in their views on intelligence. For example, people in the United States tend to focus on quickness of decision or action as a strong measure of how smart a person is. Yet, many cultures view a quick person as less intelligent than one who reflects or ponders issues deeply before acting. The lack of concern for how different cultures view intelligence might account for many of the problems we face as a nation.

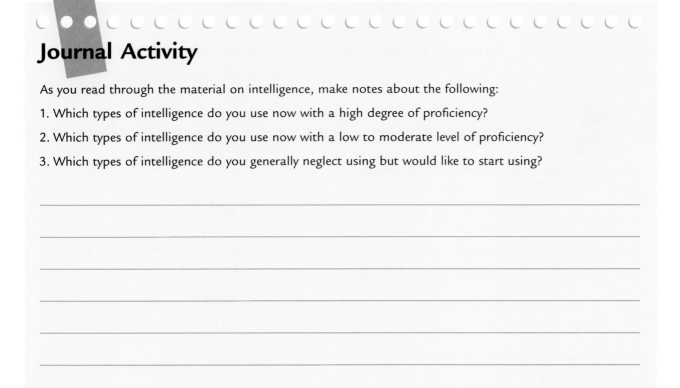

Journal Activity

As you read through the material on intelligence, make notes about the following:

1. Which types of intelligence do you use now with a high degree of proficiency?

2. Which types of intelligence do you use now with a low to moderate level of proficiency?

3. Which types of intelligence do you generally neglect using but would like to start using?

If you want to make the most of your potential, you will want to move beyond academic skills and focus on other aspects of your mental makeup. The discussions that follow summarize three recently developed theories of intelligence. This information will help you determine whether you are making the most of your mental abilities.

■ GARDNER'S THEORY OF MULTI-INTELLIGENCE

Noted educator Howard Gardner argues that people have at least seven "intelligences" rather than a single capacity:[3]

1. *Linguistic intelligence*—verbal, reading, and writing skills

2. *Logical-mathematical intelligence*—logical reasoning and quantitative skills

3. *Spatial intelligence*—ability to recognize images, to manipulate the images in space, and to recreate versions of the images when they are no longer present

4. *Musical intelligence*—ability to perform music or appreciate musical structure

5. *Bodily kinesthetic intelligence*—skillful use of the body

6. *Interpersonal intelligence*—ability to understand and work well with other people

7. *Intrapersonal intelligence*—self-awareness (who you are), self-motivation, personal growth, and capacity for change

Exercise 5.6 will help you begin to recognize where your intelligences lie.

Identifying Your Strongest Areas of Intelligence

Which are your strongest intelligences according to the Gardner model? Circle the numbers of those descriptions that you feel apply to you.

1. You easily remember nice turns of phrase or memorable quotes and use them deftly in conversations.

2. You sense quickly when someone you are with is troubled about something.

3. You are fascinated by scientific and philosophical questions like "when did time begin?"

4. You can find your way around a new area or neighborhood very quickly.

5. You are regarded as quite graceful and rarely feel awkward in your movements.

6. You can sing on key.

7. You regularly read the science pages of your newspaper and look at magazines on science or technology.

8. You note other people's errors in using words or grammar, even if you don't correct them.

9. You can often figure out how something works or how to fix something that's broken without asking for help.

10. You can readily imagine how other people play the roles they do in their work or families and imaginatively see yourself in their roles.

11. You can remember in detail the layout and landmarks of places you've visited on vacations.

12. You enjoy music and have favorite performers.

13. You like to draw.

14. You dance well.

15. You organize things in your kitchen, bathroom, and at your desk according to categories and in patterns.

16. You feel confident in interpreting what other people do in terms of what they are feeling.

17. You like to tell stories and are considered a good storyteller.

18. You sometimes enjoy different sounds in your environment.

19. When you meet new people, you often make connections between their characteristics and those of other acquaintances.

20. You feel you have a keen sense of what you can and can't do.

Now compare the numbers of the questions you circled with those in the key to help you determine your specific areas of intelligence.

Key

QUESTIONS	AREA OF INTELLIGENCE
Questions 1, 8, and 17	Linguistic intelligence
Questions 6, 12, and 18	Musical intelligence
Questions 3, 7, and 15	Logical-mathematical intelligence
Questions 4, 11, and 13	Spatial intelligence
Questions 5, 9, and 14	Bodily kinesthetic intelligence
Questions 10, 16, and 20	Intrapersonal intelligence (knowing yourself)
Questions 2, 10, and 19	Interpersonal intelligence (knowing others)

Source: Reprinted by permission of Jeremy P. Tarcher, Inc., a division of the Putnam Publishing Group from *Peak Learning* by Ronald Gross. Copyright © 1991 by Ronald Gross.

Journal Activity

Describe how the results of Exercise 5.6 might benefit you. For example, if you find that you are weak in the area of bodily kinesthetic intelligence, you might participate in sports or take dancing lessons. These activities would not only help you improve your bodily kinesthetic intelligence, but also help you get more exercise and increase your social interactions.

■ **GOLEMAN'S THEORY OF EMOTIONAL INTELLIGENCE**

Daniel Goleman proposes that you have both a rational mind and an emotional mind.[4] The rational mind is involved in the skills measured by IQ tests. Emotional intelligence, however, Goleman argues, "can be as powerful, and many times more powerful, than IQ. . . "[5] Goleman builds a model around the following five emotional attributes:

1. *Self-motivation*—the ability to manage one's own motivation rather than depend on external sources

2. *Self-awareness*—the ability to monitor one's own feelings

3. *Emotional control*—the ability to manage moods such as fear, anxiety, anger, rage, and so forth.

4. *Empathy*—the ability to attend to the emotional needs of others

5. *Interpersonal skills*—the ability to interact effectively with other people

Remember that learning involves more than performing well on tests. You will want to learn how to improve your interpersonal skills because much of what you will do in life will involve working as a member of a team. Learning how to gain more control over your emotions will help you work around many of the factors that hinder learning and even impair your health.

■ STERNBERG'S THEORY OF SUCCESSFUL INTELLIGENCE

Psychologist Robert Sternberg's model deals with a full range of mental skills that will help you achieve important life goals.[6] Thus, the Sternberg model bears a striking contrast to the concept of inert intelligence. It covers three main areas of intelligence: analytical, creative, and practical.

1. *Analytical intelligence*—the ability to apply problem-solving and decision-making skills to real-life situations

2. *Creative intelligence*—the ability to build on known information to come up with new and interesting ideas; the ability to learn from mistakes

3. *Practical intelligence*—the ability to convert concepts and ideas into practical accomplishments; also known as common sense; involves social skills and a worldly focus

Table 5.1 shows that more mental skills are involved in Sternberg's "successful intelligence" than in "inert intelligence." The Sternberg model confirms the observations of the author of this textbook over the past three decades. Many students who later excelled in their careers did not make the top grades in school. These students had high levels of successful intelligence. They would always make the most of their strengths and shore up or work around their weaknesses. Students without successful intelligence may struggle in their careers despite having received top grades in school.

There is nothing unique about this observation. Most teachers throughout the country can point to similar examples. Professor Sternberg details a story about two students that he knew (Penn and Matt) in his book, *Successful Intelligence*:[7]

(Source: Ron Chapple/ FPG International.)

Penn was one of the most brilliant students at Yale. He had strong analytical and creative skills. When he applied for jobs, he seemed to make the short list of all of the most prestigious firms in his field. Penn was the envy of his peers—but not for long. Despite his many interviews, he received no offers. Penn had two problems. The first was his incredible arrogance. His second

TABLE 5.1
*Comparison of Inert
Intelligence and
Successful Intelligence*

INERT INTELLIGENCE	SUCCESSFUL INTELLIGENCE
Verbal Reasoning	**Analytical**
Vocabulary	Comparison/contrast
Comprehension	Judgment
Absurdities	Analysis
Verbal relations	
	Creative
Quantitative Reasoning	Discovery
Number series	Invention
Arithmetic word problems	Intuition
	Insight
Figural/Abstract Reasoning	Imagination
Pattern analysis	Supposition
	Synthesis
Short-Term Memory	
Memory for sentences	**Practical**
Memory for digits	Use
Memory for objects	Application
	Adaptation
	Social competence

Source: Based on concepts from *Successful Intelligence* by Robert Sternberg. Copyright © 1996 by Robert Sternberg by permission of Simon and Schuster.

(*Source: Janeart Ltd./ The Image Bank.*)

problem was that he didn't have enough common sense to hide this flaw in his personality. Penn did receive and accept an offer from a second-rate firm, but he lasted less than two years on the job.

Contrast Penn's story with that of his classmate, Matt. Matt did not have Penn's brilliance, but he had a warm, sincere personality and high social skills. Matt ended up in the second tier of most interviews, but he received offers from seven out of eight interviews. Matt accepted one of the offers and turned it into a successful, though not stellar, career.

The message for you in the story of Penn and Matt is to realize that you cannot rely solely on your teachers' evaluations and your grades and test scores to predict your potential for success in life. For example, teachers sometimes misjudge talent. As the boxed feature shows, some of the most successful people in history did not impress their teachers (mentors) when they were students.

In addition, quantitative criteria are not the final measure of what you can become. In other words, the full extent of your abilities cannot be judged by your grades or test scores. They cannot tell you whether you will meet the challenges of life and career. They can provide useful information to help you assess your skills and find ways to compensate for your deficiencies. But they are only an aid to assessment, not the final word.

The material in the boxes on the three types of intelligence—analytical, creative, and practical—provides guidelines for moving beyond the inert intelligence that enables you to do well on tests. Review these boxes and the exercises that follow often. When you apply the strategies they address to your work as a student, you will be preparing yourself to use them as well in life outside the classroom. These strategies will help you manage most of the tasks you will face in life.

The material in the boxes shows how you can apply a specific type of intelligence to a specific situation. Be aware of events that require you to use all of your forms of intelligence—analytical, creative, and practical. Get in the habit of asking the "how" type of questions: "How can I join the fraternity and still maintain a high grade point average?"

The previous discussion focused on the use of the Sternberg model of successful intelligence in general situations. Table 5.2 shows you how to apply this approach to your specific courses.[8]

What Some Teachers and Mentors Said About Their Students

Abraham Lincoln
"When you consider that Abe has had only four months of school, he is very good with his studies, but he is a daydreamer and asks foolish questions."

Woodrow Wilson
"Woodrow is a unique member of the class. He is ten years old and is only just beginning to read and write. He shows signs of improving, but you must not set your sights too high for him."

Albert Einstein
"Albert is a very poor student. He is mentally slow, unsociable, and is always daydreaming. He is spoiling it for the rest of the class. It would be in the best interests of all if he were removed from school at once."

Amelia Earhart
"I am very concerned about Amelia. She is bright and full of curiosity, but her interest in bugs and other crawling things and her daredevil projects are just not fitting for a young lady. Perhaps we could channel her curiosity into a safe hobby."

Enrico Caruso
His teacher told him that he had no voice.

Admiral Richard Byrd
He was retired from the Navy as "unfit for service."

Louisa May Alcott
An editor told her that she would "never be able to write anything for popular consumption."

Source: From *The Power of Optimism* by Alan Loy McGinnis. Copyright © 1990 by Alan Loy McGinnis.

General Analytical Intelligence

- Identify personal goals: academic goals, personal-growth goals, financial goals, career goals, relationship goals, and spiritual goals (discussed in Chapter 4).

- Monitor your progress toward your goals.

- Monitor your thoughts and behaviors (self-assessment).

- Request feedback on your progress from trusted friends, family members, or professionals.

- Identify problems that prevent you from reaching your goals

General Creative Intelligence

- Allow for mistakes and setbacks (discussed in Chapter 2).

- Take sensible risks (discussed in Chapter 2).

- Seek out tasks that force you to be creative; that is, look for tough problems to solve.

- Allow time for creative thinking (discussed in the problem-solving section later in this chapter under "Effective Tools and Strategies for Learning").

- Tolerate ambiguity; that is, see issues in shades of gray rather than in black and white terms.

- Find ways to overcome or work around resistance to your ideas.

- Seek out opportunities to enhance your personal growth by means of books, tapes, and seminars.

- Get passionate about something and follow through; you will always perform at a higher level if you like what you are doing.

- Find and fix the problems that prevent you from reaching your goals.

- Ask "why" and "what if?"

General Practical Intelligence

- Assess your strengths and weaknesses. Remember, no one is good at everything. What do you do best? How can you compensate for your weaknesses?

- Shore up your strengths and compensate for your weaknesses.

- Keep a journal. In each learning situation, ask yourself, "How can I apply this information to other courses, to my personal life, to my relationships, to my career?"

- Focus on ways to use, apply, construct, translate, sketch, solve, express, explain, and describe.

COURSE	ANALYTICAL	CREATIVE	PRACTICAL
Science	Judging the work of other scientists	Designing an experiment yourself	Carrying out the experiment you designed; finding practical applications for experiments
Literature	Analyzing plots, themes, characters	Writing a story	Applying concepts from literature to everyday life
History	Comparing major works of the last 200 years	Imagining how you might have responded if you had been a participant in a major battle of the past	Figuring out what we can learn from the past to prevent future wars
Art	Judging an artist's work for style or form; comparing the style of art from various periods	Creating a work of art yourself	Developing a marketing strategy for your work

TABLE 5.2

Application of Sternberg Forms of Intelligence to Specific Courses

Source: Based on concepts from *Successful Intelligence* by Robert Sternberg. Copyright © 1996 by Robert Sternberg by permission of Simon and Schuster.

Journal Activity

Identify a problem that exists on your campus. Outline how you would solve the problem. Indicate at each step which form of intelligence (analytical, creative, practical, all) you would be using. Repeat the exercise for a problem that exists in your community, your country, or a global problem. Compare your results with those of some of your classmates.

In his book, *Peak Performance,* psychologist Charles Garfield relates the remarkable story of Liu Chi Kung.[9] This brilliant concert pianist placed second to Van Cliburn in the 1958 Tchaikovsky Competition. The next year, Liu was one of many individuals sent to prison during the Cultural Revolution in China. The prison officials did not allow him to play the piano at all during his seven years of confinement. When they released him from prison, Liu promptly went back on tour. The critics were amazed that his musicianship was better than ever. The secret to Liu's success was that he would practice mentally each day. Dr. Garfield observes,

> *Research has shown that imagined events imprinted deeply in the mind are recorded by the brain and central nervous system as memories. With practice and repetition, one can imagine well enough so that these memories are not distinguishable from actual physical experience.*[10]

Mental rehearsal/mental imagery: to form a picture in your mind of events and go over them as if they were real.

Scientists use several terms to describe this process: imagination, mental rehearsal, mental imagery. When you use this method, you practice desired thought patterns or habits with the mind "as if" they were real. If you have a pattern you want to change or a new skill you want to acquire, your imagination can speed up the process significantly. Many of the major insights and discoveries of our time came first through mental images. For example:[11]

- Discovery of the benzene ring by chemist Friedrich August von Kekule

- Invention of the sewing machine by Elias Howe

- Creation of the periodic table of chemical elements by Dmitry Ivanovich Mendeleyev

- Invention of the automatic flour mill by Oliver Evans

- Formulation of the theory of relativity by Albert Einstein

- Invention of the violin bow by Guiseppe Tartini

Psychiatrist Maxie Maultsby is a pioneer in the use of imagery in therapy.[12] He compares the "as if" process to ground training for pilots. Prior to flying, pilots spend hours on the ground acting "as if" they were flying the plane.

Much of the research in this field of imagery has come from studies on athletes. For example:

- Former basketball great Bill Russell would picture in his mind the moves of great players, then practice the moves over and over until he could duplicate them precisely.[13]

- Tests on basketball players during free-throw shooting showed that the performance of those who used mental rehearsal during practice was up to 15 percent higher than those who did not.[14]

- Imagined physical movement can cause muscles to react in ways that people can detect on electrical instruments.[15]

The use of imagery is more than a tool for just artists and athletes. All people can, and many do, use this process from time to time. For example, a

GROUP	ACTIVITY	RESULTS
I	Took speaking course; no mental practice	No improvement
II	Read material on speaking; moderate mental practice	Significant improvement
III	Underwent extensive training, including readings, and videotape models; extensive mental practice	The most improvement

Source: From *Peak Performance* by Charles Garfield. Copyright © 1986 by Charles Garfield. By permission of William Morrow and Co., Inc.

research team studied people who were afraid of speaking in public.[16] They divided the participants into three groups. Table 5.3 shows what each group did and the results. Note that Group III showed the most improvement. The reason for this group's success is that they practiced mentally against a norm. Through imagery, they sought to mimic the performance levels of the models they watched on videotape.

Imagery is one of the best techniques known for helping you manage your thoughts and habits. Imagery can help you

- Model successful people

- Learn new skills

- Eliminate fears

Journal Activity

Take a few minutes to brainstorm about using imagery to help you in several of the areas just listed.

_____

_____

_____

_____

_____

_____

- Overcome compulsive behavior

- Design your future

Since the mind cannot tell the difference between a real experience and one imagined vividly, your imagination can provide the basis for your new behavior.

Most successful people use a form of mental rehearsal to help them prepare for events or overcome certain challenges. You do not need any special training to master this skill. Just use it often in the following way:

1. Find a quiet place.

2. Close your eyes and focus on an issue.

3. Let your mind do the rest.

Effective Tools and Strategies for Learning

This section will equip you with tools and strategies for becoming a better learner. For example, you will learn how to take good notes and use them effectively. You will also learn how to get more out of your reading assignments. Once you have acquired good information, you need to apply some form(s) of analysis to it. These tools will take you beyond memorizing facts and help you see concepts as they relate to the big picture. Finally, you will learn how to be more effective in solving problems, writing papers, dealing with complex tasks, and preparing for exams.

ASK DIFFERENT TYPES OF QUESTIONS

Your success as a learner depends both on your attitude and on your ability to master certain cognitive skills. These are the skills involved in analysis and problem solving. The key to analysis and problem solving is asking questions. To tap more of your mental resources, you need to ask different types of questions, reflecting different levels of thinking.

As a child, you spent a large portion of your time asking questions. You questioned parents, relatives, teachers, and playmates. From the answers to this battery of questions, you formed your beliefs, gained insights into your own personality, and created a mental picture of the world around you.

If you are like most people though, you tended to ask fewer and fewer questions after you started attending school. One reason for this pattern is that many teachers lecture to the students rather than encourage them to ask questions. Another reason that people ask fewer questions is that they don't want to appear stupid. Professor James Adams, author of *Conceptual Blockbusting*, explains that this fear is based on the belief of most people that others know more than they do.[17] Thus, they feel that asking questions will expose their ignorance. Adams observes, however, "No one has all the answers, and the questioner, instead of appearing stupid, will often show his insight and reveal others to be not as bright as they thought."[18]

Indeed, Professor Adams confirmed a point that Socrates made thousands of years ago. Socrates concluded that he did not know anything, so he set out to educate himself. His approach was to learn by questioning other people that he felt knew more than he did. Every day, Socrates would stop passersby on the streets and ask them questions about basic concepts and values. He questioned everybody that entered his space. To his surprise, Socrates found out that nobody else knew anything either. But he figured he had an advantage—he knew that he didn't know anything, while others did not. Socrates' style of questioning impressed some people but offended others because he would often force them to contradict themselves and look silly.

No learned person would think of Socrates as ignorant because he asked questions. Instead, scholars agree that he was one of the greatest teachers who ever lived. His method of teaching, the *Socratic method*, is the basic model for critical inquiry in western societies.

Knowledge: in this context, knowledge simply refers to knowing facts well enough to able to recall them.

In lectures and readings, always learn in as many ways as you can. Asking any kind of questions will help you acquire **knowledge** (facts), but different types of questions reflect different levels of learning. That is, some questions will help you learn simple facts, whereas other questions address how to understand, use, dissect, create, and evaluate knowledge.

The strategy that is laid out in Table 5.4 stems from Professor Benjamin Bloom's classic system for ordering thinking skills.[19] Using this approach, you ask questions at six levels: knowledge, comprehension, application, analysis, synthesis, and evaluation. Table 5.4 shows all six levels to help you appreciate the options you have for asking questions as you do your assignments. For simplicity, you might think of two levels: 1) simple questions that reflect memory and comprehension, and 2) complex questions that reflect higher levels of thinking. The column of key words is based on Fuhrmann and Giasha's *A Practical Handbook for College Teachers*.[20] The examples in the far right column will help you tap the various levels of thinking. Note that many complex questions begin with "how" or "what if?"

Example 5.1 shows how the different levels of questions apply to a specific topic.

(Source: Patrick Clark/ Monkmeyer Press.)

LEVELS OF QUESTIONS	BLOOM'S CLASSIC LEVELS OF QUESTIONS	DESCRIPTION	KEY WORDS IN THE QUESTIONS OR IMPLIED QUESTIONS	EXAMPLES
Simple	Knowledge	Focus on recall of factual information. Answers are verifiable through reference sources.	Define, identify, label, list, match, name, outline, reproduce, record, recall, repeat, select, state, ask who, what, when, where?	List five characteristics of a goal.
	Comprehension	Understand the meaning and intent of knowledge.	Convert, defend, describe, discuss, distinguish, estimate, explain, extend, extrapolate, generalize, Give examples, infer, interpret, paraphrase, predict, rewrite, summarize, translate.	Explain the reason for having a "no drinking on campus" policy.
Complex	Application	Use knowledge in new ways, such as to generalize; detect and apply the underlying principle of knowledge.	Apply, change, compute, discover, demonstrate, illustrate, manipulate, modify, operate, prepare, predict, produce, relate, show, sketch, solve, use.	How would you design this classroom to allow access for students using wheelchairs?
	Analysis	Dissect knowledge into its component parts and see the relationships among the parts.	Compare, diagram, differentiate, distinguish, illustrate, identify, infer, outline, point out, relate, select, separate, subdivide.	Subdivide your chemistry class based on the mathematics background of your classmates.
	Synthesis	Combine knowledge from varied sources to come up with something new.	Categorize, combine, compare, compile, create, derive, devise, design, explain, generate, If . . . . then . . . what . . . ? Modify, organize, plan, propose, rearrange, reconstruct, relate, reorganize, rewrite, revise, solve, summarize, tell, write, ask what if?	What academic goals will I have to achieve if I want to graduate in four years?
	Evaluation	Judge or assess the value of knowledge based on a set of criteria.	Appraise, assess, compare, conclude, contrast, criticize, describe, discriminate, explain, interpret, judge, justify, measure, support.	Justify the use of undergraduate students as teaching assistants.

Source: Adapted from *Taxonomy of Educational Objectives* by Benjamin S. Bloom. Copyright © 1956. Reprinted by permission Addison-Wesley Educational Publishers, Inc. Adapted from B. Fuhrmann and A. Grasha: *A Practical Handbook for College Teachers*. Copyright © 1983, Little Brown & Company. Used with permission of the publishers.

TABLE 5.4
Levels of Questions

EXAMPLE 5.1

The Topic is the Civil War.

Knowledge

Name the defining battle of the Civil War.
Who was the U.S. president during the Civil War?

Comprehension

Describe the major causes of the Civil War.
Distinguish the positions of the North and South.

Application

Apply the lessons learned from the Civil War to the current U.S. political and economic framework.

Analysis

Compare the perspectives of a Southern landowner, a Northern businessperson, and a slave during the Civil War.

Synthesis

If the South had won the Civil War, what would have been the effects on the United States?

Evaluation

Assess the effects of the Civil War on the U.S. economy in the North and in the South.

●●●●●●EXERCISE 5.7

Practice Developing Levels of Questions

Choose a topic that interests you. Generate two questions for each of the levels of questions in Table 5.4.

You will find Table 5.4, Example 5.1, and Exercise 5.7 useful in writing questions for your notes as well as for your reading and writing assignments.

USE THE DNA FORMAT FOR LECTURE NOTES

Taking good notes is perhaps the most important step in the learning process. You cannot remember every thought, idea, or concept that you read or hear. You need an accurate record of your learning experiences to help you prepare for exams, term papers, and future tasks. A good notetaking system helps you recall facts as well as grasp concepts.

TABLE 5.5
DNA Format for Lecture Notes

FEATURE	COMPONENTS
Directory of Notes for one Course	▪ Title of lecture ▪ Date ▪ Concept question(s) ▪ Pages
Notes for each Class	▪ Common abbreviations ▪ Notes ▪ Focus questions ▪ Glossary
Analytical Tools	▪ Focus word links ▪ Comparison grids ▪ Thoughts and ideas ▪ Questions for professor or TA

Use the DNA Format to take notes in your lectures. This system is based on Walter Pauk's Cornell Notetaking System.[21] Just as your biologic DNA serves as a record for the characteristics that define your life, so the DNA Format is a record of your learning activities. As shown in Table 5.5, it consists of three parts: a directory (D) of notes, the actual notes (N), and some analytical tools (A). We will look at each of these parts in detail.

Directory for History 120

Date	Title	Concept Question*	Pages
	Abbreviations		1
Oct 6, 1999	Colonial Africa	Discuss the migration of Europeans to the African continent and its impact on the people of that region.	2–10

*See step 10 in the next section for a definition of *concept questions.*

The DNA Directory is like a table of contents for your lecture material. Creating a Directory section now will make work much easier when you review your notes in studying for exams or look for references to your notes in the future. Put the following items in your directory: date, listing and page numbers for abbreviations, lecture notes, and concept questions.

■ DNA NOTES

The second part of the DNA Format is the notes themselves. In the first page of your Notes section, insert a list of abbreviations that you use for taking notes on this particular subject. The following list shows samples of abbreviations that some students use. The key to abbreviating words for your notes is to leave out unnecessary vowels. Exercise 5.8 allows you to create some of your own abbreviations.

Sample Abbreviations for Notes

Word	Abbreviation
time	tm
that	tt
this	ths
ing	g e.g. going = gog
ize	z e.g. visualize = visualz
ion	n e.g. notion = notn
at	@
because	b/c
with	w/
what	wht
Biology	Bio
Chemistry	Chm
Mathematics	Mth
Psychology	Psych or ψ
political	pol
people	ppl
example	ex
function	funct
discussion	di

Developing Notetaking Abbreviations

Create some abbreviations for your own use in note taking.

WORD	ABBREVIATION

Use the following procedure for taking and processing notes in your classes:

1. Separate your paper into a Focus column and a Notes column as follows. Draw a line down the page that leaves a margin of 2½ to 3 inches from the left edge of the page (Focus column). Write all notes on the right 5½ to 6 inches (Notes column). If you prefer, you can use Cornell-style notetaking paper or buy law-ruled notebooks in your bookstore, depending on which one is available.

2. During the lecture, write down as much as you can in the Notes column. Leave space for items that you miss or don't understand. Later you can fill in missing information or add explanations to confusing information.

The student who took the notes in this example added some abbreviations to the list at the front of the notebook:

Government–govt

Independence/Independent—independ

Leadership—ldrship

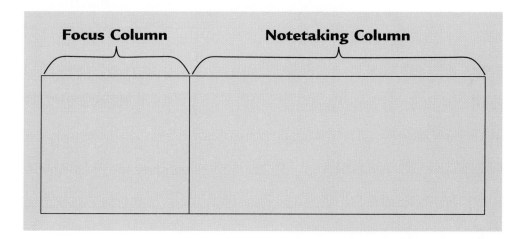

Focus Column   **Notetaking Column**

History 120
Date-Oct 8, 1999

Post-independence Africa-Prof Reynolds

Plenty of high hopes as moved towrd indep. Since indep, post-indep has to do w/ ldrshp in Africa

The nature & perform in the ldrshp in post-indep Africa

Educated Africans (elite) were referred to as elite & they were treated w/ contempt by the European colonists.

This elite took over at the time of indep 3 factors determ their performance

1) colonial heritage
2) ?
3) prob of independence

Colonial heritage, col. gov't was run by a small group of Europeans. They enjoyed privileges over & byond the masses of Africans.

Colonial gov't was very sensitive; hostile to criticism & opposition—couldn't tolerate it from anyone.

But the elite denounced the colonial rul-ings & didn't like the gov't. they still tried to imitate these values as they denounced them.

The new gov't always wanted 1 party at the end b/c they didn't like the gov't oppo-sition.

Another major problem—ethnic diversity & at the time of indep building 1 national gov't.

3. Read over your notes as soon as possible after class. Fill in the missing blanks, and clear up points of confusion after consulting the text, another student, or the instructor or TA.

4. Look in the Notes column of each page and try to identify four or five main points that the professor made during that lecture.

5. Write a focus question in the Focus column for each main point. Focus questions call your attention to the main points in the lecture.

6. Highlight focus words in the Notes column. Focus words direct your attention to central facts or concepts and cause you think of related concepts. Focus words help you memorize information.

Notes with Focus Questions

	History 120 Date Oct 8, 1999
	Post-independence Africa
	Describe the nature of post-independence problems in Africa nd the failure of the gov't to deal w/ them: is there hope?
What is the basis of post-indep problems?	Plenty of high hopes as moved towrd indep. Since indep, Post-indep has to do w/ldrshp in Africa
	The nature & perform in the ldrshp in post-idep Africa
Who are the elites in Africa & how where they treated by the Europeans colonists?	Educated Africans (elite) were referred to as elite & they were treated w/ contempt by the Euro peans colonists.
Name 3 factors that determined the performance of elites post-independently.	This elite took over at the time of indep 3 factors determ their performance 1) colonial heritage 2) the way indep came about (process) 3) prob of independence

(continued)

Notes with Focus Questions *(continued)*

How would you describe colonial heritage w/ respect to masses of Africans?	Colonial heritage, col.gov't was run by a small group of Europeans. They enjoyed privileges over & byond the masses of Africans.

Colonial gov't was very sensitive; hostile to criticism & opposition—couldn't tolerate it from anyone. |
| Explain the irony/paradox in the attitude of elites toward colonial gov't values. | But the elite denounced the colonial rulings & didn't like the gov't. they still tried to imitate these values as they denounced them.

The new gov't always wanted 1 party at the end b/c they didn't like the gov't opposition. If you agree w/ the gov't programs, how can you be in the opposition? There is no place for opposition. |
| Cite a major source of prob. In terms of unity. | Another major problem—ethnic diversity & at the time of indep building 1 national gov't. |

Notes with Focus Questions and Focus Words Highlighted

	History 120
Date Oct 8, 1999

Post-independence Africa—Prof Reynolds

Summary Q

Describe the nature of post-independence problems in Africa and the failure of the gov't to deal w/ them: is there hope? |

What is the basis of post-indep problems?	Plenty of high hopes as moved towrd indep. Since indep, Post-indep has to do w/ ldrshp in Africa
Who are the elites in Africa & how where they treated by the Europeans colonists?	The nature & perform in the ldrshp in post-idep Africa
	Educated Africans (elite) were referred to as elite & they were treated w/ contempt by the European colonists.
Name 3 factors that determined the performance of elites post-independ.	This elite took over at the time of indep 3 factors determ their performance 1) colonial heritage 2) the way indep came about (process) 3) prob of independence
How would you describe colonial heritage w/ respect to masses of Africans?	Colonial heritage, col. gov't was run by a small group of Europeans. They enjoyed privileges over & byond the masses of Africans.
	Colonial gov't was very sensitive; hostile to criticism & opposition—couldn't tolerate it from anyone.
Explain the irony/ paradox in the attitude of elites toward colonial gov't values.	But the elite denounced the colonial rulings & didn't like the gov't. they still tried to imitate these values as they denounced them.
Predict the inevitable outcome of intolerating any opposition.	The new gov't always wanted 1 party at the end b/c they didn't like the gov't opposition. I you agree w/ the gov't programs, how can you be in the opposition? There is no place for opposition.

7. Perform self-test 1: look at each focus question and try to answer it by glancing at the focus words.

8. Perform self-test 2: cover the Notes column with a piece of paper and see how well you can recall the points prompted by the focus questions. Exercise 5.9 illustrates the concept of focus words.

9. Make a glossary of new terms and their definitions at the end of the lecture notes.

● ● ● ● ●●EXERCISE 5.9

Associating Focus Words with Concepts

The first three lines give examples of focus words and the concepts that they trigger. Fill in the missing spaces on the subsequent lines. Create your own examples when you find blank spaces on both sides of the vertical line.

FOCUS WORD	CONCEPTS TRIGGERED
Stock market	Profits, losses, crashes, depression, prosperity
Rocket scientist	
Homeless	Poverty, disease, mental illness
Affirmative action	
Minority	
Healthy foods	
Family values	
Gangster rap	
	High crime, high unemployment, high illiteracy
	High taxes, regulations
	Guns, trucks, beer
	Tension, oil, war, sheiks
	Pillow, sheets, dark, bed
	Candlelight, soft music, poetry

Updated Directory for History 120

Date	Title	Concept Question*	Pages
	Abbreviations		1
Oct 6, 1999	Colonial Africa	Discuss the migration of Europeans to the African continent and its impact on the people of that region.	2–10
Oct 8, 1999	Post-independence Africa	Describe the nature of post-independence problems in Africa & the failure of the gov't to deal. Is their hope?	11–20

Concept questions: questions that capture the overall focus or central idea of a professor's lecture. Concept questions can bring related and unrelated issues together to create a big picture.

10. Derive one or two concept questions from the lecture and enter them in your Directory. A concept question asks, "What was the big picture that the instructor sought to get across in this lecture?"

■ DNA ANALYTICAL TOOLS

Many students take notes during their classes, and some of these notes even have a directory-like component. The missing feature from these notes, however, is often organization. Without organization, it is difficult to memorize material. The Analytical section of the DNA Format consists of tools to organize the material in ways that stress concepts. Two of these analytical tools are focus word links and comparison grids.

Focus word links: graphic displays of focus words showing their relationships.

Focus word links allow you to connect key words in many ways to form diagrams, maps, and flowcharts. There are many variations on the simple diagram shown in Figure 5.1. For example, Tony Buzan shows numerous ways of linking words and graphics in his books on "mind mapping."[22]

Comparison grid: a matrix that allows the comparison of several items of the same category.

Comparison grids show relationships between items of the same category. A comparison grid is similar to a multiplication table. If you want to know what 3×4 is, you look across from 3 and down the column under 4 to find the answer. Similarly, if you want to compare the policies and issues of two governments, you can put that information in a cell that is at the intersection of a column for the government and the row describing the policies or issues related to that government. Follow these steps to make a comparison grid:

1. Create a grid;

2. Put the categories or items you are trying to compare at the top of the grid;

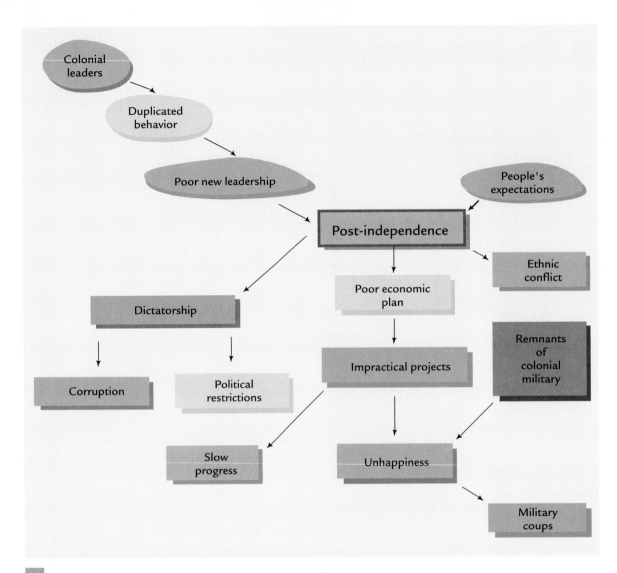

FIGURE 5.1
A diagram of focus word links.

3. Put topics or issues related to the categories along the left side of the grid.

4. Use focus words or short phrases to fill in the cells of the grid

READ WITH A PURPOSE: PQRST METHOD

Most students read with little sense of purpose. Chapter passages become random words that have little meaning. The reading approach described next will help you apply focus to your reading. When you read with a purpose, you are more likely to retain and understand more of the subject matter.

The *PQRST Method*[23] is a highly effective procedure that will help you grasp key ideas and concepts in reading material. The method gets its

Comparing Colonial and New Governments in Africa

Topics/Issues	Categories/Items	
	Colonial gov't	New gov't
Time periods	Pre-independence	Post-independence
Make-up of the leadership	Small group of leaders	Educated elites; small group
Major principles and values of the leadership	Privileges and excesses	Privileges and excesses
Reaction of the leadership to opposition	Torture/ imprisonment	Torture/ imprisonment
Results of intolerance to opposition	Colonial control	1-party; corruption; dictatorship

name from the first letter of its five steps: previewing, questioning, reading, self-recitation, and testing. Note that the letters in this acronym are five sequential letters in the English alphabet; this may help you remember the five stages of "reading with a purpose." Table 5.6 presents a description of the PQRST Method, and Figure 5.2 presents a schematic illustration.

USE TASK-ORGANIZATION STRATEGIES: TASK ANALYSIS AND TO DO LISTS

Many times during your life you might feel that you have more to do than you can possibly get done. In these situations, it is best to focus less on the big picture and more on its smaller segments. In *The Power of Optimism*, Alan Loy McGinnis credits industrialist Henry Ford with saying that any task, no matter how large, is manageable if you break it down into small enough pieces.[24] McGinnis goes on to point out that most optimists think like Henry Ford in that "they bracket their work into manageable segments." According to McGinnis, optimists say, "I don't know how we're going to lick this thing, but at least here's one thing we can do today."

You can adopt this proactive, optimistic attitude as you pursue your studies and conduct your personal affairs. The task-organization system that follows will help you achieve that goal:[25]

STEP	DESCRIPTION
Previewing	Scan headings, subheadings, graphs, tables, pictures, and diagrams to get an idea of what the chapter is all about.
Questioning	Formulate questions from the preview; that is, turn headings, subheadings, graphs, tables, and so on, into questions. If you are reading a textbook, look at the questions at the end of the chapter for clues about what you can expect in your readings. Guess at the answers to your questions in advance to stimulate your curiosity.
Reading	Read for answers to your questions, rephrasing your questions if necessary. Highlight focus words as you read.
Self-recitation	Verbalize the content that you read. Use analytical tools such as focus word links and comparison grids to help reveal gaps in your knowledge.
Testing	Answer your initial questions, or create and answer new, more appropriate questions if necessary. Teach someone else what you have learned.

TABLE 5.6

Description of the PQRST Method

Master Task Worksheet: a list of major tasks that must be done during a specific period of time, with priorities noted.

- *Step 1:* Create a **Master Task Worksheet** for a specific period of time.

- *Step 2:* Identify the big task that you have to get done.

- *Step 3:* Perform a task analysis. Subdivide the tasks into smaller segments. The size of the smaller tasks should reflect your attention span. People vary in terms of how long they can focus on a specific task. Some people have an attention span of 10–15 minutes. Others might be able to focus for 30, 40, or more minutes on a single task.

- *Step 4:* Set priorities based on how soon and for what purpose you need to do the task.

To Do List: a list of specific tasks selected from the Major Task Worksheet to be checked off as they are completed.

- *Step 5:* Create a weekly **To Do List** from the high-priority items for each category.

- *Step 6:* Check off each item on the To Do List as it gets done.

- *Step 7:* Review your Master Task Worksheet weekly, set new priorities, and create new To Do Lists.

This task-organization system might seem cumbersome at first, but it will actually save you time and help you get more done. Try it out in Exercise 5.10.

FIGURE 5.2
Schematic illustration of PQRST Method.

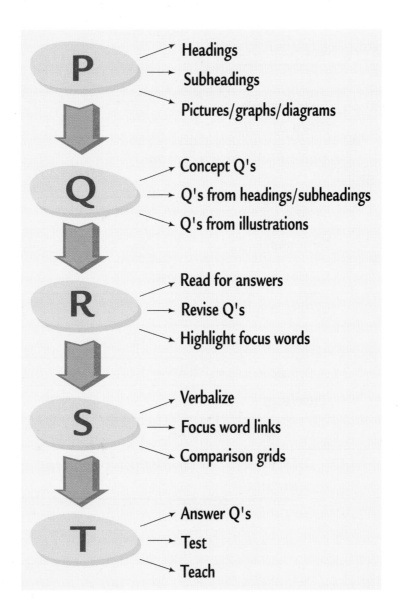

Master Task Worksheet

Task Identification (Step 2)	Task Analysis (Step 3)	Priority Level (Step 4)
Solve Money Problems	Do budget analysis.	1
	Do analysis of how to overcome deficit spending.	2
	Evaluate how options affect goals.	3
	Visit a financial counselor.	3

(continued)

Master Task Worksheet *(continued)*

Task Identification (Step 2)	Task Analysis (Step 3)	Priority Level (Step 4)
Improve Time-Management Skills	Analyze how I spend my time.	1
	Explore time-management options.	3
Assignments	**Term paper**	
	Develop list of questions.	1
	Answer questions.	2
	Organize paper, and add transitions.	3
	Complete paper.	3
	Chemistry	
	Work sample problems.	1
	Obtain feedback from instructor and teaching assistant.	1
	Work problems 1–3.	1
	Work problems 4–6.	1
	Work problems 7–10.	1
	Philosophy Chapter 4	
	Preview chapter.	1
	Generate questions from survey.	1
	Read for answers to questions.	1
	Do self-recitation on sections read.	1
	Biology Chapter 2	
	Preview chapter.	1
	Generate questions from survey.	1
	Read for answers to questions.	1
	Do self-recitation on sections read.	1

Master Task Worksheet *(continued)*

Task Identification (Step 2)	Task Analysis (Step 3)	Priority Level (Step 4)
Select Classes for Spring	Review courses in catalog.	1
	Do degree check.	2
	Consult with academic advisor.	2
	Discuss with professors their expectations.	3
	Balance courses with respect to levels of difficulty.	3
	Register for classes.	3

To Do List for Week Three (Step 5)

Money Problems
_Do budget analysis.

Time Management
_Analyze how I spend my time.

Term Paper
_Develop list of questions.

Chemistry
_Work sample problems.
_Obtain feedback from teaching assistant and instructor.
_Work problems 1–3.
_Work problems 4–6.
_Work problems 7–10.

Philosophy Chapter 4
_Preview chapter.
_Generate questions from survey.
_Read for answers to questions.
_Do self-recitation on sections read.

(continued)

To Do List for Week Three (Step 5) *(continued)*

Biology Chapter 2

_Preview chapter.

_Generate questions from survey.

_Read for answers to questions.

_Do self-recitation on sections read.

_Review courses in catalog.

Spring Semester Courses

_Review courses in catalog.

● ● ● ● ● ●EXERCISE 5.10

Creating a Master Task Worksheet

Fill in the form to make up a Master Task Worksheet for the next month of school.

STEP 2 TASK IDENTIFICATION	STEP 3 TASK ANALYSIS	STEP 4 PRIORITY LEVEL

WRITE PAPERS GOOD ENOUGH TO IMPRESS SOCRATES

Many students panic when their professors ask them to write a paper. The challenge is often not how to write but what to write. The following approach may help you work through the initial trauma of your writing assignments.

Pretend that you are going to have a meeting with Socrates. Earlier you learned that Socrates was a very demanding individual. Try to predict what questions he would ask you about the topic. Write these questions and their answers in advance of the meeting. In selecting the questions, you will want to impress Socrates with your broad thinking skills. Thus, your questions will range from those that reflect simple knowledge to those that point to higher levels of learning (refer to the discussion of

Bloom's six levels of questions earlier in this chapter under "Ask Different Types of Questions."

Once you write the answers to your questions, you can then arrange them in the proper order and add transitional phrases. The overall value of this *Socratic writing approach* is threefold:

1. You are more likely to produce your best work because you are anticipating a demanding audience.

2. You will use your imagination and thus stretch your thinking abilities; perhaps you will learn more with less stress this way.

3. This novel approach to writing can add some fun to an otherwise tedious task.

Exercise 5.11 provides an opportunity to try out this Socratic approach.

TWO PROBLEM-SOLVING STRATEGIES

Proactive students seek out ways to improve their problem-solving skills. The result is that they often have greater success in solving both academic and nonacademic problems. Add the two basic strategies described here to your list of tools. The first is called the *Successful Problem-Solving Process* and is shown in Table 5.7. This tool is a general process based on Graham Wallas's "Creative Problem-Solving Strategy"[26] and Sternberg's "Successful

● ● ● ● ● ●EXERCISE 5.11

Socratic Writing

Your professor has asked you to write a paper on "The Impact of Organic Foods on the Health of Young Children." Write questions reflecting all the levels of the cognitive skill required for writing this paper. Refer to Table 5.4 for key words associated with the different types of questions.

QUESTION LEVEL	QUESTION
Knowledge	
Comprehension	
Application	
Analysis	
Synthesis	
Evaluation	

TABLE 5.7

The Successful Problem-Solving Process

STAGE	OPERATIONS	SKILL AREA
Stage 1	Preparation	Analytical
Stage 2	Incubation	Creative
Stage 3	Illumination	Creative
Stage 4	Verification	Analytical
Stage 5	Follow Through	Practical

Source: Based on Graham Wallas: *The Art of Thought* (London: Watts, 1949), pp. 51–76; and Robert J. Sternberg: *Successful Intelligence* (New York: Simon and Schuster, 1996).

Intelligence" model[27] discussed earlier. The five stages of this process are as follows:

1. *Preparation*—fact gathering, analysis, planning, and organization

2. *Incubation*—stepping back from the problem and doing something else (during this period, the unconscious mind works on the problem)

3. *Illumination*—frequently referred to as the "aha" phenomenon; involves flashes of inspiration or insight

4. *Verification*—checking the accuracy of your solution

5. *Follow through*—taking action on the results

Stages 2 and 3 go hand in hand, but most students do not build these stages into their problem-solving schemes. Stage 3 is one of the most important but least used of the stages. The "aha" effect that occurs in this stage allows for synergy. You will recall that synergy is a combining of efforts to produce a result greater than the sum of the individual efforts. This blending of diverse facts, thoughts, and ideas into new forms can occur at any time but often requires hours, days, weeks, or longer. Scientists know very little about how synergy occurs.

You can make good use of stages 2 and 3 when you write papers and study for exams. For example, most students wait until the last minute to study for exams. Many of them find that they cannot digest enough of the material in such a short time. Also, the added stress often leads to increased anxiety. The result is that many of them do poorly. When you stay current in your courses, you allow for stages 2 and 3 to take place well before the night before the exam. With fewer demands on yourself to produce during a crisis, you can avoid some of the problems that most students face.

The second strategy is called the *Strategy for Solving Mathematics-Based Problems* and is shown in Figure 5.3. It works well when you have to solve problems in your math and science classes. The main purpose of showing this method here is to highlight a point that many students miss

FIGURE 5.3
*The strategy for solving
mathematics-based
problems.*

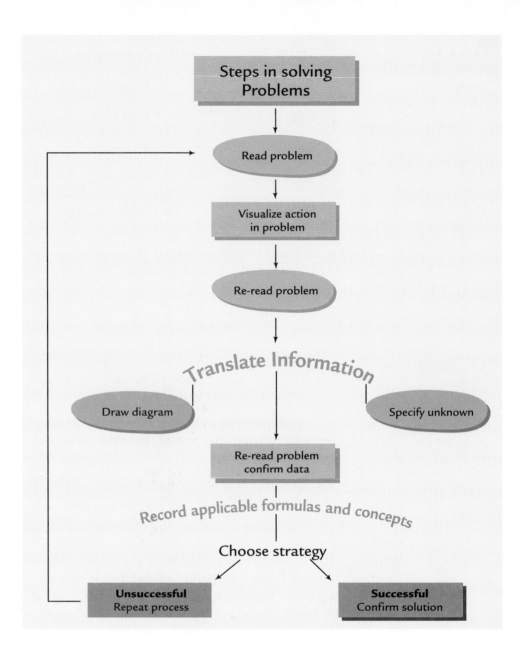

but professors often detect. The difference between success and failure in solving problems is frequently based on how many times you read the problem. When you reread a problem, you will often avoid the costly mistakes that plague many of your peers.

USEFUL APPROACHES TO EXAM PREPARATION

Proactive students think of exam preparation as an ongoing process, not just something that happens at specific times. There are no shortcuts to good exam preparation. Persistence and consistency are essential.

Proactive students exploit one of the most widely known facts about learning—that repetition improves memory. Spaced repetition is a technique based on this fact. In this technique, the lag between the learning events is the key factor. There is little retention when you learn information

Spaced repetition:
learning material over a period of time in which study time is separated by other events.

en masse. You retain much more when you learn the subject matter over periods of time separated by other events.

During exams you need to use your memory ("inert intelligence") as well your higher thinking skills. You also want to be aware of attitudes and habits that could hinder your test-taking ability and that of others. The following guidelines will help you avoid the mistakes that many students make prior to and during exams.

1. *Attend class*—you might learn what to focus on from how the professor presents the lecture.

2. *Stay alert*—find ways to involve yourself with the subject matter.

3. *Attend instructor's office hours and TA sessions.*

4. *Study independently and with a compatible group.*

5. *Take your own notes*—you will learn more.

6. *Use analytical tools* to increase understanding, such as focus word links and comparison grids.

7. *Review notes* briefly each night.

8. *Organize your tasks.*

9. *Attend to your personal needs*—for example, diet, exercise, and personal hygiene. Some students tend to neglect their personal hygiene during the periods of exams; but this issue is important to how you feel as well as to how you might affect someone else.

10. *Get a good night's sleep before exams*—you will be more alert and feel less pressure.

11. *Maintain a positive environment* to reduce anxiety. For example, put off arguments, and limit your exposure to bad news by being selective about what you read in the papers or watch on television.

In plan in Table 5.8 offers suggestions for the material that you should study for exams, with "1" being the highest priority. This plan is only a

TABLE 5.8
Plan for Exam Preparation

MATERIALS	PRIORITY
DNA Format lecture notes	1
Course syllabus	1–2
Notes from TA sessions (high priority if the TA helps develop the test)	1–2
Notes from professor's review session (if held)	1
Old tests given by the professor	1
Old tests given by another professor who taught the course	3
Textbook (priority may vary depending on the professor's emphasis; check with the professor)	1–3

guide. Check with your professor, TA, and the student "pipeline" for specifics as they may pertain to your courses.

Identifying and Correcting Thinking Problems

*T*wo major factors will dictate whether you make the most of your opportunities as a student. The first is self-motivation, and the second is your pattern of thought.

MOTIVATION

Recall from Chapter 4 that self-motivation results from the mind's attempt to satisfy the needs for

1. *Self-management*—control over one's life

2. *Connectedness*—mutual love and caring

3. *Competence*—ability to take on and complete meaningful tasks

Many students lack the degree of self-motivation necessary to perform at their best. If you have a problem in this area, this book will help you get on the right track. For example, Chapters 3 and 4 will help you feel more in control of your life (self-management). Chapter 7 will help you improve your ability to relate to people (connectedness). This chapter will help you become a better learner (competence). Together, these chapters will equip you with the tools you need for self-motivation. Act on what you learn in these chapters, monitor your progress, and self-correct as necessary.

PATTERNS OF THOUGHT

Any of the thinking problems involved in self-defeating beliefs or self-defeating values can hinder your ability to learn. Your task is to identify which thinking problems apply to you and then correct them using the Change Formula (Figure 5.4). In this process, you select a remedy (S) to change the self-defeating belief or value to a productive belief or value that will lead to productive thoughts and behaviors. Some remedies for correcting thinking problems appear in Figure 5.5.

Recall that self-defeating values (or beliefs) lead to self-defeating thoughts that lead to self-defeating behaviors (Figure 5.6). Figure 5.7 shows that you can correct self-defeating values (or beliefs) by using one or more of remedies and thereby achieve productive behaviors. Figure 5.8 shows the impact that values (or beliefs) ultimately have on life outcomes.

When you apply the Change Formula consistently to your own concerns, you will become a more proactive learner. Examples 5.2 through 5.4 show how this is done.

Exercise 5.12 allows you to identify the thinking problems in 15 different examples and select the correct remedy for each.

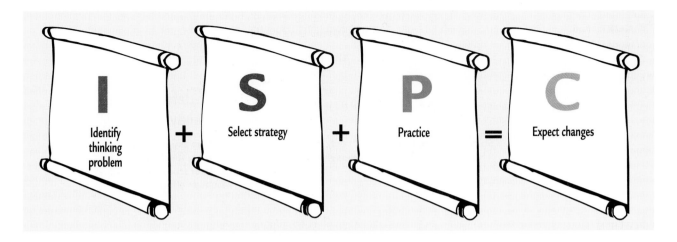

FIGURE 5.4
Change formula to apply to thinking problems.

FIGURE 5.5
Remedies for correcting thinking problems.

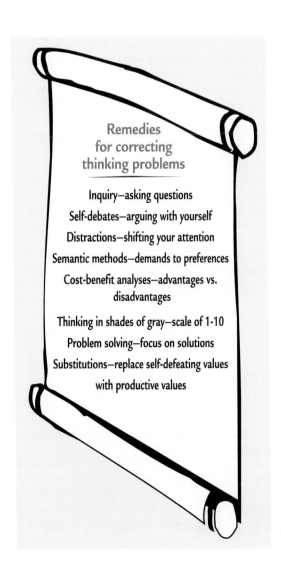

Remedies
for correcting
thinking problems

Inquiry—asking questions
Self-debates—arguing with yourself
Distractions—shifting your attention
Semantic methods—demands to preferences
Cost-benefit analyses—advantages vs. disadvantages
Thinking in shades of gray—scale of 1-10
Problem solving—focus on solutions
Substitutions—replace self-defeating values with productive values

FIGURE 5.6

How self-defeating values lead to self-defeating behaviors.

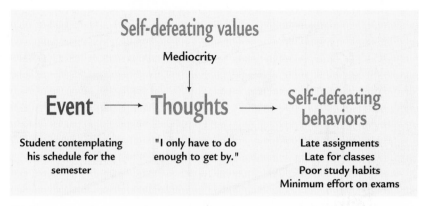

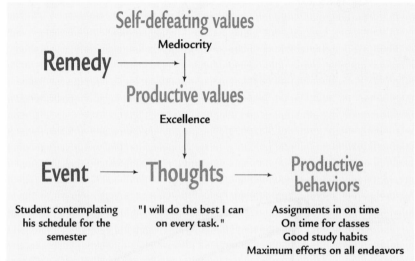

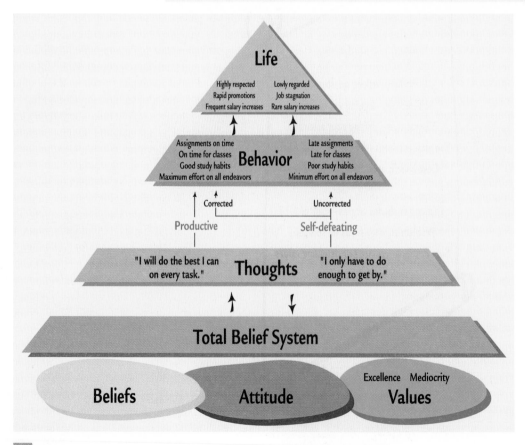

FIGURE 5.8

Impact of values on life outcomes.

EXAMPLE 5.2

Event

Todd did not pass his midterm exam in European History. He feels disappointed over these results.

Todd's Self-Statement

I would have passed the European History midterm if Professor Garcia's lectures had been better organized.

(I) Identify the Thinking Problem

Blaming others. Tod is making Professor Garcia responsible for his education.

(S) Select a Remedy: self-debate

Q. Where is the evidence that I would have done better?
A. There is none.
Q. Whose responsibility is it to learn this course, mine or Professor Garcia's?
A. My responsibility.
Q. Are there other ways of learning the material other than from Professor Garcia's disorganized lectures?
A. Yes, there are several.

(C) Productive Beliefs/Values

Self-motivation; responsibility

Productive Self-Statement

I am responsible for my own education. It would be nice if all professors presented well-organized lectures. Since that is not the case, I will find other ways to learn the material.

(P) Practice

Rehearse the remedy and the productive self-statement

EXAMPLE 5.3

Event

Rebecca is thinking about the B on her grade report for the semester.

Rebecca's Self-Statement

I'm a failure. I wanted all As this semester, but I got four As and one B.

(I) Identify the Thinking Problem

1. All-or-nothing thinking
2. Mental filter
3. Overgeneralization

(continued)

EXAMPLE 5.3 (*continued*)

(S) Select a Remedy

1. *Inquiry:* What constitutes a failure at this university? How would other students, the registrar, and professors define "failure" at this university?
2. *Thinking in shades of gray:* Anyone who can get four As in any semester is a very successful student. In some courses, even a B indicates high performance. Some of the best students do not get all As.

(C) Productive Beliefs

1. Avoid hasty judgments.
2. See all sides of an issue.
3. Avoid using one example to draw conclusions.

Revised Self-Statement

I did not get all As this semester, but I still did very well. I will keep on working to be the best that I can be.

(P) Practice

Rehearse the remedy and the productive self-statement.

EXAMPLE 5.4

Event

Roland is gloating over how much he knows.

Roland's Self-Statement

I feel that I now know enough about electrical engineering to last me throughout my career. I don't have to worry about studying hard any more now that my college days are nearly over.

(I) Identify the Thinking Problem

Value based on unsound principle of complacency

Remedy

Replace unsound principle with sound principle.

(C) Productive Belief/Value

Growth and change

Revised Self-Statement

Electrical engineering is a field that changes rapidly. I will have to stay current; otherwise, I will not be competitive.

Practice

Rehearse the remedy and the revised self-statement.

Correcting Thinking Problems Related to Learning

List the thinking problems, potential consequences, and possible remedy for each thought or behavior.

A STUDENT'S THOUGHTS AND BEHAVIORS	THINKING PROBLEMS	POTENTIAL SHORT-TERM CONSEQUENCES	POTENTIAL LONG-TERM CONSEQUENCES	PROPOSED REMEDY
1. Skips classes; reads the textbook instead				
2. Skips classes; uses other students' notes				
3. Does little studying during the semester and then crams heavily on the night before the exam				
4. Thinks professor's office hours and TA sessions are a waste of time				
5. Only contact with lecture notes is to memorize the material.				
6. Always studies alone				
7. Stays up all night, skips meals, drinks coffee, uses No-Doz				
8. Lacks a system for organizing and managing tasks				
9. Relies exclusively on grades and test scores for motivation				
10. Does only enough to keep from failing her courses				
11. Takes notes and never looks at them again				
12. Focuses on how to get good grades but lacks comprehension of and the ability to use the knowledge acquired				

(continued)

A STUDENT'S THOUGHTS AND BEHAVIORS	THINKING PROBLEMS	POTENTIAL SHORT-TERM CONSEQUENCES	POTENTIAL LONG-TERM CONSEQUENCES	PROPOSED REMEDY
13. Fails to make connections between what he learns and how this knowledge might apply to situations outside the classroom				
14. Makes excuses for poor performance				
15. Occasionally is rude in dealing with other students, professors, and staff people				

Journal Activity

Identify the thinking problems that hinder your ability to make the most of your educational opportunities. How can you use the Change Formula to correct these problems.

Many people give students advice about to live their lives. Work hard. Be more responsible. Prepare for the future. The problem with much of what students hear is that it lacks specifics about how to act on the advice. This text provides those specifics. For example, the advice to take charge of your own education is followed up with a description of tools to help you achieve that task. The tools include attitude and behavior strategies, study skills, and techniques to help you access more of your mental resources. The combined effects of these tools will help you make the most of the talents that you have. *You are in charge.*

NOTES

1. Reprinted by permission of Jeremy P. Tarcher, Inc., a division of the Putnam Publishing Group from *Peak Learning* by Ronald Gross. Copyright © 1991 by Ronald Gross.

2. Quote from *Successful Intelligence* by Robert Sternberg. Copyright © 1996 by Robert Sternberg by permission of Simon and Schuster.

3. Howard Gardner: *Frames of Mind* (New York: Basic Books, 1983).

4. Daniel Goleman: *Emotional Intelligence* (New York: Bantam Books, 1995). Copyright © 1995 by Daniel Goleman. Used with permission of Bantam, a division of Bantam Double-Day Dell Publishing Group, Inc.

5. Ibid.

6. Sternberg: *Successful Intelligence.*

7. Ibid.

8. Ibid.

9. From *Peak Performance* by Charles Garfield. Copyright © 1986 by Charles Garfield. By permission of William Morrow and Co., Inc.

10. Ibid.

11. S. Starker: *F States* (San Bernardino: The Borgo Press, 1985), pp. 91–94. Reprinted with permission of Newcastle Publishing, Inc., North Hollywood, CA, USA © 1985.

12. M.C. Maultsby, Jr.: *Help Yourself to Happiness* (New York: Institute for Rational Living, 1975).

13. B. Russell and T. Branch: *Second Wind: The Memoirs of an Opinionated Man* (New York: Random House, 1979).

14. B. Kalonay in C. A. Garfield with Zina Bennett: *Peak Performance: Mental Training Techniques of the World's Greatest Athletes* (Los Angeles: Tarcher, 1984), pp. 131–132.

15. R. M. Suinn: "Body Thinking: Psychology for Olympic Champs," *Psychology Today* July 1976.

16. Garfield: *Peak Performance.*

17. Adapted from J.L. Adams, *Conceptual Blockbusting,* pp. 105–106. Copyright © 1986 by James L. Adams. Reprinted by permission of Addison Wesley Longman.

18. Ibid.

19. Adapted from *Taxonomy of Educational Objectives* by Benjamin S. Bloom. Copyright © 1956. Reprinted by permission Addison-Wesley Educational Publishers, Inc.

20. Adapted from B. Fuhrmann and A. Grasha: *A Practical Handbook for College Teachers.* Copyright © 1983, Little Brown & Company. Used with permission of the publishers.

21. From Walter Pauk, *How to Study in College,* 6th ed. Copyright © 1997 by Houghton Mifflin Company.

22. T. Buzan: *Use Both Sides of Your Brain* (New York: Dutton/Plume, 1991); and T. Buzan and B. Buzan: *The Mind Map Book* (New York: Plume/Penguin, 1996).

23. Excerpts and figure adapted from *Introduction to Psychology,* Tenth Edition by Rita L. Atkinson, Edward E. Smith, and Daryl J. Bem, copyright © 1990, pp. 762–764, by Harcourt Brace & Company, reprinted by permission of the publisher.

24. Excerpts from *The Power of Optimism* by Alan Loy McGinnis. Copyright © 1990 by Alan Loy McGinnis. Reprinted by permission of Harper Collins Publishers, Inc.

25. From *How to Get Control of Your Time and Your Life* by Alan Lakein. Reprinted by permission of David McKay Co., Inc., a division of Random House, Inc.

26. Graham Wallas: *The Art of Thought* (London: Watts, 1949), pp. 51–76.

27. Sternberg: *Successful Intelligence.*

Read each statement and circle the number that best reflects your response.

NEVER   ALWAYS

1   2   3   4   5   6   7   8   9   10

1. I feel that I am responsible for my health.

   1   2   3   4   5   6   7   8   9   10

2. My meals conform to a semi-vegetarian diet.

   1   2   3   4   5   6   7   8   9   10

3. When I cook, I look for ways to replace unhealthy ingredients with healthier choices.

   1   2   3   4   5   6   7   8   9   10

4. I get 30–45 minutes of moderate exercise each day.

   1   2   3   4   5   6   7   8   9   10

5. My weight falls within acceptable guidelines for my height.

   1   2   3   4   5   6   7   8   9   10

6. I get enough sleep.

   1   2   3   4   5   6   7   8   9   10

7. I respond to stress in constructive ways, not by getting angry.

   1   2   3   4   5   6   7   8   9   10

8. I use a system of relaxation to help me control stress.

   1   2   3   4   5   6   7   8   9   10

9. I reduce stress by staying current in my coursework.

   1   2   3   4   5   6   7   8   9   10

10. When I experience stressful situations, I seek the comfort of close friends or relatives.

    1   2   3   4   5   6   7   8   9   10

11. I wash my hands after using the toilet.

    1   2   3   4   5   6   7   8   9   10

12. I avoid sharing eating or drinking utensils with other people.

    1   2   3   4   5   6   7   8   9   10

13. I avoid risky practices such as body piercing and tattooing.

    1   2   3   4   5   6   7   8   9   10

14. I follow safe practices during intimate contacts with other people.

    1   2   3   4   5   6   7   8   9   10

15. I avoid using chemical substances for the purpose of getting high.

    1   2   3   4   5   6   7   8   9   10

16. I can identify and correct thinking problems that threaten my health.

    1   2   3   4   5   6   7   8   9   10

Determine your relative degree of proactivity for this trait by using the following formula:

Percent Proactivity = Sum of Circled Numbers ÷ 160 × 100

(Note that 160 is the maximum sum possible. It would result in a score of 100 percent.)

Percent proactivity = _____

For example, if you checked 5 for each question, your score would be

Percent Proactivity for Health Issues = 80/160 × 100 = 50

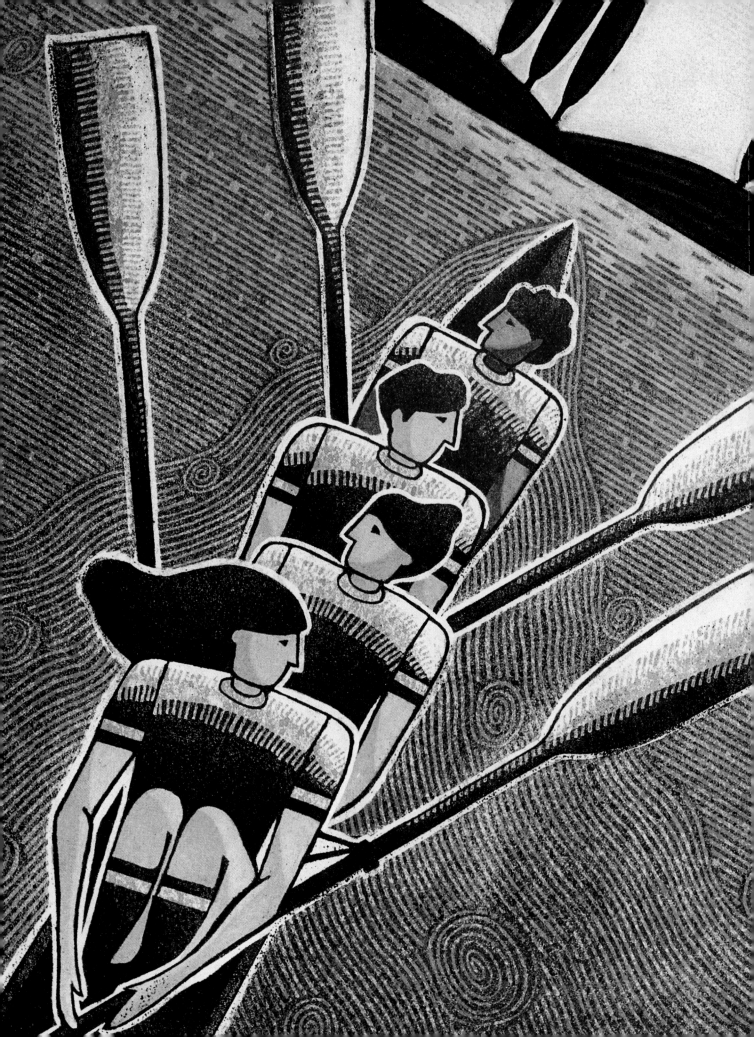

"Good health depends to a large extent on certain lifestyle choices we make that include what we eat, how active we are, whether or not we smoke, the precautions we take to avoid injuries and accident, how we deal with tension and anxiety, even how we manage the environments in which we live and work."

The New Wellness Encyclopedia[1]

Health and Wellness: Proactive Strategies for Now and the Future

OUR STATE OF HEALTH and wellness depends both on factors beyond your control and factors within your control. For example, poor health can be the result of bad genes, environmental factors, self-abuse, or a combination of these conditions. You can do nothing about bad genes. But you often can choose your environment, modify attitudes and behaviors that expose you to unnecessary hazards, and avoid situations that allow the expression of bad genes. In this respect, the state of your health and wellness is partly a choice.

The purpose of this chapter is to help you make proactive choices in the following areas:

- Attitudes about health matters

- Nutrition

- Exercise

- Sleep

- Eating habits

- Stress control

- Disease prevention

- Substance abuse

infectious diseases

modifiable factors

semi-vegetarian diet

sexually transmitted diseases (STDs)

stress

substance abuse

A few years ago, a student asked me to let her bring her dog to class. I refused on grounds that it might be disruptive, or that other students might want to follow her lead. I felt that the situation could get out of hand. A few months later, I met her dog and realized that I had made a mistake. Actually, the dog would have been a better audience for my class than some students. The dog was alert, enthusiastic, and respectful. It did not consume gallons of black coffee, nor did it use drugs or drink alcohol. Her dog did not stay up late at night or eat junk food. There was no evidence that the dog had listened to loud, deafening music through headphones or at concerts.

This student took better care of her dog than some students take care of themselves. Judging from their behavior, some students think that that they will live forever. They also think that they will stay healthy despite their bad habits. For example, Tim smokes cigarettes, uses marijuana, drinks alcohol, and experiments with cocaine. Gina eats junk food and never gets any exercise. Troy gets mad at his roommate several times a week. Ashley is furious with the administration over some of its student policies. She also makes demands on her partner, and gets upset when he doesn't comply.

Many people assume that their health is someone else's responsibility—their parents', doctor's, or government's. These people have a false sense of security in thinking their parents, doctor, or government will be able to fix any health problems they encounter, which obviously is not the case. All people will have their share of health problems and accidents. But you can help prevent many such problems by the kind of life you lead. There is no need for people to feel like victims.

In Western societies, people are living longer. But how long you live is only one issue. The other issue is of equal or even greater concern—what will be the quality of your life as you get older? When you have health problems, it is more difficult to perform at your best. Many factors affect life quality: attitude, diet, physical activity, emotions, and habits. Let's take a closer look at these issues and consider how to take a proactive stance toward your health.

Impact of Attitude and Behavior on Health and Wellness

ARE MEN MORE AT RISK FOR POOR HEALTH?

John is an arrogant, self-centered person with many self-defeating behaviors. He seldom exercises, and he has a poor diet. He hates vegetables. He never goes to the doctor unless he is seriously ill. Unless John changes, he will be part of a trend that he and many men like him could avoid.[2] Many men act like John on health and wellness matters.

What might happen to John? For starters, he can expect to live seven years less than his friend Paula does. Most people know that, on average, women live longer than men do. Fewer people know that men are more susceptible than women to most of the diseases and mishaps that lead to death.[3] For example, at most stages of their lives, men are

- Eighty-eight percent more likely to die of heart disease

- Forty-five percent more likely to die of cancer

- Eighteen percent more likely to die of stroke

- Sixty-nine percent more likely to die of pneumonia or influenza

- Almost eight times more likely to die of AIDS

There is no evidence that genes account for these statistics. However, differences in attitude and behavior might play a strong role in the differences between male and female health. Consider the following findings:[4]

1. *Men live more dangerously.* They are more likely to drive recklessly and engage in risky stunts. Consequently, they have a higher incidence of accidental death and disability. Some of these increased risks for men come from industrial or military situations that are more common for men than women. But overall their behavior patterns make them more susceptible to health problems than women are. In addition, more men than women carry through on suicide threats.

2. *As they grow up, males feel more and more invincible.* They are encouraged and feel compelled to be in charge of their surroundings and their bodies. As a result, they are more likely to shun advice. Many men avoid doctors, checkups, healthy foods, and exercise. These factors have a major impact on whether or not a person contracts or survives a chronic disease.

3. *Men and women think about and behave differently toward their health.* For example, most women see a doctor on a regular basis starting in their early teens. At first, these visits relate mostly to female reproductive issues. In time, women develop a working relationship with their doctors that focuses on broad health concerns. The upshot is that women form a pattern of preventive health care that men seldom acquire.

Attorney Ron Henry shared his insight on why men don't go to the doctor:[5]

> *In our 20s, we don't go to the doctor because we think nothing can hurt us. In our 30s we're too busy with family and jobs to go. By the time we hit our 40s we don't go because we're afraid to find out and don't want to know.*

To be fair, men are not fully at fault for the factors that make them more at risk than women. There is a difference in how our society conditions men and women in regard to health. Still, both men and women are responsible for their own health.

YOUR CHOICES CAN MAKE A DIFFERENCE

The basic principles of maintaining health apply to both genders. About half of the 2 million deaths that occur in the United States each year come from the causes listed in Table 6.1. Notice that these causes of death all involve modifiable factors, or factors that one can choose to change. For example, 300,000 deaths result from poor diet and exercise levels. A person can

Modifiable factors: factors that a person can choose to change.

TABLE 6.1

Number of U.S. Deaths per Year Due to Modifiable Factors

SOURCE	NUMBER OF DEATHS
Tobacco	400,000+
Diet and activity level	300,000
Alcohol	100,000
Infectious agents	90,000
Toxic agents	60,000
Firearms	35,000
Sexual behavior	30,000
Motor vehicles (not including crash deaths related to alcohol or drug use that are included in statistics for those causes)	25,000
Illicit drug use	20,000

Source: *U.C. Berkeley Wellness Letter* (August 1997): 7.

choose to eat a good diet and exercise regularly. For this reason, scientists estimate that most if not all of the deaths represented in Table 6.1 were preventable. This conclusion highlights the role of attitudes and behavior in maintaining health and wellness for as long as possible. The rest of this chapter discusses the proactive attitudes and behaviors you can take to improve your chances for a longer and healthier life.

Journal Activity

Write down any attitudes or behaviors that you have that might have an adverse effect on your health.

_____

_____

_____

_____

_____

_____

Attending to the Basics: Nutrition and Exercise

WHAT IS A HEALTHY DIET?

Katie is living away from home for the first time in her life. She knows little about cooking and is on a tight budget. She relies on fast foods and snacks for most of her meals. Thus, her diet consists mostly of hamburgers, potato chips, candy bars, French fries, and drinks loaded with caffeine.

Staying well is a constant struggle for Katie. During the semester, she often feels run-down and seems to catch every cold that comes along. Katie would like to improve her diet, but she knows little about the subject. She wants to find answers to many questions, such as, what is sound nutrition? How can I distinguish fact from "hype"? Is every doctor or biochemist an expert on this subject? Should I believe the ads on television? Should I believe the athletes, and movie stars—do they know what they are talking about? Whom *can* I trust?

Although experts disagree on many aspects of nutrition, there are some points of near consensus.[6] The best diet is semi-vegetarian and conforms to the U.S. Department of Agriculture guidelines shown in Figure 6.1.

Semi-vegetarian diet: a diet that includes mainly fruits, vegetables, and grains; less amounts of fish, poultry, eggs, and dairy products; occasionally meat; and small amounts of oil and refined sugar.

Definition of serving sizes:

1 slice of bread

1 piece of fruit

½ cup of cooked rice, pasta, or vegetables

3 ounces of cooked lean meat, poultry, or fish

FIGURE 6.1

USDA's food guide pyramid: a recommendation for daily choices.

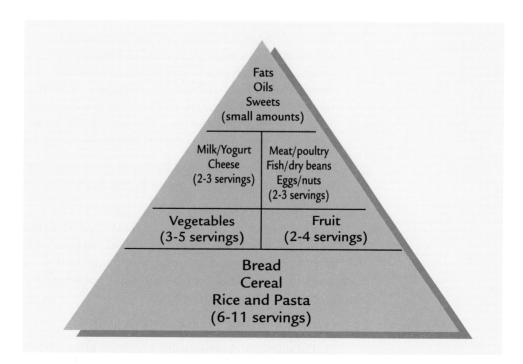

Note that the main items in this diet are fresh fruits, vegetables, and whole grains. There are lesser amounts of fish, poultry, eggs, and dairy products. Meat is an occasional item. Oils, when used, are to be low in saturated but high in monounsaturated fats. The important point is this: The common theme of the "healthy" diet is high fiber, low cholesterol, and low fat, particularly low saturated fat. Many studies show that people who consume this type of diet are more likely to enjoy good health and less likely to suffer from diseases affecting the heart and blood vessels as well as certain cancers.

"HAVE YOUR COOKIE AND EAT IT TOO": THE VALUE OF FOOD REPLACEMENTS

Proactive people always look for ways to work through or around a challenge. The challenge posed by the healthy diet is that you might frequently have to forgo many of your favorite foods. For example, many people like the taste and texture of fatty foods such as butter, eggs, sour cream, and whole milk. With some creative planning, you don't have to completely give up all the foods you like. What you can do is look for substitutes. For example:

- Instead of butter on your toast, try olive oil.

- Instead of eggs for breakfast, use egg substitutes that contain egg whites but no yolks, or remove the yolks yourself (you can buy a separator to speed up this process). When you remove the yolk, you remove all of the cholesterol (a fatty substance) associated with the egg. If you find that the egg sticks to the pan, try adding one-fourth teaspoon of lecithin per egg before you put it in the pan. You can obtain lecithin at any health food store. This product adds only a negligible amount of fat to the egg.

- Instead of sour cream and butter on your baked potato, try nonfat yogurt, and sprinkle on some Butter Buds. The latter product contains the flavor of butter but not the fat.

People rave over the texture of foods baked with butter and eggs. After all, what student does not crave a good chocolate chip cookie? The problem is that the typical chocolate chip cookie derives more than 45 percent of its calories from fat. Thus, chocolate chip cookies add a hefty amount of fat to your diet. You have four options:

1. Eat chocolate chip cookies less often.

2. Do without chocolate chip cookies altogether.

3. Find healthier cookies at a store or bakery.

4. Make healthier chocolate chip cookies yourself.

The author of this textbook tried three of the four options. After deciding to make major changes in his diet, he jumped straight to option 2. He did without chocolate chip cookies for two years before trying some of the fat-free versions available at the store. Finding these products too sweet and lacking in flavor and texture, he then decided to bake the cookies himself. After a suitable period of trial and error and tastings hosted by eager students, he settled on the recipe shown here. Notice that this cookie is described as "healthier," not healthy. No cookie is really healthy because of its fat and sugar content.

The value of the cookie project is that it proves that a person can take action on matters that are important to him and achieve results. Keep this point in mind when you face a challenge in trying to enjoy eating and at the same time stay healthy. Look for ways to "have your cookie and eat it too."

WHAT YOU CAN DO TO IMPROVE YOUR DIET

You can improve your diet by planning your meals according to the information in the food guide pyramid in Figure 6.1 and, more specifically, making smart food choices within each food category. The information presented in Table 6.2 can help you. Notice that for each food category, some foods are healthier than others. The healthiest foods are in the "anytime" category. For example, in the grains category, bread and bagels are in the "anytime" category, biscuits are in the "sometimes" category, and donuts are in the "seldom" category. To improve your diet, begin by making "anytime" foods the basis of your diet. Limit "sometimes" foods to once or twice

Journal Activity

Describe your diet. How many meals do you eat per day? Do you snack? What types of foods do you typically eat?

_____

_____

_____

_____

_____

_____

_____

Professor Brown's "Healthier" Chocolate Chip Cookies

Servings: 30   Serving size: 1 piece (3½ oz.)   Preparation time: 1 hour

2½ cups whole wheat flour (for finer texture, use whole wheat pastry flour)
½ teaspoon baking powder
½ teaspoon lecithin (granules: available at health food stores)
1 teaspoon corn syrup
½ teaspoon baking soda
½ cup Egg Beaters
3 tablespoons canola oil
⅝ cup sugar
1.22 cups brown sugar (¾ cup, packed)
2 teaspoons vanilla extract
1 teaspoon imitation butter flavor
10 ounces chocolate chips, semi-sweet

1. Prepare dry ingredients first. Sift flour before measuring. Add baking soda and baking powder. Mix well.

2. Prepare wet ingredients: combine oil, corn syrup, lecithin granules and sugar, and mix well. Add Egg Beaters last. Mix well.

3. Add dry ingredients to wet ingredients: add about a quarter of the dry ingredients, stir well, add the second quart, mix well, etc., until all of the ingredients are mixed.

4. Add rounded tablespoons of the batter to a cookie sheet. For an approximately 12×16 cookie sheet, add nine cookies, well spaced.

5. Bake 9 minutes or until crusty brown on top in a 375° convection oven or 12 minutes in a conventional oven. You might have to adjust the time for your oven by experimenting with a few batches. It will be worth the effort.

Nutritional information obtained using Nutridata Software Corp., P.O. Box 769, Wappingers Fall, NY 12590

Nutritional Information per serving

% Calories from fat	21.9%		
Calories	143.4 cal	Vitamin E	0.6 mg
Protein	2.2 g	Thiamine	0.1 mg
Carbohydrates	26.9 g	Riboflavin	0.0 mg
Total fat	3.6 g	Niacin	0.5 mg
Saturated fat	1.4 g	Vitamin B6	0.0 mg
Monounsaturated	1.3 g	Vitamin B12	0.0 mcg
Polyunsaturated	0.6 g	Folate	6.5 mcg
Cholesterol	0.0 mg	Sodium	37.5 mg
Dietary fiber	1.1 g	Calcium	32.9 mg
Caffeine	3.5 mg	Magnesium	21.5 mg
Vitamin A	9.9 RE	Potassium	131.5 mg

FOOD	ANYTIME (LOW FAT/ CHOLESTEROL)	SOMETIMES (MODERATE FAT/ CHOLESTEROL)	SELDOM (HIGH FAT/ CHOLESTEROL)
Fruits and vegetables	Any fresh, frozen, canned, or dried	Avocado, olives	Coconut, vegetables in cheese, cream, or butter; and French fried vegetables
Grains (breads, cereals, rice, pasta and baked goods)	Bread, bagels, bread-sticks, English muffins, pita bread, plain rolls, corn tortillas, hot and cold cereals, rice, bulgur, pasta, popcorn (plain or light micro-wave), pretzels, no-oil tortilla chips, fat-free and low-fat crackers and cookies	Biscuits, muffins (from mix), cornbread, low-fat granola, pancakes, waffles, French toast, packaged rice mixes, popcorn (regular microwave or buttered)	Donuts, croissants, sweet rolls, commer-cial muffins, granola, egg noodles, chow mein noodles, stuffing, chips, crackers, pies, cakes, cookies
Dairy products	Skim and one percent milk, buttermilk, nonfat dry milk, fat-free yogurt and cheese, fat-free or low-fat cottage cheese	Two percent milk, four percent cottage cheese, reduced-fat and part-skim milk cheeses, low-fat yogurt, frozen yogurt, ice milk, sherbet	Whole milk, whole milk yogurt and cheeses, ice cream (regular and gourmet)

(continued)

TABLE 6.2
Guide to Food Choices

FOOD	ANYTIME (LOW FAT/ CHOLESTEROL)	SOMETIMES (MODERATE FAT/ CHOLESTEROL)	SELDOM (HIGH FAT/ CHOLESTEROL)
Fish, poultry, meat, legumes, nuts and eggs	Any finfish or shellfish (except shrimp), water-packed tuna, poultry, skinless ground turkey, USDA choice or select beef (round, sirloin, tenderloin, flank, ground round), veal, lamb (leg), pork (center-cut ham, loin chops or tenderloin), Canadian bacon, low-fat luncheon meats, dried beans and peas, lentils, egg substitutes or egg whites	Shrimp, oil-packed fish, fish sticks, poultry (with skin), ground beef (extra lean and lean), eggs (four a week)	Fried-fish or poultry, USDA prime beef, pork or lamb (rib, brisket, shoulder, porterhouse, T-bone), organ meats, regular ground beef, sausage, bacon, most regular luncheon meats, nuts
Fats (use in limited amounts)	Polyunsaturated oils (corn, sunflower, soybean, sesame, cottonseed), monounsaturated oils (canola, olive, peanut), margarine, reduced-fat margarine and salad dressing, fat-free sour cream, peanut butter	Regular salad dressing, mayonnaise, reduced-fat sour cream, reduced-fat cream cheese, sour half-and-half	Coconut oil, palm and palm-kernel oils, shortening, lard, butter, cream, half-and-half, sour cream, cream cheese, gravy, most non-dairy creamers

Source: Adapted from "Center for Science in the Public Interest Healthy Eating Pyramid." *Nutrition Action Health-letter* 19:8–9, 1992. Copyright © 1992, CSPI.

TABLE 6.2 *(continued)*

daily, and eat small portions. If you choose to eat "seldom" foods, keep the portions small, and limit them to once or twice a week. Exercise 6.1 gives you an opportunity to review your eating habits to see whether you need to change them.

THE IMPORTANCE OF EXERCISE

Current estimates are that over a quarter of a million deaths occur each year because of physical inactivity. What is the connection between exercise and wellness? Studies show that exercise does the following:

- Reduces stress

- Improves learning and productivity

Your Eating Habits

Record what you eat for three consecutive days, including one weekend day. Include both snacks and meals. Then review your three-day record and jot down some ideas for improving your diet.

DAY	MEAL	YOUR CHOICES
	Breakfast	
	Snack	
	Lunch	
	Snack	
	Dinner	
	Snack	
	Breakfast	
	Snack	
	Lunch	
	Snack	
	Dinner	
	Snack	
	Breakfast	
	Snack	
	Lunch	
	Snack	
	Dinner	
	Snack	

Make notes below for how you will improve your diet.

_____

_____

_____

- Helps prevent obesity

- Reduces the risk for cardiovascular disease

- Reduces the risk for diabetes

- Reduces the risk for osteoporosis

- Reduces the risk for breast cancer

- Reduces the pain of arthritis

You might ignore this information in the belief that most of the diseases on the list affect older people more frequently. Your belief is correct, but remember these two points: (1) you will not stay the same age you are now forever; and (2) the habits you have now will stay with you for the rest of your life unless you do something to change them.

WHAT YOU CAN DO TO INCREASE YOUR LEVEL OF EXERCISE

You can improve your health by getting 30–45 minutes of moderate exercise each day. Activities could include the following:

- Brisk walking

- Cycling

- Jogging/running

- Swimming

- Intramural sports

- Aerobics

- Dancing

A good long-term strategy is to build physical activity into your day. Here are some steps you can take to achieve this goal:

1. Walk or bike to school instead of taking the campus shuttle or driving.

2. Meet some friends after classes for a round of basketball or volleyball.

3. Do calisthenics at home.

4. Walk rather than drive to the grocery store.

5. Climb the stairs in a building instead of using the elevator.

Most people know that exercise is good for them, but they lack the mental discipline to make this effort a part of their routine. We suggest that you review the discussion on self-motivation in Chapter 4 to help you avoid this problem. You will recall that the traits involved in self-motivation are self-management, competence, and connectedness. These traits can be applied to an exercise program. For example:

- *Self-management.* Always remember that you are in charge of your health. Your program of physical activity starts with a decision to make this issue a priority in your life. Your next step is to set goals and devise

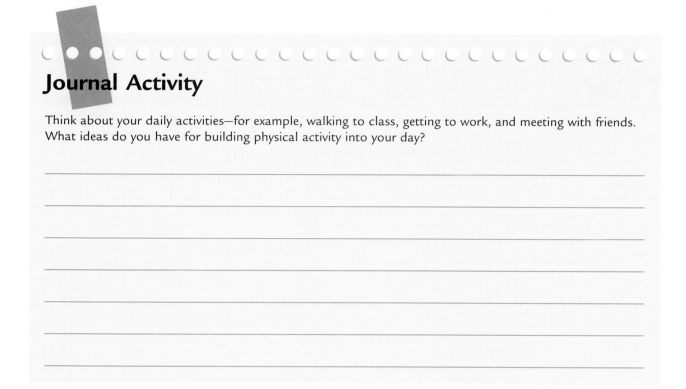

Journal Activity

Think about your daily activities—for example, walking to class, getting to work, and meeting with friends. What ideas do you have for building physical activity into your day?

_____

_____

_____

_____

_____

_____

a plan that fits your needs. The final step is to follow through on your plan.

■ *Competence.* Exercise improves learning and productivity. When you learn more and achieve more, you will have more confidence in your abilities.

(*Source: Chip Henderson/Tony Stone Images.*)

■ *Connectedness.* When you exercise with a friend or friends, you will have more fun, bond with your friend(s), and reinforce your own desire to stick to your goals.

Do Exercise 6.2 to see where you need to increase your physical activity, and decide how you will increase it. Sometimes you might find it hard to stick to your new physical activity program. When this happens, review these concepts to help motivate yourself to get back on track.

ARE YOU GETTING ENOUGH SLEEP?

If you want to be productive and healthy, you will want to think of sleep as a necessity item on your daily agenda. Many college students complain about not getting enough sleep. They are not alone. Dr. James Maas cites in his book, *Power Sleep*, that at least 50 percent of the American adult population is chronically sleep-deprived and a similar percentage report trouble sleeping on any given night.[7] Consider these statistics cited in Maas's book:

■ High school and college students are among the most sleep-deprived people in our population. Thirty percent of students fall asleep in class at least once a week.

■ Thirty-one percent of all drivers have fallen asleep at the wheel at least once in their lifetime.

■ The National Sleep Foundation reports that each year on our highways at least 100,000 accidents and 1,500 fatalities are due to the driver falling asleep at the wheel.

■ Medical residents and interns are among the most severely sleep-deprived individuals. Many work more than 130 hours per week in shifts of 12 to 60 hours' duration, and every other night they are on call.

Sleep deprivation may result in serious consequences. For example:

■ *Daytime drowsiness*—loss of energy and alertness

■ *Stress, anxiety, and loss of coping skills*—overwhelming feelings of not being able to cope even with simple problems or moderate workloads; increase in worry and frustration and nervousness; inability to maintain perspective or relax

■ *Lack of interest in socializing with others*—desire to disengage from the outside world

■ *Weight gain*—results from consumption of beverages and foods high in sugar content used to stay awake

■ *Reduced immunity to disease and viral infection*—results from the lowered activity of important immune cells that fight infections

■ *Reduced productivity*—results from problems with cognitive functions and reduced reaction time

The final item on this list is expanded on in the boxed feature. Exercise 6.3 will help you determine whether or not you are sleep-deprived.

Your Exercise Pattern

Record your exercise pattern for one week.

DAY	ACTIVITY
Monday	
Tuesday	
Wednesday	
Thursday	
Friday	
Saturday	
Sunday	

Based on an analysis of your current exercise pattern, set goals for improvement. Then devise a plan for how you will achieve your goals and for how you will keep track of your progress.

Goals:

_____

_____

_____

Plans for achieving my goals:

_____

_____

_____

Plans for keeping track of my progress.

_____

_____

_____

Effect of Sleep Deprivation on Productivity

- Reduced ability to concentrate

- Reduced ability to remember (especially short-term memory)

- Reduced ability to handle complex tasks

- Reduced ability to think logically

- Reduced ability to assimilate and analyze new information

- Reduced ability to think critically

- Reduced decision-making skills

- Reduced vocabulary and communication skills

- Reduced creativity

- Reduced motor skills and coordination

- Reduced perceptual skills

● ● ● ● ● ●EXERCISE 6.3

Do You Get Enough Sleep?

Place an X in the box to indicate whether each of the following statements is true or false.

True ❏   False ❏   1. I need an alarm clock in order to wake up at the appropriate time.

True ❏   False ❏   2. It's a struggle for me to get out of bed in the morning.

True ❏   False ❏   3. Weekday mornings, I hit the snooze button several times to get more sleep.

True ❏   False ❏   4. I feel tired irritable, and stressed out during the week.

True ❏   False ❏   5. I have trouble concentrating and remembering.

True ❏   False ❏   6. I feel slow with critical thinking, problem solving, and being creative.

True ❏   False ❏   7. I often fall asleep watching television.

True ❏   False ❏   8. I often fall asleep during boring meetings or lectures or in warm rooms.

True ❏   False ❏   9. I often fall asleep after heavy meals or after a small amount of alcohol.

True ❏   False ❏   10. I often fall asleep while relaxing after dinner.

True ❏   False ❏   11. I often fall asleep within five minutes of getting into bed.

True ❏   False ❏   12. I often feel drowsy while driving.

True ❏   False ❏   13. I often sleep extra hours on weekend mornings.

True ❏   False ❏   14. I often need a nap to get through the day.

True ❏   False ❏   15. I have dark circles around my eyes.

If you answered "true" to three or more of these items, you are probably not getting enough sleep. You might be able to increase the amount of sleep you get by improving your level of organization. The section on task organization in Chapter 5 might help you achieve this goal.

Source: From *Power Sleep* by James Maas, Ph.D. Copyright © 1998 by James Maas, Ph.D. Reprinted by permission of Random House, Inc.

Asleep in the College Classroom

Ivy League college tuition is approximately $29,000 per year. If a student takes four courses per semester that meet three hours a week for 15 weeks, that's $80 per lecture hour. If the student falls asleep in the classroom, it's an expensive hourly rate for a bedroom that's not very quiet, dark, or comfortable.

Source: From *Power Sleep* by James Maas, Ph.D. Copyright © 1998 by James Maas, Ph.D. Reprinted by permission of Random House, Inc.

Maintaining Control over Your Eating Habits

WEIGHT CONTROL

Some students tend to eat too much once they leave home and attend college. This problem is often more acute for students who live on campus and eat at the cafeteria. An attractive display of already prepared food and the possibility of getting second and third helpings tempt some students beyond their power to resist. Even students who prepare their own meals might load up on snacks between meals. The end result in both cases is often excessive weight gain.

Studies suggest that if you are overweight, you are more at risk for heart disease. Extra weight can exacerbate ailments such as lower-back pain and arthritis. If you are very overweight, you have a higher risk for diabetes and certain cancers. Also, overweight people have low self-esteem because our society favors thin people over those who carry extra pounds.

How do you know if you are overweight? The *University of California at Berkeley Wellness Encyclopedia* describes a method called the *body mass index:*[8]

1. To convert your weight to kilograms, divide the pounds (without clothes) by 2.2: _____

2. To convert to meters, divide your height in inches (without shoes) by 39.4: _____, then square it: _____.

TABLE 6.3

Interpretation of the Body Mass Index

GENDER	DESIRABLE WEIGHT	OVERWEIGHT	SERIOUSLY OVERWEIGHT
Men	22–24	Above 28.5	33
Women	21–23	27.5	Above 27.5

3. Divide the result of step 1 by the result of step 2: _____. This is your body mass index.

Table 6.3 shows the standards for men and women.

If your index indicates a weight problem, see the strategies for weight control in the boxed feature.

EATING DISORDERS

Among the many students who tend to overeat, a small but growing number have serious eating disorders. Two such disorders are anorexia nervosa and bulimia.[9] Both of these disorders occur mostly in females.

People with *anorexia* tend to starve themselves because they have an intense fear of obesity. This disease is most prevalent in teenagers. Obsessed

Weight-Control Tips

- Eat slowly.

- Clear your refrigerator and pantry of high-calorie foods and snacks; stock only what you intend to eat on your new diet.

- Eat less fat and more complex carbohydrates (whole grains, fruits, and vegetables).

- Limit your intake of butter, ice cream, cheese, salad dressings, and oils.

- Avoid packaged snacks, cookies, and high-fat baked goods.

- Use nonstick cooking utensils so that you don't have to add butter or oil in your cooking.

- Bake, broil, or poach meats and steam vegetables (instead of frying or sautéeing them in fat).

- Switch from whole milk to skim milk, and make sure all other dairy products are low-fat.

- Exercise regularly.

- Take up enjoyable activities that don't involve food (such as gardening or sports).

- Get counseling or join a support group on a long-term basis.

Sources of Help for People with Anorexia and Bulimia

American Anorexia/Bulimia Association
418 East 76th St.
New York, NY 10021
212-734-1114

National Association of Anorexia Nervosa and Associated Disorders
P.O. Box 2771
Highland Park, IL 60035
708-831-3438

National Anorectic Aid Society
1925 East Dublin-Granville Rd.
Columbus, OH 43229
614-436-1112

with having a slender figure, they refuse to maintain normal body weight and lose 25 percent of their body weight or more. They deny any impulse to eat or enjoy food. Often malnutrition results, with its consequent health problems, even death.

While people with anorexia eat too little, people who have *bulimia* sometimes eat too much. The symptoms of bulimia are binge eating, preoccupation with body weight, and repeated efforts to lose weight, sometimes by purging, vomiting, or excessive use of laxatives. Bulimics may also engage in fasting behavior that might involve weight fluctuations of 10 pounds or more. These patterns of alternating fasts and binges take their toll on the body and produce various health problems.

If you struggle with an eating disorder, seek professional help immediately. The counseling center on your campus is the best place to start. See the accompanying box for other sources of help.

PROFILE FOR SUCCESS

Kelly Brett

Once upon a time, a young woman wanted to be a princess. She longed for the long, flowing hair, bright blue eyes, and, especially, the trim, perfect figure of all the heroines in the stories she read, movies she saw, and commercials she watched on television. Like Snow White in the famous story, she found herself desiring the "wishing apple" that would magically bring her all that she desired. One plump, juicy,

red apple decided Snow White's fortune, and in this real-life fairy tale, a single apple became a young woman's path to supposed perfection.

I was that young woman, and when I turned 15 years old, anorexia and

(continued)

bulimia became my way of life. My eating habits became just as methodical as rising out of bed every morning. A typical day's menu consisted of a bowl of Special K for breakfast, a salad for lunch, and an apple for dinner. If, by chance, I failed to follow my strict dietary code, I would resort to the laxatives hidden under my mattress. Regardless of how many calories I consumed in one day, I spent my nights on the StairMaster at the gym, dizzy with hunger. Despite the appearance of my 100-pound body, I refused to acknowledge how withered and emaciated I had become. My hair fell out in chunks, my bones protruded from my hips, and my once sparkling eyes were clouded by nightmares of becoming fat. The clues were numerous, yet it was easier to disregard the abuse I inflicted on my own body than to admit that I had a problem.

My life progressed in this ritualistic manner until the day my doctor finally threatened to put me into the hospital for my eating disorder. I took my first real look in the mirror. The person staring back at me was a complete stranger. Surely this hollow-cheeked girl with dark bags under her eyes could not be me. After all, I was an "A" student with a level head who made excellent decisions, right? I realized that I had lost control of my life, that the food had won the battle. I had thought that my weight was the only aspect of my life that I had control over, and the realization that I had ironically caused damage to myself by controlling it dumfounded me. If I wasn't even capable of deciding when to eat, what could I do? I could not answer this question, and this terrified me. I needed help because I knew that I could not overcome this problem on my own.

Slowly, I began talking to my mother and my close friends about my feelings, thoughts, and perceptions. I thank God every day that I have had a solid support group on which to rely in my time of need. Now I am to the point where I am conscious of the food I eat, but not obsessive. I can go out with friends and eat a meal at the mall without feeling as though I need to go to the gym and burn off the calories from it. I know I am a beautiful person who does not deserve any type of abuse, especially self-inflicted abuse. I have gained 15 pounds and limitless amounts of inner strength and confidence. Although I have not forgotten my past, I have overcome my fear of not having control of my life, the root of my eating disorder. Today, I am the commander of my life.

Although I am not 100 percent perfect like the women in fairy tales, I have found a connection to one in particular. Both Snow White and I bit into apples and, consequently, escaped the rest of the world. A prince awakened Snow White with a kiss, whereas a mirror with my own reflection awakened me. However, I don't need to model myself after this princess any longer. She was not able to save herself; the prince had to save her. In contrast, I was able to make the decision to save myself.

Because I have experienced the consequences of poor health, I realize how vital good health is to being a successful college student. Nobody is here to watch over my shoulder to make sure that I am eating properly, exercising regularly, and maintaining good health. It is all up to me. I know that if I do not eat a balanced diet, exercise, or get enough sleep, I will not have the energy that I need to deal with my strenuous college lifestyle.

In order to accomplish everything that I need to get done in a day, I plan what I am going to do the next day before I go to bed each night. For example, if I need to be in class at 10:10 AM, I plan to wake up at 9:00 AM so that I will have time to eat breakfast, shower, and get to class on time. Instead of taking the shuttle to class, I walk. This gives me time to clear my mind, relax, and even get some exercise! By leaving myself enough time to accomplish all of this, I reduce the amount of stress in my day. Another stress-relieving technique that I use is to set aside a certain amount of time for each activity in my day, which includes going to class, studying, doing homework, and socializing with friends.

The key in planning my day is knowing how much I can reasonably accomplish in a given amount of time. First, I started out only planning to do a little bit at a time until I got a good estimate of my true capabilities. I am now a calm and collected person who manages to get a great deal done each and every day.

Throughout my first quarter in college, I found that the results of good health are infinite and truly play a key role in my life. I feel energized, excited, and hopeful at the start of each day. This positive attitude enables me to work to my full potential on a regular basis. What more can I really ask for?

Stress: The Good and the Bad

Stress: a mentally or emotionally disruptive state of the body often characterized by increased heart rate, a rise in blood pressure, muscular tension, and irritability.

Many definitions have been offered for the term stress. Dr. Hans Selye, often referred to as the founding father of stress studies, called it "the rate of wear and tear on the body."[10] Others have referred to stress with some variation of the following words: "the body's response to outside forces." One factor that complicates definitions is that different people often respond to the same outside force, or "stressor," in different ways. Thus, the tendency of workers in this field of research is to focus on how humans *respond* to stress rather than what stress *is*.

You might think of the body's response to stress in the following way: Suppose you are walking in the forest, and suddenly you come upon a large black bear. Your body would perceive the bear as a threat and undergo some dramatic physiological changes: increased blood pressure and heart rate, muscle tension, and possibly intestinal upset. This is known as the *fight-or-flight reaction,* common to both human and nonhuman animals. These changes prepare you to fight for your life or run for it. The same reaction protected the caveman from the dangers of his day. Modern threats and perceived threats usually do not come from wild animals but rather from noise pollution, interpersonal conflicts, traffic problems, and demanding professors. The body's response is often the same as if you had encountered a wild animal.

Your success as a student and in the rest of your life will depend on your ability to manage stress. There are both good and bad aspects to stress. Let's look at both.

THE GOOD SIDE OF STRESS

The good side of stress is that it causes you to attend to basic needs. For example, you are more likely to eat when you get hungry, drink water when you are thirsty, or go to sleep when you get very tired. Another good side is that stress helps you stay on task. For example, you are more likely to focus on your assignments when your instructor gives you a deadline.

THE BAD SIDE OF STRESS

The bad side of stress shows up when the stress is intense or of long duration. This kind of stress can have adverse effects on the immune system, which can lead to increased sensitivity to infections and other abnormalities. Some fairly recent findings follow:[11]

- Whereas mild stress can enhance, high stress can suppress innate system functions.

- Stress triggers the release of compounds that activate allergic reactions such as asthma.

- Scientists at Ohio State University gave injections of the hepatitis B vaccine to two groups of medical students, one under more stress than the other. The low-stress group had a more intense immune response (and thus more resistance) to the virus than the high-stress group.

- In another study, the stress of interpersonal conflicts made volunteers more susceptible to the cold virus

Finally, consider the results of studies on senior citizens showing that high levels of stress-induced hormones such as cortisol lead to memory loss. The subjects with high concentrations of cortisol in the blood remembered what they learned long ago but forgot things they were just told. The researchers concluded that stress might be a major reason why some older people remain quite sharp while other seemingly healthy individuals become more forgetful as they age. These studies are relevant to your situation in the following way. If stress affected memory loss to the same degree in younger people, it could seriously hinder your performance in school.[12]

Complete Exercise 6.4 to assess your level of stress during the last year.

HOW PEOPLE RESPOND TO STRESS

There are positive and negative ways to respond to stress. Often people choose a negative response such as anger. For example, Larry is angry with his roommate who fails to do his share of the housecleaning. Lea is angry

College Readjustment Rating Scale

To determine your level of stress during the past year, add up the number of Life Change Units corresponding to the events listed below that you have experienced. If your score is 160 or more, you have about a 50-50 chance of experiencing an adverse health change. If your score is below 150, you have a 30 percent chance of becoming more vulnerable to illness.

LIFE EVENT	LIFE CHANGE UNITS
Death of spouse	100
Female unwed pregnancy	92
Death of parent	80
Male partner in unwed pregnancy	77
Divorce	73
Death of a close family member (other than parent)	70
Death of a close friend	65
Divorce between parents	63
Jail term	61
Major personal injury or illness	60
Flunk out of college	58
Marriage	55
Fired from job	50
Loss of financial support for college (scholarship)	48
Failed important or required course	47
Sexual difficulties	45
Serious argument with significant other person	40
Academic probation	39
Change in major	37
New love interest	36
Increased workload at college	31
Outstanding personal achievement	29
First quarter/semester in college	28
Serious conflict with instructor	27
Lower grades than expected	25
Change in colleges (transfer)	24
Change in social activities	22
Change in sleeping habits	21
Change in eating habits	19
Minor violations of the law (e.g., traffic ticket)	15
Total	_____

Source: From C.L. Otis & R. Goldingay, In *Campus Health Guide* (New York: College Entrance Examination Board, 1989).

with her professor because of the low grade she received on her art project. Larry could try to negotiate with his roommate. Lea could visit with her professor and find out the reasons for the low grade. Those would be better responses than getting angry.

Moderate anger does little harm, but intense or long-term (chronic) anger can do the following:

- Depress the immune system, leaving a person more susceptible to many diseases

- Make a person less effective because she might focus more on revenge than on solving problems or achieving high productivity

- Damage interpersonal relationships

People who frequently resort to anger are often rigid in their dealings with others. This pattern makes them less attractive socially. So in addition to harming your body and your productivity, excessive anger can harm your popularity!

You can manage anger in the same ways that you manage other forms of stress, as discussed shortly under "How You Can Manage Stress."

WHO IS MOST SUSCEPTIBLE TO BAD STRESS?

Most of what we know about how stress affects humans comes from studies on the workforce. These studies show that people at the bottom of the job ladder have more heart attacks and other diseases than those at the top. The risks for illness for those at the bottom are two to four times that of those at the top, independent of all other risk factors.[13] The issue is one of control. People at the bottom have less decision-making power than those at the top. The more control a person has over his life and what he does, the less likely he is to suffer the ill effects of stress.

As a student, you might feel more at risk because of a perceived lack of control. You might feel that the administration of your school controls your life through its policies and that professors control you by the demands that they place on your time. We will offer some suggestions for how to buffer the effects of this stress next.

HOW YOU CAN MANAGE STRESS

You will encounter stressful situations often as you pursue your education and go about your daily life. You cannot avoid stress, but you can take steps to help you stay more in control of your life:

1. *Learn to relax.* You can benefit from a having a regular relaxation program designed to help you reduce the ill effects of stress. One useful approach is the *relaxation response* described in the boxed feature.

2. *Maintain a regular exercise program.* In one study, researchers showed that aerobic exercise reduced anxiety and muscle tension and improved coping skills. The scientists studied two groups of college students, one group that exercised and another that did not. Both groups took a test containing problems that mostly could not be solved and were told that the test was a good indicator of how they were likely to perform in college. The

The Relaxation Response

1. Pick a focus word or phrase that is rooted in your personal belief system (for example, peace or love).

2. Sit quietly in a comfortable position.

3. Close your eyes.

4. Relax your muscles.

5. Become aware of your breathing, and breathe very slowly and naturally. Simultaneously, repeat your focus word or phrase as you exhale. Use one word or phrase during your sessions so that you'll automatically come to associate it with the calming impact of the relaxation response.

6. Assume a passive attitude, and if other thoughts intrude in your mind, gently disregard them.

7. Continue for 20 minutes.

8. Practice the technique once or twice daily.

Source: Herbert Benson: *The Relaxation Response* (New York: Times Books, 1984), p. 122.

nonexercising students showed increased blood pressure, muscle tension, and anxiety when told they did poorly on the test. The exercising group also showed increased muscle tension and anxiety but not as much as the nonexercisers, and the exercising group showed no increase in blood pressure.

3. *Stay current in your coursework.* Many students create stress for themselves by procrastinating. Once they get behind, their only option is to stay up all night to study for their exams. The result is often high anxiety, temporary memory blocks, and increased risk for disease. You can avoid this common problem by staying current in your coursework. You might want to review the learning strategies in Chapter 5. For example, the notetaking strategies encourage you to review your notes often, not just before exams. The task-organization system helps you break big tasks into small, manageable segments. When you can do a number of small tasks and check them off your list, you feel more in control of your schedules. A sense of increased personal control reduces stress.

4. *Maintain a network of support.* Strong social support can have a profound effect on a person's ability to cope with stress. Studies show that people who have strong social networks made up of family and friends live longer and are healthier than people who isolate themselves from others. Dr. Leonard Syme of the University of California at Berkeley and Dr. Lisa Berkman of Yale University followed the health and social habits of 7,000 men and women for nine years.[14] The results showed that lonely women have about three times the risk and lonely men twice the risk of illness and death than those who have a strong support network.

5. *Be a proactive student.* Previously we discussed how many students might experience stress because of a perceived lack of control over their

lives. A proactive approach to life gives you more control. One proactive approach is to share ownership of your classes with your professors. For example, if the professor provides a syllabus, you can choose to read ahead. Or you might read related material to expand your knowledge of the subject. During office hours, you might share what you have learned with your professor. She might even incorporate some of your ideas into her lecture, or she might ask you to share some of your findings with the class. Your involvement will help you become a participant rather than just a recipient in the class. Students who become more involved in their education feel more in control and thus suffer fewer ill effects from stress.

Managing the Risks of Infectious Disease

Infectious disease: a disease that can be transmitted by ordinary physical contact.

One issue that you will always face is how to protect yourself from infectious diseases. You face threats from general diseases, such as colds, flu, urinary tract infections, and diarrhea. Under certain conditions, you might risk infections from sexually transmitted diseases.

GENERAL DISEASE RISKS

For decades medical research has focused on chronic diseases such as cancer and heart disease. In recent years, though, researchers have paid less attention to infectious diseases caused by bacteria and viruses. Health professionals and policymakers have considered infectious diseases to be under control because of (1) improved sanitation and hygiene, (2) the advent of antibiotics, and (3) the widespread use of vaccines. Today, however, we face new threats from newly discovered diseases as well as from old diseases that just won't go away. In *The Coming Plague*, author Laurie Garrett outlines a likely scenario:

> *The history of our time will be marked by recurrent eruptions of newly discovered diseases (most recently, hantavirus in the American West); epidemics of diseases migrating to new areas (for example, cholera in Latin America); diseases which become important through human technologies (as certain menstrual tampons favored toxic shock syndrome and water cooling towers provided an opportunity for Legionnaires' Disease); and diseases which spring from insects and animals to humans, through manmade disruptions in local habitats.* [15]

One current issue of concern is contaminated food. Modern lifestyle choices play a role in many food-related outbreaks. For example, many Americans have busy lifestyles. The result is that they more frequently rely on fast-food restaurants for their meals. Mass production often leads to foods tainted with *Salmonella* and *E. coli*, bacteria that can cause illness and sometimes death.

As the leading infectious killer in the world, tuberculosis (TB) represents the return of a disease once under control, at least in Western countries. This ancient disease still plagues mankind, accounting for more than 9,000 deaths per day worldwide. Over one third of the world's people are infected. About 10 percent of these infected individuals will develop an active case of the disease at some point during their lifetimes. In the recent past, TB was more of a problem in developing countries. But during the 1980s, the incidence increased sharply in Western countries. A person can contract this disease by ordinary physical contact (usually prolonged) with an infected person who talks, coughs, or sneezes.

Although you cannot completely eliminate the risks of infections, you can take the steps shown in the boxed feature to help protect yourself and others. Exercise 6.5 also focuses on the subject of protection against infectious diseases.

Guidelines for Reducing the Risks from Infectious Diseases

1. *Stay healthy.* A healthy body is a poor prospect for harmful disease agents. Eat well; get plenty of rest and exercise; manage stress; avoid habits such as smoking and excessive drinking.

2. *Always cover a cough or sneeze.* Use a tissue; stick your head into a coat, shirt, blouse, sweater, or bended elbow. If you have to use your hands, wash them as soon as possible after you finish coughing or sneezing.

3. *Wash your hands often.* Dirty hands are a major source of infection; always wash your hands well after using the toilet.

4. *Avoid sharing eating or drinking utensils with other people.* A person might transmit to you an infectious agent that causes them no harm but could make you sick. You could do the same to someone else.

5. *Be aware of food hazards.* Products sold at food outlets such as salads, cole slaw, and prepared meats carry special risks. Sometimes food handlers contaminate these products with their dirty hands, dirty water, or dirty utensils. Also, avoid all raw or undercooked meat or fish.

6. *Take antibiotics only on orders from a physician.* Also, finish taking all of the antibiotic prescribed unless the doctor instructs you otherwise.

7. *Educate yourself.* Take a course on health and hygiene; stay abreast of current hazards through newspaper and magazine articles.

8. *Get expert advice before you travel to foreign countries.* The best source of information is the Center for Disease Control (CDC) website.

9. *Avoid risky trends and fashions.* Practices such as tattooing and body piercing carry special risks such as infection by hepatitis viruses carried on dirty instruments. One form of hepatitis (Type C) might not show up for up to 20 years, and no treatment or cure is available for this type of hepatitis.

10. *Be clear about your values, and know what is important to you.* Sometimes you might have to make a choice between self-preservation and your concern for others. For example, community service might be high on your list of values. But if you frequent a homeless shelter, you might contract TB or some other disease. On other occasions, you might have to choose between self-preservation and social acceptance. For example, you might have to decide whether you will get a tattoo or pierce your body in order to fit in with your social group. Your values will dictate the choices you make in these situations.

Checking Out the CDC Website

Think of a country or region you would like to visit. Check the CDC website for a list of precautions you should take before and during travel in that area.

SEXUALLY TRANSMITTED DISEASE (STD) RISKS

··········
Sexually transmitted diseases (STDs): diseases transmitted by some form of sexual contact, frequently intercourse.

You risk infection from diseases such as colds and diarrhea at anytime. But there are certain diseases that you get only if you have sexual contact with another person. We refer to theses as sexually transmitted diseases (STDs). STDs are typically transmitted from one person to another person during sexual intimacy. The list of possible diseases includes syphilis, gonorrhea, AIDS, and genital herpes. In a recent survey of college students, 9 percent of the women and 4 percent of the men said they had been diagnosed with an STD.[16] The authors citing this statistic suggested that the lower number for men might reflect the fact they are less likely than women to have regular checkups, allowing diseases to go undiagnosed.

Table 6.4 lists some common STDs with brief descriptions. Table 6.5 deals specifically with the HIV virus. The boxed feature offers guidelines for how to avoid STDs.

DISEASE	TRANSMISSION	SYMPTOMS	CONSEQUENCES	TREATMENT
Chlamydia (bacteria)	Usually sexual intercourse	Often, no symptoms; when present, causes painful urination and discharges from the penis or vagina.	Untreated cases can lead to severe infection of female sex organs	Antibiotics
Gonorrhea (bacteria)	Sexual intercourse; oral-genital and anal-genital sexual contact	In males causes painful urination and urethral discharge. In females causes vaginal discharge or bleeding, painful urination, fever, painful intercourse, and pelvic pain. No symptoms in 10% of men and 80% of women.	Untreated cases lead to sterility; also can affect the heart and joints and can lead to severe infection of sex organs	Antibiotics

TABLE 6.4

Common Sexually Transmitted Diseases

DISEASE	TRANSMISSION	SYMPTOMS	CONSEQUENCES	TREATMENT
Syphilis (bacteria)	Sexual intercourse; kissing; intimate body contact as through sores	Untreated disease occurs in four stages: *primary*—sore at point of contact; *secondary*—rash; symptoms that might mimic a cold or flu; joint pains; *latent*—no overt symptoms; *late or tertiary*—permanent damage to vital organs	Blindness, insanity, heart disease, and death	Antibiotics effective only in first two stages
Genital warts (human papilloma virus)	Sexual or nonsexual contact	Initially small, round elevations on skin; later, blend together to form cauliflower-like growths	Possible cancers of the vagina, vulva, cervix, and penis	Physicians can remove visible warts by cutting away, freezing, laser treatment, and surgery; no treatment for invisible lesions; no vaccine available
Genital herpes (herpes virus)	Genital-to-genital or genital-to-mouth contact	Sores commonly on the genitals	Virus remains in system for life	No vaccine; Drugs shorten or decrease frequency of outbreaks
Viral hepatitis (a family of viruses, e.g., A, B, C, D, E)	Sexual and nonsexual transmission: vaginal and penal secretions, urine, other bodily fluids such as blood, sweat, tears; fecal matter; contaminated instruments and needles used in body piercing and tattooing; contaminated razors and toothbrushes	Two stages: *early*—flu-like symptoms; nausea; abdominal pain; *Later*—jaundice (yellow skin and eyes); darkened urine	A type rarely fatal and never chronic; B type sometimes deadly and often chronic in children; chronic in about 10% of infected adults; can cause liver cancer	Vaccines available only for types A and B

(continued)

TABLE 6.4 *(continued)*

DISEASE	TRANSMISSION	SYMPTOMS	CONSEQUENCES	TREATMENT
HIV/AIDS (human immuno-deficiency virus)	Most common route is through sexual contact, either oral, anal, or genital; also blood transfusions; needles contaminated with the virus; mother-to-baby transmission during childbirth	HIV infection follows a course of infection as shown in Table 6.5.	Eventually fatal	Drugs can reduce severity of symptoms and prolong life.

Source: Adapted from S. Althoff, M. Svoboda, and D. Girdano: *Choices in Wellness for Life,* 3rd ed. Copyright © 1996. All rights reserved. Adapted by permission of Allyn and Bacon. W.G. Weinburg: *No Germs Allowed! How to Avoid Infectious Diseases at Home and on the Road* (New Brunswick, NJ: Rutgers University Press, 1996), p. 144.

TABLE 6.4 *(continued)*

TIME AFTER INITIAL INFECTION	DIAGNOSIS	MOST COMMON PROBLEMS
3 weeks	Acute HIV	Fever Swollen glands Rash
6 weeks to 8 years	Asymptomatic HIV	None
8 years	AIDS	Pneumonia Yeast infections
10 years	Advanced AIDS	Chronic diarrhea Weight loss Tuberculosis Rare infections Vision loss Loss of mental function

Source: Adapted from W.G. Weinberg: *No Germs Allowed! How To Avoid Infectious Diseases at Home and on the Road.* New Brunswick, NJ: Rutgers University Press, 1996), p. 165.

TABLE 6.5
Average Course of HIV Infection

Universal Guidelines for Preventing STDs

1. Have unprotected sexual intercourse (that is, without using a male latex condom) only if you know that your partner

   - Is your only sexual partner and is faithful

   - Was never an injecting drug user

   - Tested negative for HIV (blood drawn six months after the last unprotected exposure to someone else)

   - Has no undiagnosed genital problems, including no visible genital sores, rashes, discharges, or other symptoms

2. For all other sexual contacts involving any penetration of any body cavity (mouth, vagina, anus), use a male latex condom properly and consistently.

3. Ordinary kisses are safe, but partners in deep (French) kissing should meet the same criteria as listed in number 1.

4. Activities considered safe without extra precautions: hugging, caressing, fondling, and masturbation.

   For more information on STDs, check with your campus health service or one of the following hotlines:

Toll-free: National STD Hotline 1-800-227-8922
(8 AM–11 PM EST M–F)

Toll-free: National AIDS Hotline 1-800-342-AIDS (2437)
(open 24 hours)

Herpes Resource Center Hotline 1-919-361-8488
(9 AM–7 PM EST M–F)

Avoiding the Perils of Substance Abuse

Substance abuse: excessive use of addictive substances.

Widespread substance abuse is one of America's most severe problems. Abusers cause serious problems for themselves and their families and also overload our legal and health care systems. In this section we will discuss what drugs are, the major classes of drugs, why people abuse substances, and what you can do about the problem.[17]

WHAT ARE DRUGS?

Drugs are chemicals that, when they gain access to the body, enter the bloodstream and travel to the brain. They alter the chemicals in the brain and affect you in one or more of the following ways: (1) causing a floating sensation, (2) dulling or heightening your senses, (3) relieving pain, or (4) creating mood swings or changes in personality and judgment. Drugs get into the body by inhalation, injection, snorting, or swallowing.

Table 6.6 describes the major classes of drugs and their effects.

DRUG GROUP	EXAMPLES	MAJOR EFFECTS	SIDE EFFECTS AND PROBLEMS
Stimulants	Caffeine, nicotine, all forms of amphetamines, all forms of cocaine, all prescription diet pills	Feelings of energy, happiness, power, a decreased desire for sleep, and a diminished appetite	Physical addiction; considered one of the most dangerous and difficult to control of the drugs that people abuse
Depressants	Alcohol, almost all antianxiety drugs (such as Valium), all prescription sleeping pills	Feelings of relaxation and sleepiness	Physical addiction; can cause problems in coordination and thinking clearly; can cause death at high doses
Opiates	Almost all prescription pain pills (such as Darvon, Percodan), codeine, demerol, heroin, methadone	Pain relief; feelings of moderate drowsiness, floating, euphoria; changes in mood	Physical addiction; can cause death at very high doses
Cannabinals	All forms of marijuana	Feelings of euphoria, floating, or mellowness; increased appetite; some mild feelings of suspiciousness and paranoia; a mild tremor or shaking of the hands; dry mouth	Slowing of decision-making and reaction times (which can interfere with driving abilities); impaired ability to think clearly (which can interfere with school and work performance)
Hallucinogens	LSD, "magic mushrooms," MDMA ("ecstasy"), mescaline, peyote, psilocybin; phencyclidine (PCP, not a true hallucinogen but mimics the effects of these drugs)	Sensations of intensified feelings and perceptions, including heightened perceptions of the impact of colors, sounds, and touches	Slightly higher than usual doses of PCP, the most prominent of these drugs, can cause severe confusion and agitation that often results in violence.

TABLE 6.6
Major Classes of Drugs and Their Effects

DRUG GROUP	EXAMPLES	MAJOR EFFECTS	SIDE EFFECTS AND PROBLEMS
Solvents or Inhalants	Acetone, aerosol gases (hydrocarbons), benzene, ether, gasoline, glue, paint thinner, toluene, Wite Out or Liquid Paper	Giddiness and lightheadinesses	Interference with cell-membrane functioning and normal brain activity; prolonged heavy use can cause permanent brain damage and also damage to the heart, liver and kidneys

Source: Adapted from M. Shuckit: *Educating Yourself About Alcohol and Drugs: A People's Primer* (New York: Plenum, 1995).

TABLE 6.6 *(continued)*

WHY PEOPLE ABUSE SUBSTANCES

Although the reasons for substance abuse vary according to the individual, statistics allow certain conclusions to be drawn.[18]

First, people are more likely to try alcohol or drugs when society signals that it is acceptable for them to do so. For example, television ads show images linking feeling good with taking pills or drinking. Some images link drinking with success, wealth, or enjoyment but seldom link alcohol abuse with its destructive results. Also, opinions of relatives and peers can have a strong impact on whether or not a person takes the first step toward substance abuse. Still another factor is ease of availability. Substance use is highest when substances are cheap and readily available. For teenagers, a desire for status is often the motivation. Many start smoking because they see this habit as something that will help them achieve adult status.

Once a person decides to try substances, other factors influence the type and degree of problems that he may encounter. For example:

1. *Nature of the drug.* A person is much more likely to have difficulties if the first drug is a potent stimulant such as cocaine, because these drugs cause marked behavioral changes even at low doses.

2. *Frequency of use.* The risks increase the more one uses a substance. For example, a person who drinks alcohol every day is more likely to get drunk frequently than one who drinks only on special occasions. The first person is more likely to drive while drunk or miss classes or exams because of drinking.

3. *Costs and ease of availability.* Low cost and general availability encourage more frequent use of drugs and alcohol, which increases the risk that a person will abuse them.

Some people curtail or end their use of drugs after they experience problems such as a DUI (driving under the influence) conviction or

(Source: Timothy Shonnard/Tony Stone Images.)

difficulties in school. Others continue their use and advance to dependency.

People vary in their vulnerability to dependency once substance abuse begins. Some of the factors that might influence this pattern are as follows:

1. *Genetics.* Studies show that sons and daughters of alcoholics have a fourfold higher risk of developing severe alcohol problems than those of nonalcoholics. Thus, some people have a predisposition for alcohol abuse. Studies are underway to determine if the same patterns exist for other substances.

2. *Biological factors.* Some studies suggest that differences in brain chemistry might play a role in determining a person's risk for severe drug-related problems.

3. *Psychological factors.* Some people might develop dependency because of a prior psychiatric disorder such as schizophrenia, mania, or antisocial personality disorder.

The boxed feature examines 12 reasons why people smoke cigarettes.

CONSEQUENCES OF SUBSTANCE ABUSE

Some potential consequences of substance abuse are:

- Cancer

- Heart disease

- Stroke

- Liver disease

- STDs

Why Do You Smoke?

This test, based on one by the U.S. Department of Health and Human Services, will help you determine why you smoke. Jot down your answers as you go.

True or False: I smoke . . .

1. Because I light up automatically and don't know I'm doing it.

2. Because it's relaxing.

3. Because I like handling cigarettes, matches, and lighters.

4. To help deal with anger.

5. To keep from slowing down.

6. Because it's unbearable not to.

7. Because I enjoy watching the smoke as I exhale it.

8. To take my mind off my troubles.

9. Because I really enjoy it.

10. Because I feel uncomfortable without a cigarette in my hand.

11. To give myself a lift.

12. Without planning to—it's just part of my routine.

Results: "True" answers to 5 and 11 indicate that you smoke for stimulation; to 3 and 7, that pleasure of handling is important; to 2 and 9, that you seek relaxation; to 4 and 8, that you need a tension-reducing crutch; to 6 and 10, that you have a physiological addiction; to 1 and 12, that you smoke from habit. No doubt you smoke for a combination of these reasons.

Substance abusers often reject traditional principles and values. Instead, they favor anything that will help them keep their drug habit. Thus, they live by the code that anything is permissible. Instead of cooperation, they choose selfishness. Immediate gratification is more important to them than hard work, consistency, and patience. Abusers are individualistic to the point of lacking any concern for family or community. Finally, they are in danger of becoming criminals.

WHAT YOU CAN DO ABOUT SUBSTANCE ABUSE

As mentioned, some people have a genetic predisposition for alcohol abuse. Although the studies are not as complete on predisposition for use of other substances, let's assume that the same pattern might exist for them. For your own benefit, you will want to keep the point in mind that predisposition does not mean predestination. Even if you have a predisposition to use alcohol (or chemical substances) you can still decide what to do about the temptations. You can avoid gatherings where the substances are available. In the case of alcohol, you can limit your drinking, or you can abstain altogether. If you feel that you are at risk for substance abuse, we suggest you speak with someone at your counseling or health center immediately. Other sources of information and advice include the following:

- Dr. Marc Schuckit's excellent and authoritative book, *Educating Yourself About Alcohol and Drugs: A People's Primer* (New York: Plenum, 1995).

- National Institute on Drug Abuse: 800-662-HELP

- Cocaine help line 8000-COCAINE

- Families Anonymous 888-989-7841

- Al-Anon/Alateen 212-302-7240

Identifying and Correcting Thinking Problems

*T*hinking problems often lead to health problems. Self-defeating beliefs or self-defeating values can hinder your ability to take care of your health. Your task is to identify which of the possible thinking problems apply to you and then correct them by using the Change Formula in Figure 6.2.

In this process, you select a remedy (S) to change the self-defeating beliefs or values to productive ones. Remedies are shown in Figure 6.3. Recall that Self-defeating beliefs (values) lead to self-defeating thoughts that lead to self-defeating behaviors, as shown in Figure 6.4. Figure 6.5 shows that you can correct self-defeating beliefs (values) by using one or more of the remedies. This process results in productive behaviors. Figure 6.6 shows the impact that values (or beliefs) can have on life outcomes.

Examples 6.1 through 6.3 show how the Change Formula applies to health issues. With practice, you will become more proactive in how you manage your health issues.

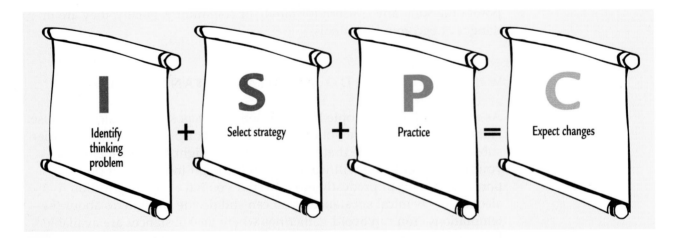

FIGURE 6.2

Change formula for correcting thinking problems.

FIGURE 6.3
Remedies for correcting thinking problems.

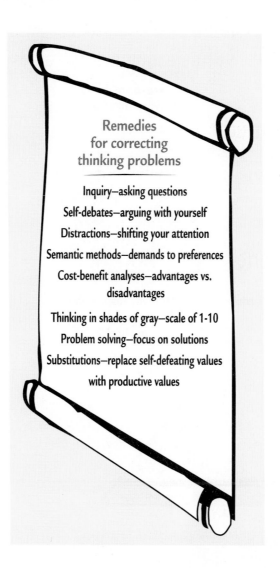

Remedies for correcting thinking problems

Inquiry—asking questions

Self-debates—arguing with yourself

Distractions—shifting your attention

Semantic methods—demands to preferences

Cost-benefit analyses—advantages vs. disadvantages

Thinking in shades of gray—scale of 1-10

Problem solving—focus on solutions

Substitutions—replace self-defeating values with productive values

FIGURE 6.4
How self-defeating beliefs and values lead to self-defeating behaviors.

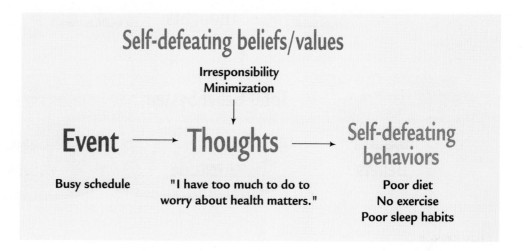

Self-defeating beliefs/values

Irresponsibility
Minimization

Event → Thoughts → Self-defeating behaviors

Busy schedule

"I have too much to do to worry about health matters."

Poor diet
No exercise
Poor sleep habits

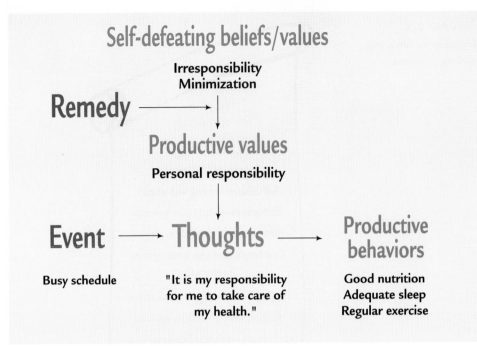

FIGURE 6.5
How corrected self-defeating beliefs or values lead to productive behaviors.

Self-defeating beliefs/values

Irresponsibility
Minimization

Remedy ⟶

Productive values

Personal responsibility

Event ⟶ Thoughts ⟶ Productive behaviors

Busy schedule

"It is my responsibility for me to take care of my health."

Good nutrition
Adequate sleep
Regular exercise

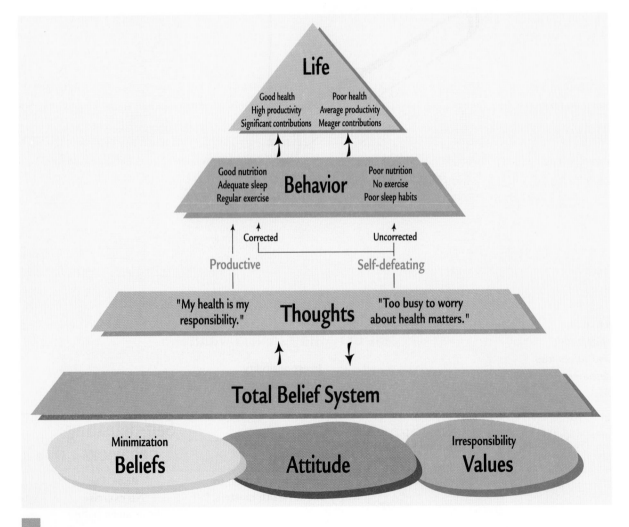

Life

Good health   Poor health
High productivity   Average productivity
Significant contributions Meager contributions

Good nutrition   Poor nutrition
Adequate sleep   Behavior   No exercise
Regular exercise   Poor sleep habits

Corrected   Uncorrected

Productive   Self-defeating

"My health is my responsibility."   Thoughts   "Too busy to worry about health matters."

Total Belief System

Minimization   Irresponsibility
Beliefs   Attitude   Values

FIGURE 6.6
Impact of beliefs on life outcomes.

244   CHAPTER SIX

EXAMPLE 6.1

Event

Dave reflects on his attitude about his health.

Dave's Self-Statement

I don't worry about staying healthy. After all, if I get sick, I'll just go to the doctor. She will give me some medicine that will make me well.

(I) Identify the Thinking Problem

Minimization

(S) Select a Remedy: self-debate

Q. Is there a difference between worrying about being sick and acting responsibly toward my health?
A. I guess there is a distinction.
Q. What does it mean to act responsibly?
A. To do everything under my power to prevent getting sick.
Q. Why should I go through all of that effort when it is so easy to just go to the doctor and get some medicine.
A. That would be placing too much of the responsibility for my health on the doctor.
Q. Isn't that what doctors are for—to make people well?
A. Doctors can help people get well. But it is up to the individual to do everything possible to stay well.
Q. Why is that true?
A. The doctor has more patients than me to think about.
Q. Who benefits most from the state of my health?
A. I do.

(C) Productive Belief

Personal responsibility

Dave's Productive Self-Statement

My health is my responsibility. I should visit and expect attention from my doctor when I get sick. But I should focus more attention on my responsibility to prevent disease.

(P) Practice

Rehearse the productive belief and the productive self-statement.

EXAMPLE 6.2

Event

Nelson is tempted to smoke cigarettes to be accepted by his friends.

Nelson's Self-Statement

I have to do what my friends do to be accepted, but I value good health

(I) Identify the Thinking Problem

Conflict in values

(S) Select a Remedy: self-debate

Q. Why do I have to smoke to fit in with my friends?
A. Because they all do.
Q. Will they not accept me if I don't smoke?
A. No, they will not.
Q. What is the worst thing that could happen to me if my friends did not accept me?
A. I would be without friends for a while until I found some new friends.
Q. Could I live with that possibility?
A. Yes, I could.
Q. What is most important to me, social acceptance or good health habits?
A. Good health habits.

(C) Productive Belief

Value good health

Nelson's Productive Self-Statement

I value my health more than activities that would endanger my health. Therefore, I will look for friends who accept me for who I am.

(P) Practice

Rehearse the productive beliefs and the productive self-statement

EXAMPLE 6.3

Event

Alan feels angry because he strongly disagrees with a campus policy.

Alan's Self-Statement

What a dumb policy. No alcohol in the dormitories. I'm ticked.

(I) Identify the Thinking Problem

Imperatives—I make the rules
Mind-reading—jumping to conclusions

EXAMPLE 6.3 *(continued)*

(S) Select a Remedy: self-debate

Q. In what manner is no drinking in the dorms a dumb policy?
A. The dorm is our place of residence, and we should be able to do anything there we want to do.
Q. Is there a reason for this policy, or is it arbitrary?
A. Just arbitrary, I guess.
Q. How can I find out for sure?
A. I can talk to the dean of students.
Q. What if I find that the policy was due to injuries following drinking incidents?
A. I would think the administration acted wisely.
Q. Should I talk to some officials in the administration before blasting this policy?
A. Yes.

(C) Productive Beliefs

Demands become preferences
Keep an open mind
Get the facts

Alan's Productive Self-Statement

I don't agree with all of the policies at this institution. But to be fair, I will first try to find out if they make sense before I reject them as being "dumb."

Practice

Rehearse the productive beliefs and the productive self-statement.

Journal Activity

List the thinking problems that you think threaten your health. Use the Change Formula to correct the thinking problems as shown in the preceding examples.

_____

_____

_____

_____

_____

_____

_____

Most students on college campuses want to achieve success in life. They want to perform well in school, obtain a meaningful job or profession, have satisfying personal lives, and make significant contributions to society. These goals are sound and obtainable. The problem is that far too many students take their health for granted, and health problems can pose serious obstacles to these goals. Many students have poor eating habits, get too little sleep and exercise, experiment with chemical substances, risk avoidable infections, and have no plans to manage the stress of daily living. Left unattended, these issues can threaten an otherwise promising future.

Use the concepts in this chapter to help you get started, or help you improve, in taking care of your health. The impact of your actions might extend beyond your responsibility to yourself. For example, when you take good care of your health, you inspire those around you to follow your lead. Your choice to adopt better health habits will contribute to a healthier and more productive society.

NOTES

1. Excerpt from *The New Wellness Encyclopedia*. Copyright © 1995 by Health Letter Associates. Reprinted by permission of Houghton Mifflin Company. All rights reserved.

2. "For Men Only," *Nutrition Action Healthletter* 22, no. 5 (June 1995). Copyright © 1995, CSPI. Reprinted/adapted from Nutrition Action Healthletter (1875 Connecticut Ave., N.W., Suite 300, Washington, DC 20009-5728. $24.00 for 10 issues).

3. Ibid.

4. Ibid.

5. Ibid.

6. Information on diet came from the following sources: "Importing the Pacific Rim Diet," University of California at Berkeley: *Wellness Letter* 10, no. 2 (1993): 1–2, B. Schardt, B. Liebman, and S. Schmidt: "Going Mediterranean," *Nutrition Health Letter* 21, no. 10 (1994): 1;5–7;9; and C. Rucker: "Why Seventh-Day Adventists Live Longer," *Bottom Line Personal*, October 15, 1991, pp. 11–13.

7. From *Power Sleep* by James Maas, Ph.D. Copyright © 1998 by James Maas Ph.D. Reprinted by permission of Random House, Inc.

8. University of California at Berkeley: *The New Wellness Encyclopedia*.

9. Adapted from S. Althoff, M. Svoboda, and D. Girdano: *Choices in Wellness for Life*, 3rd ed. (Scottsdale, AZ: Gorsuch Scarisbrick Publishers, 1996).

10. J. Carpi: "Stress," *Medical World News*, May 1993, p. 27.

11. "Anxiety Impinges on an Immune Response," *ASM News* 63, no. 3 (1998): 128.

12. E. Pennisi: *Science News* 144 (November 20, 1993): 332.

13. University of California at Berkeley: *The New Wellness Encyclopedia*.

14. Ibid., p. 453.

15. Laurie Garrett: *The Coming Plague: Newly Emerging Diseases in a World Out of Balance* (New York: Farrar, Straus and Giroux, 1994).

16. L. Elliott and C. Brantley: *Sex on Campus: The Naked Truth about the Real Sex Lives of College Students.* (New York: Random House, 1997), p. 74.

17. This discussion is based on concepts and data from M. Schuckitt: *Educating Yourself about Alcohol and Drugs: A People's Primer* (New York: Plenum, 1995).

18. National Institute on Drug Abuse: *National Household Survey on Drug Abuse. Population Estimates* (Rockville, MD: U.S. Department of Health and Human Services, 1992).

PRE-CHAPTER SELF-ASSESSMENT

Read each statement and circle the number that best reflects your response.

NEVER   ALWAYS

1   2   3   4   5   6   7   8   9   10

1. When I encounter a conflict with my parents, I consider the interests of both my parents and myself in reaching an agreement.

   1   2   3   4   5   6   7   8   9   10

2. In resolving conflicts between others and me, I look for win/win solutions.

   1   2   3   4   5   6   7   8   9   10

3. I choose friends who have compatible beliefs, values, goals, and aspirations.

   1   2   3   4   5   6   7   8   9   10

4. I can resist pressure from others who to engage in negative and self-destructive behaviors.

   1   2   3   4   5   6   7   8   9   10

5. When I discuss issues with other people, I try to put myself in the other person's place and figure out how she might think and feel.

   1   2   3   4   5   6   7   8   9   10

6. When I engage in a dispute with another person, I do not label that person but instead seek to separate the issue of dispute from the person.

   1   2   3   4   5   6   7   8   9   10

7. I am honest about my feelings and emotions when I try to resolve conflicts with other people.

   1   2   3   4   5   6   7   8   9   10

8. I base my evaluation of a professor mainly on my own observations and impressions.

   1   2   3   4   5   6   7   8   9   10

9. I am open-minded when I listen to and consider the religious perspectives of other people.

   1   2   3   4   5   6   7   8   9   10

10. I feel secure enough about my own abilities to attend instructors' office hours and initiate conversations with them.

    1   2   3   4   5   6   7   8   9   10

11. I can ignore the ridicule of other students who might accuse me of "sucking up" to instructors.

    1   2   3   4   5   6   7   8   9   10

12. I have a detailed plan (including a list of questions to ask) for attending the office hours of each of my instructors.

    1   2   3   4   5   6   7   8   9   10

13. Most of my questions during office hours reflect a deeper understanding of the material rather than simple recall of facts.

    1   2   3   4   5   6   7   8   9   10

14. I can identify and correct specific thinking problems that hinder effective interactions with parents.

    1   2   3   4   5   6   7   8   9   10

15. I can identify and correct specific thinking problems that hinder effective interactions with peers.

    1   2   3   4   5   6   7   8   9   10

16. I can identify and correct specific thinking problems that hinder effective interactions with my professors.

    1   2   3   4   5   6   7   8   9   10

Determine your relative degree of proactivity for this trait by using the following formula:

Percent Proactivity = Sum of Circled Numbers ÷ 160 × 100

(Note that 160 is the maximum sum possible. It would result in a score of 100 percent.)

Percent Proactivity = _____

For example, if you checked 5 for each question, your score would be

Percent Proactivity for Outlook = 80/160 × 100 = 50

"If you are very strong in problem solving but you have no common sense about interacting with other people, there are going to be all sorts of paths to success that will be closed to you."

Jack Lochhead[1]

Relationships: Constructive Interactions with Peers and Authority Figures

YOU CANNOT EXPECT TO reach your full potential unless you have good social skills. A large part of what you do in life involves people. Therefore, in addition to academic plans, you need a plan that will help you develop effective interactions with peers, authority figures, and people of diverse cultures.

Improved negotiation skills will help you in all situations involving people. A proactive approach to diversity issues will contribute to a better society as well as benefit you as a person.

Your choice of friends and romantic partners will have a profound impact on your academic performance and overall success. You can choose a reactive or proactive approach to this issue. Reactive students make friends randomly with little selectivity. They are more likely to follow the crowd. Proactive students choose friends based on compatible goals, aspirations, and study habits. As discussed in Chapter 4, proactive students have strong personal goals and values, and these goals and values help them resist peer pressure. They live by a set of guidelines that helps them interact effectively with their peers.

Interactions with authority figures pose an area of special concern. A student's relationship with his parents can be a challenge because he has adult freedoms on campus while his parent(s) might still treat him like a child. The reactive student rebels against his parents' treatment and thus invites frequent family conflicts. The resultant situation can increase personal stress and hence poor academic performance. The proactive student learns to understand her parent's point of view and seeks to negotiate with them on matters of mutual concern.

On campus, reactive students avoid instructors because of misconceptions about them, personal insecurities, or fear of ridicule from fellow students. As a result, most reactive students fail to attract mentors or receive strong letters of recommendation. Proactive students are less concerned about student perceptions than they are about achieving their goals. They believe that it is their responsibility to get to know and be known by their instructors. They attend and have a plan for how to get the most out of their instructors' office hours. Proactive students know the importance of mentors to their career success. Thus, they conduct themselves in a manner that will attract mentors.

This chapter will help you:

- Resolve conflicts effectively

- Understand the importance of diversity and promote and benefit from an appreciation of its value

- Develop effective and satisfying relationships with parents, peers, romantic partners and instructors

- Identify and correct any thinking problems that hinder effective and satisfying social interactions

The electronic revolution brings the issue of relationships to center stage. Why? Because many of us spend a large amount of our time interacting with computers, and this practice can hinder a person's social development. For example, a teenager in Berkeley, California, who started on his path to computer literacy at the age of three now has great Internet skills but cannot hold a face-to-face conversation with another person.

How can people acquire the social skills to become responsible members of society if they spend most of their free time in front of a computer? How will they as students negotiate college life? Have you given any thought to your own situation? A large part of your success as a student involves people (Figure 7.1). You must interact with your parents, other students, and—very important—your instructors. You will make new friends and meet new acquaintances. Also, you may establish a romantic relationship with someone.

FIGURE 7.1
Relationship issues.

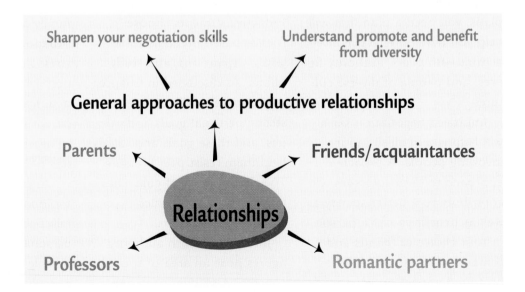

As we become a more multicultural society, you will be challenged to accept others from different backgrounds. After school, you will find it difficult to advance in your career unless you find effective ways to communicate with people of different races, ages, and cultures. Two general approaches to productive relationships are (1) to sharpen your negotiation skills and (2) to value diversity among people (Figure 7.1).

Two Key Approaches to Productive Relationships

SHARPEN YOUR NEGOTIATION SKILLS

As you pursue your goals, you will have to negotiate with other people frequently. Figure 7.2 shows six negotiation strategies.[2] We will refer to these strategies throughout this chapter.

1. *Win/win*—provides mutual benefits to all parties concerned. There are no losers in this approach. Everybody gets the satisfaction needed to support the plan. People who use the win/win approach are more likely to cooperate than to compete; they use principles instead of power or position to convince others.

2. *Win/lose*—I win, you lose. This is perhaps the most widely used approach in our society. People who use the win/lose approach depend on power, prestige, and possessions to get their way at the expense of others. You see win/lose at work in college if the grading system is on a bell curve. Only a few members of the class can receive As while other students get lower grades.

FIGURE 7.2

Covey's negotiation strategies.

Stephen R. Covey's Negotiation Strategies

Win/Win—provides mutual benefits to all parties concerned

Win/Lose—I win, you lose

Lose/Win—I lose, you win

Lose/Lose—everybody loses, nobody wins

Win—the only consideration

Win/Win or no deal—both parties agree or both walk away

3. *Lose/win*—I lose, you win. People who use the lose/win approach often put themselves at the mercy of someone else. They often see themselves as losers. They give in easily and will do anything to make peace. These people lack the courage to stick up for their points of view. You see the lose/win approach at work when students let instructors intimidate them. People fixed on lose/win solutions tend to suppress their true emotions. The result is often anger and hostility toward others.

4. *Lose/lose*—everybody loses; nobody wins. This situation often happens when two people who use the win/lose approach encounter conflict. People who use the lose/lose approach have a mentality of "if I can't have it, you can't either." They often resort to revenge and get-even tactics.

5. *Win*—the only consideration is to win. People with this approach give no thought to whether the other person wins or loses. They take care of their own interests and leave others to fend for themselves.

6. *Win/win or no deal*—both parties agree or both walk away. In other words, if the parties cannot agree on a solution, they agree to disagree. Since there is no pressure to agree, the parties in this approach can preserve their relationship no matter what the outcome of an issue.

Except for sports and games, the win/win approach is the best approach for most situations.

UNDERSTAND, PROMOTE, AND BENEFIT FROM DIVERSITY

Diversity: a mix of people who differ in ethnicity, race, religion, socioeconomic class, gender, sexual orientation, geographic origin, values, and any other traits that define groups of people.

Diversity will be an issue in many of your relationships. Your success in school and in life will often depend on your understanding the importance of diversity, promoting it when possible, and benefiting from an appreciation of its value.

UNDERSTANDING THE IMPORTANCE OF DIVERSITY

Your college campus probably includes people from a variety of backgrounds. For example, people may be from different geographic regions, such as other parts of the United States or other countries. Also, students may represent different ethnic heritages, practice different religious faiths, and speak different languages. Students also may come from a variety of socioeconomic levels. Some students on your campus may have physical disabilities or learning disabilities. Your campus probably has both female and male students, and both heterosexual and homosexual students. All of these factors combined create a campus life rich with diversity.

Here are a few points about valuing diversity:[3]

Valuing diversity is

- Understanding cultural differences

- Listening to a variety of perspectives

- Sharing your thoughts, ideas, and opinions with others

- Being honest

Valuing diversity is not

- "White male bashing"

- "Political correctness" (whatever that is)

- A lecture on how you should think, feel, or act

- Saying what you think others want to hear

Because we are becoming a more and more diverse society, diversity is becoming a more and more important issue. Consider the following statistics based on the 1990 census:

- By the year 2000, one in three of the total population in the United States will be a person of color.

- By 1990 one in three businesses in the United States already had international connections. Based on continued talks with other nations, the ratio will likely jump.

- During the next decade, 80 percent of the entering workforce will consist of women, people of color, and immigrants.

- In the 20 largest school districts in the nation, all the student population counts tally more than 50 percent for students of color.

- By 1990, one in seven students spoke a language other than English at home.

In addition to the United States becoming more diverse, the world is becoming smaller and more accessible as we can more easily communicate with people in other parts of the world. People need to be prepared to work with people of diverse backgrounds and of different cultures, both in their professions and in daily social interactions with others.

As a college student, you have an opportunity to interact with people representing this diversity. You can learn to be open to different individuals' worldviews, or the way people see and interpret the world.

Worldview: the overall perspective from which one sees and interprets the world; a collection of beliefs about life and the universe held by an individual or group.

■ PROMOTING DIVERSITY

Here are some guidelines for what you can do to help promote diversity:

- Be willing to interact with and learn from people of other cultures. Many campuses have a cross-cultural center that provides materials, workshops, and programs for this purpose.

- Identify and eliminate stereotypes about other people in your thinking.

- Be willing to see life from someone else's point of view. For example, if you are a Christian, imagine how a Jew would view a certain issue. If you have no physical limitations, think about what it would be like for a person in a wheelchair to navigate your campus.

Think of diversity as a win/win situation. We all gain when we share with and learn from each other. People of diverse cultures, often with great success, share food, music, art, literature, and dress. Exercise 7.1 helps you explore this idea.

(Source: Gary Buss/FPG International.)

Understanding and Promoting Diversity

Prepare a personal plan for how you will learn to understand and promote diversity. Use the following topics as a guide:[4]

1. Information I plan to seek out to help further my understanding of racism, prejudice, and discrimination:

_____

_____

2. Information I plan to seek out to help further my understanding of different cultural groups:

_____

_____

3. A topic of conversation I would like to have with my friends or family:

_____

_____

4. A cultural group(s) that I would like to learn more about:

_____

_____

5. Events or activities I plan to participate in to increase my awareness of diversity on my campus:

_____

_____

6. An action I can take (through a leadership position, student organization, or class project) that will enhance diversity on my campus:

_____

_____

■ BENEFITING FROM AN APPRECIATION OF DIVERSITY

When you understand the value of diversity and help promote it on your campus, you will find your college career more fulfilling. While you are studying academic subjects such as history, English, and math, you will also learn about other groups of people. This can be an interesting time as you see how your beliefs, values, customs, ideas, and perspectives often differ significantly from others. You will find that this broader understanding of diversity gives you a wider lens from which to view the world. Although your beliefs, values, and so forth may not be changed—in fact, they may be strengthened—what you will gain is an to appreciation of other viewpoints. As a result, you will be able to overcome any self-defeating attitudes and behaviors stemming from prejudice and discriminatory thinking. When you replace such self-defeating beliefs with productive beliefs, you will help improve society through your example.

When you gain skill in working in multicultural situations, you will have an added value in the workforce. An increasing number of tasks today require teamwork. Because of the changing demographics in this country, many teams will be diverse. People who can work with and manage multicultural teams will have career advantages over individuals who lack these skills. Furthermore, you can expect a richer social life when you share experiences with people of different backgrounds.

Relationships with Parents

Parent: one who nurtures and raises a child; a mother, father, or guardian.

Your **parent** is the person or persons who nurtured and raised you. You may have a single parent, two parents, several parents, or a guardian. For simplicity, in this text we use the term to refer to all possible situations.

While you are in college, you may resent the fact that your parents still seem to be trying to control what you do. Before you came to college, you were probably "under their wings," and they took responsibility for most of your activities. Now your college considers you an adult. All of a sudden, you have unprecedented freedom. Yet most parents are not ready to give up their authority so quickly. To them, you probably are still a child, and they may treat you accordingly whether you live at home or away from home. You cannot change your parents' behavior. They have developed and hardened their beliefs over a long period of time. By now, they probably believe that their way is the right way. When conflicts arise, some parents will pull rank and say: "I raised you. I know what's best for you. You will do as I say." As one student puts it, "Once you start pushing, you can affect other aspects of the family. You start tampering with family values, with history, heritage, the way it is, was, the way it's going to be. They might often remind you that you are just one person in the family—that you are part of a unit, and that you can't break the unit for just one person."

For these reasons, interacting with parents can be one of the most difficult challenges for young adults. Moreover, you may feel homesick for your parents and other family members, especially if this is your first time away from the family. It may be that you miss the company of your family and you long for home-cooked meals. Or perhaps you are adjusting to having to assume some new responsibilities, such as managing your finances and making other decisions for yourself. Moving away from home can be stressful for these and other reasons.

Journal Activity

If you are struggling at college because you are separated from your family and miss them, discuss what you miss about your family. What are you currently doing to maintain a tie with your family? What can you do to help yourself become used to living apart from the family?

_____

_____

_____

_____

_____

_____

There are both proactive and reactive approaches possible to conflicts with parents. The reactive student often sees only her own side. This stance leaves the door open for frequent family conflicts, which in turn might lead to personal stress and hence poor academic performance. The proactive student tries to be sensitive to his parents' point of view. He seeks to forge new areas of communication and collaboration with them. Figure 7.3 shows three guidelines for a proactive approach to conflicts with parents.

Penny's story points out how a student's goals can conflict with those of her parents. Penny was the youngest of four children in her family. Toward the end of the second semester, Penny beamed with pride as she reflected on her life and first year of college. A communications major, she was on the dean's list each semester. She was a member of a foreign language club and was elected to the student government during the second semester. Penny plays the piano and reads classic literature for recreation. She communicates well and has excellent "people" skills.

Penny was the top candidate for a summer internship at a local television station. They made her an offer, and she wanted to accept the offer. The problem was that Penny was not totally free to make her own decisions. Her parents had much to say about what she did. They put strong pressure on her to find a summer job closer to home. How did Penny resolve this serious conflict? Did she ignore her parents or give in to their demands? Analyze Penny's situation in Exercise 7.2.

Penny's story highlights the point that although your college might treat you like an adult, your parents might still expect to make the major decisions that affect you. Your challenge is to find effective ways to pursue your own goals without alienating your parents. Following are examples of the three proactive approaches shown in Figure 7.3 as they were used by several different students to help resolve family conflicts.

FIGURE 7.3

Guidelines for productive relationships with parents.

Guidelines for productive relationships with parents

1. Appeal to your parents' values

2. Seek help from third parties

3. Get creative

Analyzing a Family Conflict

1. Describe your immediate reactions to Penny's dilemma.

    _____

    _____

    _____

    _____

    _____

2. Discuss the possible impact on Penny's emotions if she does the following:

    a. Ignores her parents

        _____

        _____

        _____

        _____

    b. Gives in to her parent's demands

        _____

        _____

        _____

        _____

3. Discuss the possible impact on Penny's parents' emotions if she does the following:

    a. Ignores her parents

        _____

        _____

        _____

    b. Gives in to her parent's demands

        _____

        _____

        _____

4. Propose alternative solutions that might satisfy the concerns of both parties.

_____

_____

_____

_____

APPEAL TO YOUR PARENT'S VALUES

Phillip lived on campus and was in his second year at the university. His grades were not what he or his parents had expected, given that he had been an "A" student in high school. His main problem was time management. He had trouble getting everything done, and this problem showed up as poor academic performance. His parents proposed that he move back home so that they could help him manage his time better. Phillip understood his parent's concerns, but he was not ready to give up his independence. He countered his parent's proposal with one of his own.

First, Phillip applied what he had learned in one of his workshops on optimal productivity. At the beginning of each week, Phillip made a detailed list of all the projects he had to complete in that week. He updated this list daily. As he completed each project, he crossed it off the list. After several weeks of using this technique, he noticed a distinct improvement in his performance. Next, he showed the lists and some of his recent test scores to his parents. They could see clearly that he was making progress and thus did not object to his plans to stay on campus.

Phillip understood what was most important to his parents. Their main concern was that he make steady progress as a student. That was the only reason that they wanted him to move back home. Phillip's approach offered a win/win situation for both him and his parents.

Let's return to Penny's story. Penny was eager to be an intern at the television station, but she also did not want to offend her parents. Penny proposed a plan to her employer that would allow her to work ten-hour rather than eight-hour days. This plan would allow her to build up hours that she could convert to several three-day weekends during the summer. She planned to spend those weekends at home with her family. Her employer approved of the plan, and her parents also liked the idea. In this way, Penny used a win/win strategy to resolve her family conflict.

SEEK HELP FROM THIRD PARTIES

Madge came from a very protective family background. She lived at home but did most of her studying with a group on campus. Late one afternoon she called home to inform her mother that she would be studying late.

(Source: Bob
Daemmrich/The Image
Works.)

Madge's mother got angry and ordered her to come home. Madge did not
object to her mother's orders even though she had to forgo a valuable session with her study group. As a result, she was not as well prepared for the
exam. Did Madge have any other options?

Mimi had a similar background in that her parents were very protective.
But Mimi took a different approach from that of Madge. Mimi took her
group home with her a couple of times for their study session. Later,
when she wanted to study late with the group, her mother did not object.
Her mother had already met, fed, and chatted with Jill, Alice, and Tom.
She was less concerned about Mimi's safety because her study partners all
seemed like nice, responsible young adults. In this case, Mimi's friends
acted as a third party that was able to gain the respect and trust of Mimi's
mother.

Basil's approach demonstrates another way of using a third party to help
sway parents. His parents expected him to attend the university in his city.
But Basil had his sights set on a sister institution 500 miles away. By visits
and by phone, he talked to professors, administrators, counselors, and staff
at the distant school. When he announced his decision, his parents thought
that he was crazy. They wondered how he could leave his family and attend
school so far away. Basil had prepared for this reaction. He did not try to
persuade his parents all by himself, instead, he sought the help of his new
contacts at the school he planned to attend. He had his parents talk to them.
The result was that his parents changed their minds and let Basil attend the
university of his choice.

If your concern is that you feel homesick, you can ask third parties for
help in this regard, too. Try sharing your concerns with your roommates or
friends. Get ideas from them. After all, they may be feeling the same way
you do. Try to fill the void of the time you miss spending with family by

developing friendships, or have a friend help you get involved in organizations that provide a social outlet. Volunteer your time to help in causes that interest you.

GET CREATIVE

Basil's parents went along with his decision and helped him get settled on campus. But they still had trouble adjusting to the fact that he was so far away from home. Although they now live in the United States, they still hold many beliefs and values that they brought with them from their country of origin. Basil was the first to break with the tradition that the family stayed together.

Basil tried to understand his parent's dilemma. They wanted him to get a good education but at the same time uphold family traditions. But Basil had his own dilemma. He wanted to please his parents, but he really did not want to attend college in his hometown and live at home. Basil did not have an immediate answer to these conflicts. What he did over time, however, turned out to be a very clever solution.

Throughout his college years, Basil stayed in close contact with his parents. He shared with them the results of his tests. He also shared details about his social activities. When they visited the campus, he introduced them to his professors. When he went on trips, he took pictures of what he did and saw and added them to a scrapbook that he prepared for them.

Thus, Basil took a creative approach to working through his family conflict. His parents reacted favorably because he took the time and made the effort to understand their concerns. Exercise 7.3 gives you a chance to explore how you might work through a variety of family conflicts.

●●●●●●EXERCISE 7.3

Working through Family Conflict

For each of the following family conflicts, write down how you would respond.

1. Your mother calls you every weekend and makes unfounded charges about your study habits and social activities.

_____

_____

_____

_____

(continued)

2. You have a midterm exam scheduled the day after your parents want you to come for a weekend cultural celebration.

_____

_____

_____

_____

3. Since you live only 20 miles from home, your parents want you to be involved in all of the family activities.

_____

_____

_____

_____

4. Your parents want to have final approval over all of your choices of friends.

_____

_____

_____

_____

5. Your parents want you to major in a technical area because they believe this path will give you more opportunities. You prefer one of the humanities.

_____

_____

_____

_____

This section has stressed how you can be more proactive as you work through family conflicts. That is, you can

■ Appeal to your parent's sense of values.

■ Seek help from third parties.

■ Use your own creativity to resolve the concerns.

Journal Activity

Think of a conflict that you might have with your parents. How might the conflict affect your mood, your academic performance, and your relationship with your parents? What ideas do you have for resolving this conflict?

_____

_____

_____

_____

_____

_____

This last approach, the creative approach, works equally well for students who are missing their parents. They could ask their parents to visit them at their new "home away from home." Another way to combat homesickness would be to join a club at school, participate in intramural sports, or attend a church near campus. These and other social activities can provide opportunities for building close, supportive friendships. Of course, the new relationships would not replace family relationships, but they could serve as a "family away from home."

Relationships with Friends and Acquaintances

Consider this comment by a student:

You come into this world with no idea of who you are or where you are going. You constantly look for feedback for where you are in relationship to the rest of the universe. I'm here, everybody else is doing this, and maybe I should be too. It takes somebody who has strong values and clear goals to ignore that influence. It is extremely rare for an 18- or 19-year-old to be that mature.

The students you spend time with can either enhance or hinder your overall success. For example, some students value television time over study time. Others give television time a lower priority. Often you will have to balance your time between two groups of students so that you can both have fun and study as much as think you should.

Peers: other students around you, such as friends. classmates, roommates, and team-mates.

This section will focus on your relationship with your **peers:** (1) friends and acquaintances and (2) romantic, or intimate, partners. *Acquaintances* are people you interact with—roommates, teammates, or members of clubs—who are not close enough to be friends.

CHOOSING FRIENDS

All through high school, Sam made friends at random. His close associates ranged from partygoers to honor students. He would get advice from all of his friends and try to follow it all. He maintained this same pattern during his first year of college. The turning point came when he was a close friend with a student who was very negative about the university they were both attending and about careers in medicine, which was Sam's career choice. Sam found his overall attitude toward life changing from enthusiastic to negative. At the end of the year, he no longer wanted to be a doctor, and he wanted to transfer to another university.

Sam's experience highlights an important point. Your choice of friends has a strong impact on your academic performance and overall success. Prior to college, your parents set the stage for who your friends will be. They choose where you live, go to school, and where you worship. They also choose many of your social activities. Some of the individuals you met in the course of your daily life in this setting will remain your friends for life.

Once in college, you encounter new opportunities for friendships as you go to class or participate in other campus activities. Now *you* make the choices. These are among the most important decisions you will make in your entire lifetime. The old adage, "a man is known by the company he keeps," is as true today as it was many years ago.

Among the many issues that you might consider when choosing friends are (1) the value of choosing friends that have goals and values compatible with your own and (2) the importance of quality versus quantity in friend-ships.

■ COMPATIBLE GOALS AND VALUES

Exercise 7.4 will help you appreciate importance of your friends having goals and values that are compatible with your own.

Did Exercise 7.4 reveal any conflicts in your values? If so, you will want to review Chapters 1,2, and 4. To avoid conflicts, you need to have a clear idea of who you are, what you think is important, and what you want to do in life. The earlier chapters will help you make independent judgments about how you live your life. When you have your own set of guidelines, you will be less pressured to follow those of your friends.

■ QUALITY VS. QUANTITY

Consider another student comment: "You could have a million friends, but you would be lucky to have one or two true friends." This comment addresses the issue of quantity versus quality. Some students value quantity of friends over the quality of the friendships. Darlene's story illustrates this point. She knew Mary, a student who had a lot of friends. Everybody

Resolving Conflicts with Friends

Write down how you would react in the following situations:

1. You want to be a good student, but your closest friends pressure you to party with them every night.

   _____

   _____

   _____

2. You want to be an engineer, but your friends think that all engineers are nerds.

   _____

   _____

   _____

3. You have strong religious beliefs, but your friends often criticize them.

   _____

   _____

   _____

4. You value good health and safety, but your friends have poor health habits and make fun of you for being too careful.

   _____

   _____

   _____

seemed to know Mary. Everywhere she went, people seemed to flock around her. Darlene felt really bad and insecure around Mary, because, in comparison, Darlene had only two friends with whom she was close. Then Darlene discovered that out of all those people, Mary really had only one close friend. All the other people were acquaintances, not close friends. Exercise 7.5 gives you an opportunity to reflect on the characteristics of a close friend.

PEER INFLUENCE

Choosing friends is one aspect of interacting with your peers. Another issue is dealing with peer influences, or *peer pressure*. Most students find it difficult to resist peer pressure. They want their peers to accept them. They fear that other students will judge them and find them inadequate. Certainly,

What Do You Look for in a Friend?

List what you consider to be the five most important characteristics in a close friend.

1. _____

2. _____

3. _____

4. _____

5. _____

when you choose not to give in to peer pressure, you risk isolation and may miss out on many social activities. And it is important to have fun and develop relationships. But it is also important to conform to your own values and stay on track toward your goals. Many young adults do not have enough self-esteem to manage these conflicting circumstances.

Oscar's story highlights this point.

When Oscar came to the campus, he had clear goals and set out to achieve his goals by having a regular study time and getting enough sleep. When he found himself left out of the activities others participated in, he felt rejected. He associated all the positive things he did with being rejected by his peers. During the second quarter, Oscar began to lower his academic standards. He stayed up later and studied less. After he failed three midterm exams, Oscar realized that he had made a mistake. He was comparing himself against others—but only the 20 or so people who were right around him on his floor in the dorm. None of these people seemed to share his goals. Eventually, Oscar realized that sometimes you have to look for people with compatible interests and goals. Later, he did meet people that he could relate to on many different levels, and he was able to balance his academic and social pursuits.

In some ways, Betty's story is similar to that of Oscar. Betty's roommate, Eve, changed her behavior during their sophomore year. She spent less time studying and more time having fun than she had before. Not only did she change her own behavior, but she also tried to bring Betty down to her level. She criticized Betty for studying so much, and pressured her to surf the Internet or hang out with Eve and her friends. When Betty said no, Eve would take it personally and feel hurt.

Betty's story is different from Oscar's in that she handled the problem before it did damage to her attitude or performance. At the same time she was under pressure from Eve, Betty was developing a good friendship with Le, whom she had met freshman year. Le was a psychology major and took her classes seriously. She would propose study sessions with Betty such as at the library or coffee shop. Betty chose to spend more time with Le than with Eve. In this way Betty was able to insulate herself from the pressure that Eve might put on her. The reason was that Betty had developed a friendship with someone who had goals more compatible with her own.

Now that you have read about how two students dealt with peer influence, complete Exercise 7.6.

Your responses to the preceding questions indicate how well you can manage peer influences. If you give in to your friends in every situation, you might find that this pattern hinders your success in school. On the other hand, if you say no to every invitation, you will have little or no social life. The key is to keep your goals and values in focus as you balance your time between academic and social activities. The task-organization system in Chapter 5 will help you improve your ability to manage tasks so that you will also have time for social activities.

● ● ● ● ●●EXERCISE 7.6

Negotiating Peer Pressure

Propose solutions to the following hypothetical situations:

1. You attend classes, stay current in all of your courses, and go to the instructor's office hours and teaching assistant (TA) sessions. Your classmates accuse you of trying to set the curve and make them look bad.

   _____

   _____

   _____

   _____

2. Students on your end of the dorm get together every Thursday evening to watch a popular television program. They pressure you each week to join them, but you prefer to spend time getting ready for the next day's classes.

   _____

   _____

   _____

   _____

3. Your friends are trying to get you to join them for spring break in Cancun, Mexico. Your parents will not pay for the trip. You have some savings from a part-time job, but you had planned to pay off your credit card for the books you bought this semester.

   _____

   _____

   _____

   _____

Journal Activity

Think of a situation when you were under extreme pressure from friends to do something that was in conflict with your values. Try to recall your thoughts at the time. Explain how you reacted, and describe the consequences, if any. If a similar situation arose now or in the future, how would you respond?

_____

_____

_____

_____

_____

_____

CONFLICTS WITH PEERS

Now that we have covered how to choose friends and manage peer influences, it is time to discuss the issue of when things go wrong with peer interactions. Friends often disagree on issues, and sometimes these disagreements will lead to conflicts. Conflicts can hinder your success because they divert your attention from the tasks of the moment.

Conflicts can lead to good or bad relationships, depending on how the parties respond. There are many potential sources of conflict for students. For example, in group living, roommates tend to clash over a wide range of issues. Relationships can also be a fertile source of tension. Sometimes students have to find ways to deal with peers who cheat or pressure them for unethical favors. Finally, students might clash over little things like parking too close to one another.

You can view each conflict as a pain or as an opportunity for personal growth. The point to remember is that you are not a victim. You can control your response even though you can't control the response of another person. The most successful students view conflicts as an opportunity for growth. They adhere to the guidelines of open communication, honesty, mutual respect, and flexibility. Let's take a closer look at each of these guidelines.

■ OPEN COMMUNICATION

Proactive students keep the lines of communication open. For example, some suitemates set up a list of guidelines at the beginning of the term. They then sit down periodically and vent their concerns. They each might talk about what they like and what they don't like. These students often solve problems before they get out of hand. Good listening skills are essential to this

(Source: Stewart
Cohen/Tony Stone
Images.)

process. The best communication occurs when a person seeks to understand, not just hear, what the other party is saying. She puts herself in the
other person's place and tries to imagine how the other person feels.

■ HONESTY

Students are more likely to resolve conflicts when they are honest with each
other. Also, honesty builds trust, an essential component of a good relationship. Consider how the situation in Example 7.1 would have benefited from
some honesty.

EXAMPLE 7.1

Bob, George, and Alice are assigned to work together on a group project. They
meet every week to update each other on their individual tasks. Even though he
has fallen way behind, Bob says he is up to date on his task and doesn't ask for
help from the others. By the time their presentation is due, Bob's portion is still
not complete, and George and Alice suffer with a lower grade.

EXAMPLE 7.2

Kenya and Ashley decide to become study partners and share information.
Kenya shares information generously, but Ashley doesn't contribute much to
the study sessions even though she knows the material well. She fears that
Kenya might outscore her on the exam. Ashley takes much but gives very little.

■ MUTUAL RESPECT

Some people tend to attack other people during heated disputes. This tactic can damage the other person's self-esteem and do much harm to the relationship. Astute students avoid this practice. They know or learn how to separate the activity from the individual, that is, how to criticize the behavior but not the person. For example, "You are a jerk" is criticism of the person. "I don't like the way you leave a mess in the kitchen" is criticism of the activity.

■ FLEXIBILITY

Relationships work best when all members of the group are willing to compromise. People often find solutions to problems when they are willing to see things from each other's point of view. Suppose some roommates like to study to music while others like quietness when they study. A compromise solution would be to agree to play music only between the hours of 6 PM and 9 PM during weekdays.

Now complete Exercise 7.7 with the guidelines of open communication, honesty, mutual respect, and flexibility in mind.

● ● ● ● ● ●EXERCISE 7.7

Applying Guidelines of Good Friendships to Problem Situations

How would you respond to the following situations?

1. You spent weeks preparing for your midterm exams. You put together complete notes, outlines, diagrams, and note cards. Your friend, who takes many of the same classes, waited until the last minute to study. He fears that his lack of preparation will cause him to fail the exam. He wants to borrow your material.

_____

_____

_____

2. You often observe cheating on exams and wonder whether or not you should tell the instructor about it.

_____

_____

_____

3. Your roommate plays her stereo too loud, leaves dirty dishes and clothes around, and talks on the phone excessively.

_____

_____

_____

4. You and one of your friends express interest in the same girl. The girl can't decide which one of you she likes best.

_____

_____

_____

5. You are willing to compromise on most issues, but your roommate is more rigid.

_____

_____

_____

Journal Activity

Think about a conflict that you might have had with one of your peers. Also think about how the conflict affected your mood, your academic performance, and your relationship with your significant other. Describe your role in trying to resolve the conflict. For example, what negotiation strategies or other measures did you use? On reflection, what would you do differently if the conflict occurred again? How might you use the information in this chapter to resolve a current or future conflict with your peers?

_____

_____

_____

_____

_____

_____

_____

This section stressed how you can be more proactive in choosing friends, managing peer influences, and working through conflict with your peers. Now let's focus on relationships with romantic partners.

Romantic Relationships

Romantic relationships can affect your schoolwork and the rest of your life in some important ways. When you have a relationship on your mind, you tend to lose track of time. As a result, you may forget about your schoolwork and neglect your other friendships. Romantic relationships also require you to assume additional responsibilities for your actions. Let's consider a few specific concerns related to romantic relationships.

TIME MANAGEMENT

When people enter romantic relationships, they sometimes lose interest in their college goals and forget priorities. What they really want to do is spend time with their boyfriend or girlfriend. So, for example, instead of studying for a test the next day, they may choose to go out on a date, and their test grade suffers as a result.

Although developing social relationships is an important part of college life, academic goals are more important. The primary reason for attending college is to obtain an education. Maintain your study time by scheduling it when your romantic interest is in class or at a job. If you want to study with him or her, consider meeting in a public place, where your focus is more likely to stay on your schoolwork.

MAINTAINING OTHER FRIENDSHIPS

Most people have a given amount of time and energy to devote to social activities and relationships with friends. A person who has a boyfriend or girlfriend may spend most of this time with the boyfriend or girlfriend, and as a result, have less time for other friends. Be sensitive to your other friends, and be careful not to neglect close friendships that are sources of support and camaraderie.

RESPECT OF PRIVACY

Everyone needs to have private time. If you have a boyfriend or girlfriend, remember to give that person space and time to spend with other friends and to pursue individual interests. You do not have to share everything to have a good relationship. Also, be sure to preserve time for yourself and your other friends and interests. Some introspection can result in a healthier relationship and a better awareness of your individual needs.

TAKING RESPONSIBILITY FOR YOUR ACTIONS

Make every effort to maintain control of your actions at all times. Your status as a college student gives you adult freedoms. Along with these freedoms, you have adult responsibilities—to yourself and to society. Stay in touch with your values, and be aware of the consequences of what you might say or do. Being responsible does not mean you don't have fun.

If you reach a point in your relationship where you and your partner are considering sexual intercourse, remember that abstinence is a choice. The decision to engage in sexual intercourse can have drastic effects on your future, especially when you consider the possibility of an unplanned pregnancy or of contracting an STD or AIDS (discussed in Chapter 6). If you do decide to engage in sexual intercourse, wearing a condom can help decrease (but not eliminate) these risks. Additional forms of protection are available for birth control.

OPEN COMMUNICATION IN ROMANTIC RELATIONSHIPS

Open communication is essential for building trust in a romantic relationship. If you are uneasy and feel pressure from your partner to do something you do not want to do, be honest with the other person. Staying true to yourself and your values and being open about your feelings helps to ensure you are involved in a relationship that is satisfying to both of you. If you are open, you are more likely to discover areas where you and your partner disagree. Then you have an opportunity to see how well the other person works with you to resolve disagreements and conflicts.

CAUTIONS TO TAKE IN ROMANTIC RELATIONSHIPS

Date rape occurs when sexual assault is committed in a dating relationship. *Acquaintance rape* refers to sexual assault by a person known by the victim. Results of a recent survey show that 11 percent of men and 29 percent of women respondents had experienced forced sexual activity by a date, sexual partner, or friend.[5] Gay and bisexual females reported an even higher rate of sexual coercion—40 percent. Perhaps the most important point to remember about sexual coercion is the relationship between this act and the use of alcohol or drugs. Researchers found that most cases of sexual coercion occurred when either one or both partners were under the influence of drugs or alcohol. The accompanying box provides specific guidelines to help you avoid a situation that escalates to rape.

Rape Prevention Guidelines

1. Be clear about what you want; make sure your body language is reinforcing what you are saying.

2. Don't fall for, "If you loved me, you would."

3. Minimize drinking, avoid drugs, and avoid socializing with people who take drugs.

4. Set sexual limits for yourself, and communicate those limits clearly to your date.

5. Don't do things you don't want to do just to be polite. Be assertive by clearly expressing what you want and what you don't want.

6. Protest loudly and clearly if things get out of hand.

7. Avoid isolated settings.

8. Contribute financially to the date so that neither "owes" anything to the other except "thank you for a nice time."

9. Double-date or meet your date at the event (e.g., movie theater, game) until you feel totally comfortable with that person.

Note: These guidelines are applicable to men seeking to avoid unwanted intimacy as well.
Source: Reprinted from S. Althoff, M. Svoboda, and D. Girdano: *Choices in Wellness for Life*, 3rd ed. Copyright © 1996. All rights reserved. Adapted by permission of Allyn and Bacon.

Laurel Krank

I cannot begin to describe what a standard college romantic relationship is like. There is a certain euphoric feeling associated with the beginning of all relationships, especially those that start in the first year of college, before experience makes you a bit more jaded and cynical, when the prom and Friday night football games seem more real than graduate school and a career. Somehow everything during that time seems newer and maybe even a bit more innocent, which lends itself so easily to romantic notions of the perfect companion . . . out there waiting just for you.

I know this is a little like how I felt when I met Bob during the first week of my freshman year in our chemistry class. It is so amazing to think back to those first few weeks and remember how little I thought about the future, how much it didn't matter.

Doing well in school was important to both of us, and neither of us really understood how much of a time commitment another person can be (especially when you care about the other person!). It is difficult to get all your readings and problem sets done, attend all your club meetings or practices, find time for volunteer work, and spend quality time with each other that feels like more than just a "designated hour" on both of your schedules. Trying to carry on a meaningful relationship as a college student is the ultimate exercise in time management. This is probably why so many of our friends still don't have a steady boyfriend or girlfriend—they just don't want to be caught up in the juggling act! (Well, some of them just haven't found a person who's worth the juggling, either.)

If someone were to ask me, "What have you learned?," I suppose this would be my reply: Respect each other's need for privacy. This means to respect each other's need for separate activities and time for being by yourself. What you learn and experience on your own you can bring back to share. Happiness with the relationship is dependent on both of you feeling satisfied and fulfilled with what you do. Trust each other, and know you always have choices with what you do with your life.

As for school, set priorities! Relationships don't have to interfere with work, especially if you use your time well. Try not to take each other (or yourself) too seriously. Remember how to be silly and have fun; it'll get you out of some sticky situations if you can laugh things off.

Lastly, learn to enjoy small things—sometimes that's all you'll have time for.

Journal Activity

In a romantic relationship, which of the topics discussed in this section do you think may be of special concern to you? What strategies have you used to address this concern? What strategies do you think you could use in the future?

_____

_____

_____

_____

_____

_____

Relationships with Instructors and Professors

Josh spent several hours per day studying for the four courses that he was taking. During the week he spent only a few hours socializing with friends. Occasionally he would take a break and watch a television program. He always sat in one of the first few rows in class, stayed alert, and took good notes. Unfortunately, these good habits did not translate into high academic performance. Josh often missed the point in lectures, and he felt very insecure when he took exams. After three quarters of mediocre grades, he knew he had to do something different.

Josh had done almost everything right, but he had not interacted at all with his instructors. His advisor brought this point to his attention. Josh's story highlights a major point that many students miss. It is difficult to succeed in college or advance to the next stage of your career without help. One of the best sources of that help is your instructor. Yet, the lack of student-instructor contacts is one of the biggest sources of complaints on many campuses. Students complain that instructors are not approachable. Instructors complain that they hold office hours and students don't show up. Admittedly, some instructors are not very friendly. But you need to get beyond personalities to break through this barrier to success. This section will help you acquire the skill and confidence levels that lead to productive interactions with your instructors.

(Source: David Shopper/Stock Boston.)

WHY STUDENTS AVOID INSTRUCTORS AND PROFESSORS

Many students avoid instructors and professors for three main reasons: (1) misconceptions, (2) personal insecurities, and (3) peer pressure.

■ MISCONCEPTIONS

Students get their information about instructors from two main sources: (1) published student course reviews and (2) word-of-mouth information from other students. Often the latter source of information is second- or third-hand. Students often form conclusions based on these two sources without checking out the situation for themselves. Remember, your experience might not be the same as that of another student. Keep in mind that instructors are like any other group of people. They have different personalities, teaching styles, and ways in which they interact with students. Examples 7.3–7.8 give some arguments that students make to avoid interaction with their instructors, together with counterarguments.

EXAMPLE 7.3

Argument: Instructor Jones is too busy. I don't want to bother him.

Counterargument: Most professors take their responsibilities to students seriously. They hold office hours, and many will meet with you by appointment. Don't assume that Instructor Jones doesn't want to meet with you. Ask him. And attend his office hours.

EXAMPLE 7.4

Argument: I have a busy schedule, with school, work, and other activities. My professor only teaches three classes, so why can't she meet on my schedule?

Counterargument: Instructors and professors may have a variety of responsibilities outside their teaching responsibilities. Here are some activities they perform that you may not be aware of:

- *Advising and counseling*
- *Community service*—working with local schools and nonprofit agencies; serving on local, national, and sometimes international committees and panels
- *Varying amounts of administrative work*—preparing and grading tests; serving on departmental and campus committees
- *Creative activity*—the major research institutions as well as some others require professors to carry out some form of scholarly activity. For example, professors in the science-based disciplines conduct research and publish the results of their findings. Professors in the humanities write books and articles for publication.

Add to this list the duties that many instructors have to perform in connection with their personal relationships and families. When you put all of this information in context, it is easy to see why instructors are busy.

EXAMPLE 7.5

Argument: Instructor Crowe is not very friendly with students.

Counterargument: It might be that Instructor Crowe is not very friendly with anybody, including nonstudents. Or perhaps she is very friendly with students she gets to know. How would you know? You cannot judge a person by outward appearance or superficial contacts. Some instructors seem cold but have a warm heart that is revealed when you begin working with them. Also, remember that your experience with Instructor Crowe might not be the same as that of another student.

EXAMPLE 7.6

Argument: Professor Song is so highly educated that he makes me feel like a a nobody.

Counterargument: Do you think that Professor Song expects you to be complete at this stage? Perhaps you are a Professor Song in progress. Will he judge you based on what you know now at your young age or on your skills as a life-long learner? Do you base your self-worth solely on what you perceive that people think you know?

EXAMPLE 7.7

Argument: I don't know any good questions to ask Instructor Perez. She might label me a stupid student.

Counterargument: Can you learn how to ask better questions? You might seek the help of successful students in finding ways to ask better questions.

EXAMPLE 7.8

Argument: I don't want the other students to think that I am "sucking up" to my instructors.

Counterargument: Concerns over student perceptions will not help you achieve your goals. Getting to know and becoming known by instructors is essential to your education and development for the reasons discussed in the following section.

■ PERSONAL INSECURITIES

Students often feel insecure when they compare themselves with their professors. Consider the arguments and counterarguments of Examples 7.6 and 7.7.

■ PEER PRESSURE

Many students fear ridicule from fellow students who might misread their intentions when they attempt to establish a relationship with their instructors. Example 7.8 addresses this issue.

BENEFITS OF PRODUCTIVE INTERACTIONS WITH INSTRUCTORS AND PROFESSORS

Getting to know your instructors is important to your success. This section discusses six major benefits of engaging in productive interactions with your instructors.

1. *They promote accountability.* Prior to your entering college, someone else took care of you and assumed responsibility for you, usually a parent. Your teachers and counselors also took some responsibility for you. Now you are in charge of yourself. College life is in many ways impersonal. You can get lost in the large classes and dormitories of many of today's colleges and universities.

Here are two points to keep in mind: First, many students act more responsibly when they make it a habit to report to somebody. Second, students often feel more connected to the campus when they know that somebody in authority there knows them and perhaps cares about their success. When you establish a relationship with one or more of your instructors, they will notice you and might even lend a word of encouragement just when you need it most. The habit of discussing your progress with them may inspire you to perform at your best. We all hate to disappoint someone who cares about us. Making yourself accountable to somebody may motivate you to try harder in your studies. And this brings us to the next point.

2. *They provide a potential source of motivation and feedback.* An instructor might be the person who provides the spark that unlocks your potential. Either positive or negative experiences may motivate you. Consider this story from a large engineering school: The dean, addressing the freshman class, says, "Look to your right and look to your left. Only one of you will be here four years from now." Obviously, this comment discourages some students. But it challenges others to do their best.

The defining moment for this author came from a healthy dose of positive motivation. When I was a college student, I had no clear concept of my abilities. I worked hard but had no idea of my career prospects or potential for graduate work. One day, near the end of my senior year, I had a talk on the sidewalk with Mr. Jenkins, my English professor. I had visited his office often during the course, as I did with all of my professors. But the conversation I had with him that day changed my whole concept of my abilities.

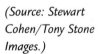

(Source: Stewart Cohen/Tony Stone Images.)

Mr. Jenkins detailed how I had impressed him as a student. He concluded our talk by saying that he thought that I was going to "be somebody." It was clear that Mr. Jenkins had confidence in me before I had confidence in myself. I have often thought of that conversation and used it to propel me through difficult times. But I wonder what would have happened to me if I had not made the effort to establish rapport with him? Will a "Mr. Jenkins" have the opportunity to provide this kind of positive affirmation for you?

3. *They yield vital course information and direction.* Some instructors give clues during office hours that help you focus on the important points and what they might cover on exams. You will never benefit from this information unless you visit your instructors during their office hours. Another point is that students and instructors often differ in terms of how they view the subject matter. Most students focus on memorizing facts. Instructors focus on key concepts and questions that reveal patterns in a particular field. You might miss the patterns if you only attend lectures or rely on the notes of other students. This difference in approach between instructors and students explains why many students score poorly on exams. Those who meet with instructors on a regular basis are more likely to align their thinking with that of the instructors. When you approach the subject in the same way as your instructor, you will find fewer surprises on exams.

4. *They provide a source of varied opportunities.* Interactions with instructors can lead to various opportunities. For example, students who get to know their instructors may

- Be invited to serve as teaching assistants

- Be invited to join the professor on a research project

- Be referred to a job that the professor knows about

- Learn about academic enrichment opportunities such as the summer research programs that take place at many institutions around the country.

- Receive help in preparing and submitting their original books and articles for publication.

Although these opportunities may not come during your freshman year in college, they could occur later on in your college career.

6. *They may result in your instructor becoming your mentor.* Do you want to make the most of your college experience? Then do everything in your power to attract a mentor. What can a mentor do for you? Let's take a look:

- *Provide general advice and counseling.* In some cases, a mentor acts like a surrogate parent, someone older and presumably wiser who can guide you as you grow.

- *Make referrals when necessary to campus specialists.* Usually a mentor does not handle specific problems but is able to refer you to someone on or off campus that can help you.

- *Assist in career planning.* Mentors sometimes serve as career role models. They might also be the source of ideas about careers that you might want to look into.

- *Provide evaluation and feedback.* It is often difficult to know where you stand in terms of progress toward your goals. With a mentor you can expect an honest evaluation of whether you are on track or need course correction. Mentors can also provide the moral support and encouragement you need to perform at your best.

- *Provide letters of recommendation for jobs and or advanced study.* Your strongest letter of support would most likely come from a successful mentoring relationship.

So how can you find a mentor? It is more likely that you would attract a mentor than be successful in setting out to "find" one. The following proactive characteristics may help you attract a mentor:

- Attend all classes.

- Show up on time for lectures.

- Sit near the front of the class or at eye level to the professor.

- Ask questions and contribute to class discussions as appropriate.

- Show interest and enthusiasm during lectures.

- Show politeness and tact in dealing with people.

- Attend office hours and TA sections on a regular basis.

- Contribute to discussions during office hours and TA sections.

- Ask for feedback on study habits and career plans.

- Demonstrate intellectual curiosity and ambition.

(Note that some of these characteristics appeared on an earlier lists, a point that confirms their importance.)

The key to attracting a mentor is consistency of performance. If you make a favorable enough impression, your instructor might start to show a special interest in your success. This is the beginning of a mentoring relationship. Keep doing what you were doing and let the process develop further. On the other hand, if you are unsuccessful in attracting a mentor, you can always *ask* an instructor to mentor you. He can only say yes or no.

Now that we have covered some of the benefits of interacting with instructors, let's turn to a discussion of office hours, the best opportunity for such interactions.

OFFICE HOURS

If you have never visited your instructors during office hours, it is time to start! If your reluctance stems from fear, remember that office hours are time slots that your instructors have set aside to visit with their students. In a sense, they are waiting for you to visit them. Here are two suggestions that might help make your first few visits easier:

- 1. Go with a friend or experienced student until you feel more comfortable going by yourself.

- 2. Walk by the office and see if other students are there asking questions; if so, join them. If no students are there, try another time.

Note that these suggestions apply only when professors meet students in groups, not one on one. The tips in the boxed feature will help you develop enough confidence to visit your instructors on a regular basis. These tips will also help you make the best use of your time and that of your instructor when you are there.

Checklist for How to Get the Most Out of Instructors' Office Hours

Before You Go
- Understand why you need to go (review the previous section).

- Review notes, assignments, and reading material.

- Develop a list of questions about material you don't understand or for which you need further clarification.

- For problem-solving courses, work through five or six examples of each assigned problem.

- Develop a list of questions based on your problem-solving exercises.

- Prepare mock exams on the course material.

- Collect relevant articles from sources other than those recommended.

- Familiarize yourself with some of the professor's publications or scholarly interests.

While You Are There
- Ask questions about the course material.

- Ask for an evaluation of your notes and study aids.

- Ask whether the notes and mock exams reflect the essential points of the course.

- Ask questions about your problem-solving exercises.

- Bring to the instructor's attention the articles that you've collected, and ask for his or her comments.

- If time permits, ask questions about the professor's scholarly interests.

- Ask questions about career possibilities.

- Look for potential study partners among any other students visiting the instructor at the same time.

After You Leave
- Write down suggestions made and any lessons learned.

- Contact any students you met who might be good study partners.

- Plan for the next office visit.

(continued)

**Checklist for How to Get the Most Out of Instructors'
Office Hours** *(continued)*

Additional Points

Point 1: For questions that you might ask about the material, try to have at least a basic understanding. Then your questions might sound like the following:

> *I didn't understand all of the lecture, but let me show you what I did get.*
>
> *I'm okay here and here, but now I am lost. Can you help me out?*

Point 2: Try to move beyond simple questions into questions that reflect a deeper understanding. Here are some examples:

> *How would this affect . . . ?*
>
> *What do you think about . . . ?*
>
> *How would you approach. . . . ?*
>
> *How is this concept related to . . . ?*
>
> *How would I apply this principle to . . . ?*
>
> *Would you be willing to evaluate my approach to . . . ?*

Point 3: Seize the moment. Many times during office hours, nobody shows up. If you are the only one there, you are likely to get a lot of attention. If you make a good impression, you could move closer toward a mentor relationship.

LETTERS OF RECOMMENDATION

Most of your instructors will not know you well enough to write a strong letter of recommendation for you unless you have attracted them as mentors. Therefore, you need to give them enough information about you to ensure convincing letters to support your applications. To get the best letters will require that you do most of the work. Provide instructors with a packet of background information that will form the basis of a meaningful interview. Your packet should contain the following:

- Transcript

- Detailed personal statement (a brief summary of your background, goals, values, career objectives, etc.)

- Summary statement of personal qualifications (see Worksheet 7.1)

- Self-evaluation of personal characteristics (see Worksheet 7.2)

Some highly proactive students even include a draft of what they might say if they were writing the letter. You might offer this draft to the instructor as points that she might want to consider in her own letter. Many instructors appreciate this gesture since it both gives them ideas and saves them time. Some actually use your letter after making some minor changes.

As you write your draft, be honest. Do not overstate or understate who you are. Describe your characteristics exactly as you believe them to be.

Start this process as far in advance as possible—ideally a few weeks. A few days before the agreed upon deadline, send the instructor a note thanking him for the letter of support. The note serves two purposes: (1) provides

WORKSHEET 7.1. SUMMARY STATEMENT OF PERSONAL QUALIFICATIONS

Prepared for Instructor _____

My Name _____

Recommendation requested for _____

Telephone _____

1. What classes have I taken with this instructor, when did I take the classes, and what grade(s) did I receive?

2. What qualities and experiences do I have that qualify me for this particular career or area of further study?

3. What are my strengths?

4. What are my weaknesses, and what am I doing to overcome them?

WORKSHEET 7.2. SELF-EVALUATION OF PERSONAL CHARACTERISTICS

Circle the appropriate number in each category

POOR   EXCELLENT

1 2 3 4 5 6 7 8 9 10

1. **Self-discipline**—drive, work habits

   1 2 3 4 5 6 7 8 9 10

2. **Interpersonal skills**—manners, tact, poise

   1 2 3 4 5 6 7 8 9 10

3. **Leadership**—ability to inspire others

   1 2 3 4 5 6 7 8 9 10

4. **Intellectual curiosity**—interest in learning

   1 2 3 4 5 6 7 8 9 10

5. **Motivation**—for chosen career

   1 2 3 4 5 6 7 8 9 10

6. **Reliability**—dependability with regard to commitments?

   1 2 3 4 5 6 7 8 9 10

7. **Social values**—sensitivity to the needs of others

   1 2 3 4 5 6 7 8 9 10

8. **Integrity**—morals, productive values,

   1 2 3 4 5 6 7 8 9 10

9. **Maturity**—self-control, judgment and choices

   1 2 3 4 5 6 7 8 9 10

10. **Autonomy**—degree of independence; initiative

    1 2 3 4 5 6 7 8 9 10

11. **Enthusiasm**—overall attitude; degree of optimism

    1 2 3 4 5 6 7 8 9 10

12. **Perseverance**—degree of persistence in the pursuit of goals

    1 2 3 4 5 6 7 8 9 10

13. **Imagination**—creativity

    1 2 3 4 5 6 7 8 9 10

evidence of your appreciation and (2) reminds the instructor to write the letter if he forgot to do so.

If your college has a service for this purpose, have all of your letters placed on file before you graduate. Instructors see a lot of students and might forget you. If you don't do this, at least send a photograph with the request. *Do not expect instructors to subsidize your career. If your letters are to go to a place other than your campus, include enough stamps in your package to cover the postage.*

Identifying and Correcting Thinking Problems

Thinking problems often lead to problems in relationships. Remember, you have no control over another person's thinking. But you can evaluate whether your thinking contributes to the problem or to the solution. Many of the thinking problems that can hinder your ability to form and maintain effective relationships are in the form of self-defeating beliefs or self-defeating values. Your task is to identify which of the problems apply to you and correct the problems using the Change Formula shown in Figure 7.4. In this process, you select a remedy (S) to change the self-defeating beliefs or values to productive beliefs or values. Remedies appear in Figure 7.5. Recall from Chapter 2 that self-defeating beliefs (values) lead to self-defeating thoughts that lead to self-defeating behaviors, as shown in Figure 7.6 Figure 7.7 shows that you can correct self-defeating beliefs (values) by using one or more of the remedies. This process results in productive behaviors. Figure 7.8 shows the impact that a person's values (or beliefs) can have on life outcomes.

Examples 7.9–7.11 and Exercises 7.8–7.14 will give you practice in working with the Change Formula as it applies to relationships. With practice, you will become more proactive in how you relate to people.

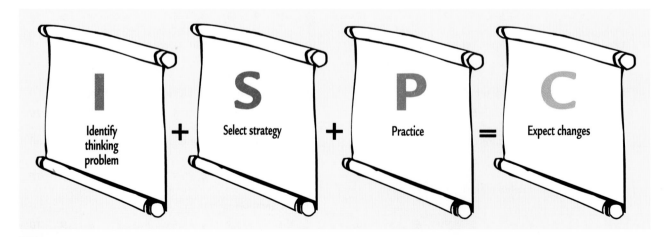

FIGURE 7.4

Change formula for correcting thinking problems.

FIGURE 7.5
Remedies for correcting thinking problems.

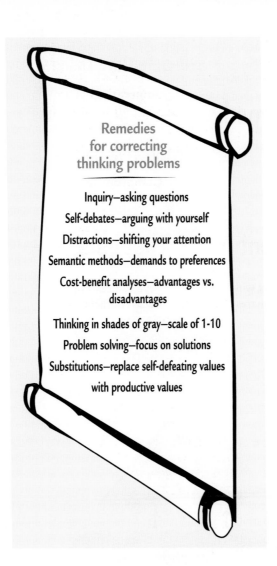

Remedies
for correcting
thinking problems

Inquiry—asking questions

Self-debates—arguing with yourself

Distractions—shifting your attention

Semantic methods—demands to preferences

Cost-benefit analyses—advantages vs. disadvantages

Thinking in shades of gray—scale of 1-10

Problem solving—focus on solutions

Substitutions—replace self-defeating values with productive values

FIGURE 7.6
How self-defeating beliefs lead to self-defeating behaviors.

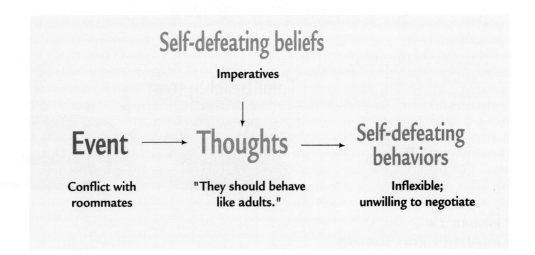

Self-defeating beliefs

Imperatives

Event   →   Thoughts   →   Self-defeating behaviors

Conflict with roommates

"They should behave like adults."

Inflexible; unwilling to negotiate

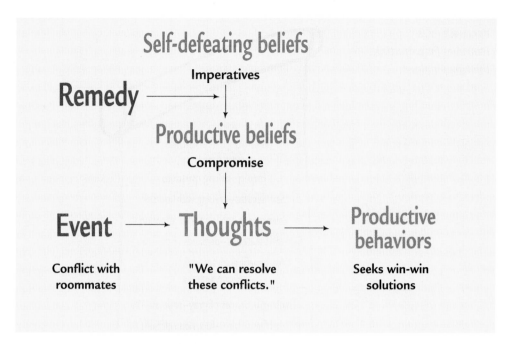

FIGURE 7.7
How corrected self-defeating beliefs lead to productive behaviors.

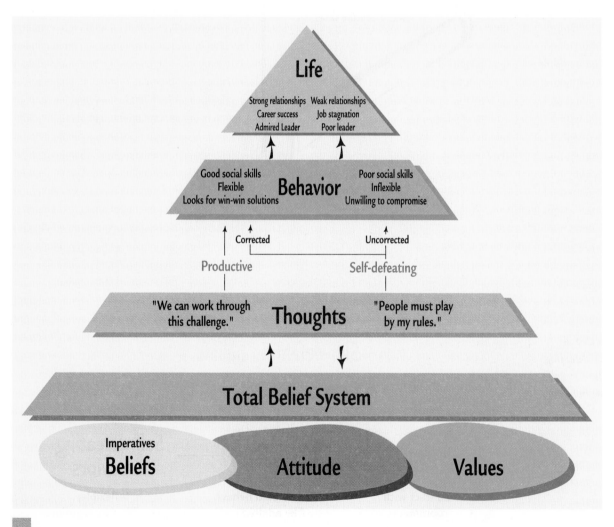

FIGURE 7.8
Impact of beliefs on life outcomes.

EXAMPLE 7.9

Event

Nema attends a large research university. Her best friend, Arnold, attends a community college in Nema's hometown 100 miles away. Nema's mother is pressuring Nema to stop seeing Arnold because (1) he has a different racial background and (2) she feels that Arnold does not measure up to Nema in terms of native ability. She feels that since Arnold only attends a community college, he has poor chances of success. Nema's mother wants her daughter to spend more time with Jed, whom Nema dated a few months earlier. Nema does not love Arnold as her mother thinks but wants to remain his friend. She has no interest in Jed. Nema faces a dilemma. She has to conform to her mother's desires or ignore her mother and think only about herself and what she wants to do. (Can you think of other possibilities?)

Nema's Self-Statement

My mother should not meddle in my personal life. I am going to call and tell her to mind her own business.

(I) Identify the Thinking Problem

Self-defeating beliefs: imperatives
Self-defeating values: arrogance; contempt; lack of tact

(S) Select a Remedy

1. Semantic methods
2. Cost-benefit analysis

Nema identified the main issue as related to her values (I). If she were to follow through on her automatic thoughts, she would be tactless and show a lack of respect for her mother.

   Nema did a cost-benefit analysis (S) to help her resolve the conflicts in her mind.

(C) Productive Beliefs/Values

Change demands to preferences
Choose tact and respect over arrogance and lack of diplomacy

Productive Self-Statement

1. I prefer that my mother let me handle my own personal affairs.
2. I will try to convince my mother that it is important for me to make my own decisions.

(P) Practice

Nema reviews the benefits section (P) repeatedly to enhance her beliefs.

Costs	Benefits
Loss in my independence	My mother would be happy with me.
Unhappiness over losing my best friend	My mother would know that I love and respect her.
Possible boring relationships with Jed	
Stress-induced negative impact on my grades and performance	

Journal Activity

How would you respond in a similar situation?

_____

_____

_____

_____

_____

_____

_____

_____

Applying the Change Formula to Family Conflicts

Fill in the blanks with the missing information, using Example 7.9 as a guide.

Event

Joe has a conflict with his father.

Joe's Self-Statement

My father is unreasonable because he refuses to pay my college expenses unless I get all As.

(I) Identify the Thinking Problem

_____

_____

_____

(S) Select a Remedy

_____

_____

_____

(C) Productive Beliefs/Values

_____

_____

_____

Productive Self-Statement

_____

_____

_____

(P) Practice

Practice the productive beliefs/values and self-statements.

Analyzing a Conflict with Your Parents

Describe a conflict that you have had or might have now with your parents. Write your self-statement and any automatic-self statements that might interfere with resolution of the problem. Identify the thinking problem that might need correcting and the productive beliefs or values that would apply. Finally, write your productive self-statement.

Event

_____

_____

_____

Self-Statement

_____

_____

_____

(S) Identify the Thinking Problem

_____

_____

_____

(S) Select a Remedy

_____

_____

_____

(C) Productive Beliefs/Values

_____

_____

_____

Productive Self-Statement

_____

_____

(P) Practice

Practice the productive beliefs and self-statement.

EXAMPLE 7.10

Event

Ryan is criticized by someone at a party.

Ryan's Self-Statement

Last Saturday night, I went to a party with some friends. One of the partygoers criticized me for not using drugs with them. He said that I was a party pooper, an insensitive person, and someone who made the other students feel uncomfortable. His comments made me feel very bad about not fitting in.

(S) Identify the Thinking Problem

Uncritical acceptance of criticism.

(S) Select a Remedy: Self-Debate

Q. Who was the person that criticized me?
A. Another student.
Q. Had the student met me before?
A. No.
Q. Did the student know anything about my abilities?
A. No.
Q. Did the student know anything about my interests?
A. No.
Q. Did the student know anything about my goals?
A. No.
Q. Did the student know anything about my values?
A. No.
Q. Did the student know anything about my concern for people?
A. No.
Q. How could a person who knows nothing about me be qualified to evaluate me?
A. He is not qualified. He only expressed his opinion.

(C) Productive Belief

Some people will criticize you even if they don't know you.

Productive Self-Statement

I am not concerned about criticism from people who don't know me and don't share my values.

(P) Practice

Practice the productive belief and self-statement.

Applying the Change Formula to a Conflict with a Roommate

Fill in the blanks with the missing information, using Examples 7.9 as a guide.

Event

Susan has a strong opinion about what she considers to be responsible behavior in a living situation.

Susan's Self-Statement

My roommate should clean up after herself.

(S) Identify the Thinking Problem

_____

(S) Select a Remedy

_____

(C) Productive Beliefs

_____

_____

Productive Self-Statement

_____

_____

(P) Practice

Practice the productive belief and self-statement.

Analyzing a Conflict with Your Peers

Describe a conflict that you have had or now have with your peers. Write your self-statement and any thinking problems that might interfere with resolution of the problem. Select a remedy that might increase the chances of a win/win solution.

Event

_____

_____

_____

Self-Statement

_____

_____

_____

(S) Identify the Thinking Problem

_____

(S) Select a Remedy

_____

(C) Productive Beliefs

_____

_____

Productive Self-Statement

_____

_____

(P) Practice

Practice the productive beliefs and self-statements.

RELATIONSHIPS WITH PROFESSORS

EXAMPLE 7.11

Event

Rayford has a strong negative opinion about a professor.

Rayford's Self-Statement

I think Professor Smith is a jerk.

(I) Identify the Thinking Problem

Overgeneralization

(continued)

EXAMPLE 7.11 *(continued)*

(S) Select a Remedy: self-debate

Q. What is a jerk?

A. I don't know for sure. I have heard other people use the term. Maybe it refers to a lousy person.

Q. What is a lousy person? What specific aspects of Professor Smith's behavior make him a jerk or lousy person?

A. I can't point to any specifics.

Q. Then why do I call him a jerk?

A. Because many students say so.

Q. How do I know that these students know what they are talking about?

A. I don't know.

Q. Is it possible that students have that opinion because Professor Smith gives hard tests?

A. It is possible.

Q. Is the fact that a Professor gives hard tests enough evidence to brand him a jerk?

A. No.

Q. Have any students spoken of Professor Smith's positive qualities?

A. Yes they have.

Q. What did they say?

A. They say that he works hard, treats students with respect, and presents clear lectures.

Q. Would it be fair to call someone a jerk who had these qualities?

A. No.

(C) Productive Beliefs

One characteristic does not make the total person.

Productive Self-Statement

Some students call Professor Smith a jerk because he gives hard tests. Other students confirm that he has some strong positive traits. It makes no sense to think of someone as a jerk unless he is totally bad. I will not call Professor Smith a jerk again.

(P) Practice

Practice the productive beliefs and self-statements.

• • • • • •EXERCISE 7.12

Applying the Change Formula to an Opinion about Instructors

Fill in the blanks with the missing information, using Examples 7.10 as a guide.

Event

Gretchen has a strong negative opinion about instructors in general.

Self-Statement

I think instructors should be more congenial when students visit their office hours.

(I) Identify the Thinking Problem

_____

(S) Select a Remedy

_____

(C) Productive Beliefs

_____

_____

Productive Self-Statement

_____

_____

_____

(P) Practice

Practice the productive beliefs and self-statement.

GENERAL ESSAYS AND EXERCISES

●●●●●●EXERCISE 7.13

Brainstorming for Relationship Conflicts Associated with Thinking Problems

Create a scenario for a relationship conflict that might emerge from the thinking problems listed in the table.

THINKING PROBLEM	CONFLICT
Overgeneralization	
Jumping to conclusions	
Personalization and blame	
All-or-nothing thinking	
Comparative thinking	
Imperatives	

Implementing the Change Formula

In rows 1–5, list the appropriate self-statements associated with the given situations. Identify the thinking problems and select remedies. In rows 6–12, propose a situation to fit the thinking problems and remedies listed.

SITUATION	(I) IDENTIFY THE THINKING PROBLEM	(S) SELECT A PROPOSED REMEDY
1. Student adopts risky behavior of friends to fit in with them.		
2. Student is unwilling to compromise—insists on a win/lose solution in all situations.		
3. Student plays stereo too loud over the objections of his roommate.		
4. Student cheats on exams.		
5. Student is reluctant to meet with instructors.		
6.	Magnification or minimization	Self-debate
7.	Imperatives	Semantic methods, self-debate
8.	Moral corruption	Replace with integrity
9.	Arrogance	Replace with modesty or respect
10.	Immaturity	Replace with maturity
11.	Unaccountability	Replace with reliability
12.	Rudeness	Replace with courtesy

CHAPTER SUMMARY

The concepts in this chapter address a critical issue for college students—relationships. Most of what you learn in college will strengthen your academic skills. There are few programs or courses that offer you specific guidelines for how to improve your relationships with your parents, peers, and professors. Few programs address how to negotiate with people or how to function in an increasingly diverse society.

The proactive approach to learning how to improve relationships takes the following course: (1) assess what key "people" skills you need in life; (2) learn everything you can from your academic courses; (3) find out what else you need to know; and (4) learn whatever else you need to know on your own. The material in this chapter serves only as a beginning to learning how to develop good relationships. Commit yourself to a lifelong effort to improve your interpersonal skills. As you gain competence in this critical area, you will have advantages over people who leave this part of their development to chance. These advantages might show up as better career opportunities, better social relationships, and a higher quality of life. A person's overall quality of life often improves when he makes a commitment to improve his social skills.

In previous chapters you learned how to become more proactive with respect to your outlook, performance, learning, health and now your relationships. In the last chapter, you will learn how to be more proactive in managing your finances.

NOTES

1. Jack Lochhead: "Teaching the Brain New Tricks," *Esquire,* March 1983, p. 61.

2. Adapted from Stephen R. Covey: *The Seven Habits of Highly Effective People* (New York: Simon and Schuster, 1989), © 1989 Stephen R. Covey. Used with permission. All rights reserved.

3. Adapted from an article by S. Birdine: "Diversity Made Simple," University of Indiana.

4. Adapted from S.L. Schmidt: "Talking About Race: Facilitation Guide." Iris Films.

5. From L. Elliott and C. Brantley: *Sex on Campus* (New York: Random House, 1997).

Read each statement and circle the number that best reflects your response.

```
        NEVER                                ALWAYS
        1   2   3   4   5   6   7   8   9   10
```

1. I feel that I responsibly manage my financial affairs.

   1   2   3   4   5   6   7   8   9   10

2. I pay credit cards in full each month to avoid interest charges.

   1   2   3   4   5   6   7   8   9   10

3. I avoid late charges by paying my bills on time.

   1   2   3   4   5   6   7   8   9   10

4. I drive in a manner that lets me avoid spending money for fines, parking tickets, and high insurance rates.

   1   2   3   4   5   6   7   8   9   10

5. I resist impulse buying, such as buying something in response to a frustration.

   1   2   3   4   5   6   7   8   9   10

6. When I buy clothing, I take quality, versatility, and cost of care into consideration, and I don't necessarily pay extra for the labels and fashions.

   1   2   3   4   5   6   7   8   9   10

7. I manage my phone budget in a responsible manner by limiting long-distance calls and making use of night-time and weekend rates.

   1   2   3   4   5   6   7   8   9   10

8. I limit computer-time charges by monitoring the time I spend online or by using free education access.

   1   2   3   4   5   6   7   8   9   10

9. I save money on automobiles by buying used vehicles.

   1   2   3   4   5   6   7   8   9   10

10. I use public transportation as often as possible.

    1   2   3   4   5   6   7   8   9   10

11. I avoid or limit the use of substances such as alcohol, tobacco, and narcotics.

    1   2   3   4   5   6   7   8   9   10

12. I take a preventive approach to health and dental care.

    1   2   3   4   5   6   7   8   9   10

13. I understand the impact of ads that claim to help me look better, have a better social life, and feel more secure, and I make informed choices.

    1   2   3   4   5   6   7   8   9   10

14. Whenever I receive any money, I follow a well-planned method for allocating my resources, which might include saving a portion.

    1   2   3   4   5   6   7   8   9   10

15. I have a savings account, and I make deposits into it whenever possible.

    1   2   3   4   5   6   7   8   9   10

16. I can identify and correct thinking problems that threaten my financial health.

    1   2   3   4   5   6   7   8   9   10

Determine your relative degree of proactivity for this trait by using the following formula:

Percent Proactivity = Sum of Circled Numbers ÷ 160 × 100

(Note that 160 is the maximum sum possible. It would result in a score of 100 percent.)

Percent Proactivity = _____

For example, if you checked 5 for each question, your score would be

Percent Proactivity for Financial Affairs = 80/160 × 100 = 50

"The relationship between people and their money (or lack of it) is not about economics. Instead, we have discovered that the state of your finances is really controlled by your state of mind and emotions."

Ron and Mary Hulnick, psychologists[1]

Finances: Understanding and Managing Your Money

WHETHER OR NOT you envision yourself becoming wealthy after you finish college, chances are one of the reasons you chose to attend college is that you are more likely to be financially secure with a college degree under your belt. A college degree is a good start toward financial security, but it is only the beginning. Many students discover the pitfalls of using credit cards and find themselves in a difficult financial situation as they exit college. Many people never learn to take responsibility for their finances, and the sad result can be little savings, much debt, and even bankruptcy. You can avoid the financial problems that most people face if you become more proactive *now* in how you handle money matters. This chapter will provide you with the thinking skills to take charge of your finances in the same way that a proactive person will manage other aspects of his life. You will learn how to

- Evaluate your spending patterns

- Identify and correct thinking problems that can threaten your financial security

- Employ sound strategies for accumulating and managing wealth

financial aid   low frustration tolerance   overspending   underspending

lifetime income

This chapter will help you increase your level of proactivity in handling money matters. The first step is to examine your beliefs and spending habits in the context of established trends. The next step is to predict whether your present pattern will help or hinder progress toward your financial goals. The final step is to identify and correct the thoughts and behaviors that threaten your financial well-being.

You might not relate now to some of the examples in this chapter. But remember the point that this book is about now *and* the future. Keep in mind that the habits you form now will stay with you for the rest of your life unless you change them. The purpose of this chapter is to help you develop productive habits of earning and spending money and provide you with suggestions for both what to do and what not to do.

The first part of Kari's story shows what not to do. Later on you will see that Kari takes steps to become more proactive about spending patterns.

Kari came to the campus with financial aid and some assistance from her mother to cover housing and tuition. She did not perform well during the first quarter and ended up dropping all of her classes. But Kari chose to spend the money anyway and allow her mother to believe that she was still attending classes. Kari went on a spending spree. Instead of going to classes, she went to the local mall every day. One day she bought an $800 stereo system for her apartment. On another day she charged an elaborate computer system to her credit card. By the end of the quarter, she had used up all of her financial-aid money and had charged the maximum on three credit cards. The only way that she could keep up with her payments was to withdraw and deposit money every month between credit cards.

The sad truth is that Kari's story is not uncommon. Money can play a pivotal role in a person's life for good or for ill. In Kari's case, money problems are related to larger issues such as

- *Self-defeating values*—immediate gratification leading to deception and dishonesty

- *Relationship conflicts*—the potential serious problems that might occur between her and her mother

- *Wasted opportunity*—failure to attend classes and learn, and failure to make use of professional help from professors, academic advisors, and psychological counselors

- *Potential legal problems*—resulting from misuse of funds

- *Long-term financial insecurity*—resulting from fiscal irresponsibility

The thoughts and behaviors that led Kari to this state of affairs will trouble her for a lifetime unless she takes steps to change them now. She needs to resolve a major issue that plagues many students in her situation: the ability to manage money responsibly. If she has trouble handling the small amount of money she has now, how will she manage the fortune that she might acquire over her lifetime?

Advertising: How Do We Respond?

Ads are everywhere—in newspapers, magazines, on television, and on the radio. Give examples of five different ads. Then describe how people might respond to each ad.

DESCRIPTION OF AD	RESPONSE
1.	
2.	
3.	
4.	
5.	

- *Health matters*—buying good-quality food even if it is more expensive; buying adequate health care insurance

- *Personal growth*—buying books; taking courses; attending seminars

- *Financial planning*—paying for advice from professionals on money management

- *Education*—buying books; taking courses to continue learning

- *Cultural enrichment*—spending money on travel, plays, concerts, and other activities that enrich a person's life

Ways to Resist the Messages of Ads

List five steps that you can take to help you resist advertising.

1. _____

2. _____

3. _____

4. _____

5. _____

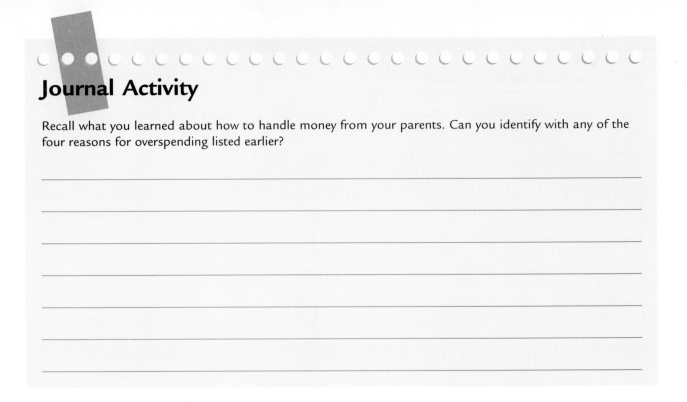

Journal Activity

Recall what you learned about how to handle money from your parents. Can you identify with any of the four reasons for overspending listed earlier?

_____

_____

_____

_____

_____

_____

CONTROLLING OVERSPENDING AND UNDERSPENDING

One approach to the control of spending problems is to ask yourself some hard questions that cause you to reflect on your habits. For example, if you tend to *overspend*, ask yourself the following:[6]

- Do I really need this item, or do I just want it?

- What bad things will happen to me if I don't buy this thing now?

- How can I achieve the same results by spending less money?

- If I really need this item now, why didn't I need it three or four weeks ago?

  If you tend to *underspend*, ask yourself the following:

- How can I adjust my spending so that I will have a frugal but comfortable lifestyle?

- How much money should I devote to activities that will enhance my personal growth?

- How can I make the best use of professionals (lawyers, accountants, and financial planners) to help me manage money?

To avoid both overspending and underspending, ask yourself:

- How can I balance my priorities so that I will avoid overspending or underspending?

  People make choices about how they spend their money. Their values often dictate these choices. Thus, they might underspend on health matters if this issue ranks lower on their priority list than having fun. The last section of this chapter provides proactive strategies for changing this pattern.

Proactive Financial Strategies for Your College Career

A s a student, you face two major tasks that will affect your financial well-being. The first task is to obtain the money you need for your academic and personal expenses. The second task is to make sound judgments about how to manage the money you obtain.

OBTAINING MONEY FOR COLLEGE

At the start of and during your college career, you will need a financial-support program. The financial-aid officer at your college can help you put together a financial-aid package that suits your needs. The package will involve three major contributors: the institution, your parents, and you. (Figure 8.1). Each contributor to your financial support program has special responsibilities. Let's look more closely at the role of each contributor.

■ YOUR INSTITUTION

The basic role of your institution is to help you plan and manage the cost of your education. Your college administers various financial-assistance programs for which you might be eligible. These programs include grants, scholarships, loans, and student employment. Some financial-aid programs require that you qualify according to federal regulations, while others do not. Your financial-aid advisor will try to find the right mix of grants, scholarships, and employment that will enable you to (1) make steady progress

FIGURE 8.1
Contributors to your financial-support program.

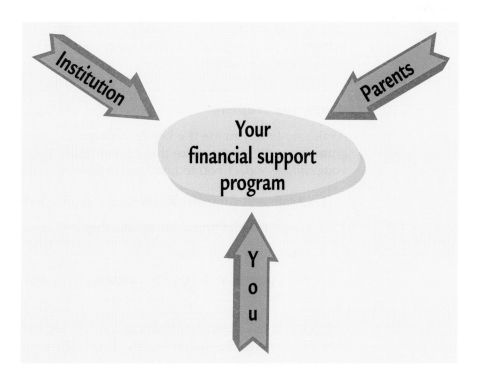

toward your degree and (2) make timely payments on your loans after graduation.

The sources of funds that colleges administer include federal, state, and local governments; businesses and foundations; community groups; and the college itself. Financial aid may be of two basic types: gift aid and self-help aid.[7] Gift aid does not need to be paid back. It consists of either of the following:

1. *Grants.* These are based on financial need.

2. *Scholarships.* These are usually based on merit but sometimes on need as well. You can use scholarship funds to pay tuition, fees, and other required education costs, but usually they are not sufficient to cover living expenses.

Self-help aid consists of the following:

1. *Loans.* These normally need to be repaid with interest. Some do not need to be repaid until after you leave college.

2. *Student employment.* Jobs are of two types:

    a. Federal and state work-study programs, which are often career oriented, part-time and often limited to less than 10 hours per week

    b. Regular part-time employment, either during the academic year or the summer months, or both

■ YOUR PARENTS

In putting together your aid package, your college expects your parents to contribute based on their income and assets. Students whose parents have low income and meager assets receive more grant money than do students whose parents are well off.

If you do not have parental help, check with your financial-aid officer before you declare yourself as an independent. There are strict guidelines that govern this category.

■ YOU, THE STUDENT

As the student, you are the key contributor to your financial-support program. You will want to take this responsibility seriously. Your parents and your college expect you to take the lead in doing the following:

1. Obtain and complete financial-aid application materials.

2. Search for and apply for scholarships.

3. Take out student loans.

4. Work part-time during the academic year and full-time during the summer.

Once you have obtained financial aid for college, you will want to be sure you manage the money wisely. This is the topic of the next section.

(*Source: Michael Krasowitz/FPG International.*)

MANAGING MONEY IN COLLEGE

A strong measure of your proactivity is the degree to which you set goals that affect all areas of your life. If you want to improve your overall level of productivity, you will want to set goals for how you manage your finances, as follows:

1. *Main Short-Term Goal:* Visit a financial counselor on campus in the next week to one month The author recommends this step for every student unless they have had extensive coaching on how to manage finances from a prudent parent or other responsible adult. Your financial-aid office will likely have someone who can help you. Your responsibility is to do the following:

- Arrange for an appointment.

- Show up for the appointment on time.

- Ask questions and take notes during the session.

- Take action on what you have learned.

The remaining goals in this section are to be completed in the next one month to four years.

2. *Main Intermediate Goal: Develop and implement a plan for fiscal responsibility.* Your financial aid office will provide you with a statement of your total allocation for the school year. Complete Exercise 8.3 to analyze the funds you have or will have. Then set subgoals as listed below to help you manage these funds.

Subgoal 1: Conduct a preliminary analysis of basic budget funds. As your first step toward fiscal responsibility, you will want to find out how you might use the funds you receive. Your financial-aid office can provide you with typical expense estimates for students at your college. Recall from the beginning of this chapter that Kari made some unwise choices in how she managed her money during the first year. Table 8.2 shows the major categories of expenses for Kari. On the advice of a friend, she visited a counselor so that she would not make the same mistakes during her second year.

A preliminary analysis of Kari's budget in Figure 8.2 shows that 80 percent of the items are beyond her personal control (fixed), and 20 percent are under her personal control (flexible).

Subgoal 2: Develop a budget for flexible expenses. Kari has $2,597 to work with for the year. Her estimate for how she should spend the money is as shown in Table 8.3. Based on these numbers, Kari determined that her monthly budget for flexible expenses was about $217 (Table 8.4). Exercises 8.4 and 8.5 allow you to work on your budget.

● ● ● ● ●●**EXERCISE 8.3**

Where Do I Get My Money?

List the amounts of money you have received or will receive from various sources:

SOURCE OF FUNDS	AMOUNT OF FUNDS
Loans	
Grants	
Scholarships	
Work-study program	
Parents' contribution	
Your own contribution	
Part-time job	
Total funds for college	

TABLE 8.2

*Major Categories of
Expenses for Kari*

EXPENSE CATEGORY	AMOUNT	PERCENT OF TOTAL EXPENSES (APPROXIMATE)
Tuition and fees	$ 4,198	30
Room and board	6,750	50
Books and supplies	630	5
Transportation	644	5
Personal expenses	1,323	10
Total for year	13,545	100

FIGURE 8.2

*Analysis of Kari's major
budget items.*

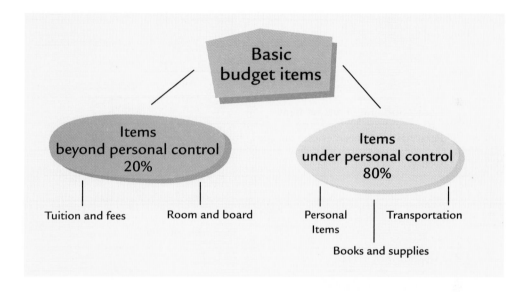

TABLE 8.3

Kari's Annual Budget

YEARLY BUDGET ITEM		AMOUNT
Books and Supplies		$ 630
Transportation		644
Personal		1,323
Clothing	$500	
Telephone	200	
Recreation and Entertainment	400	
Personal Care (cosmetics, toiletries, etc)	100	
Other	123	
Total		2,597

Preparing a Budget

Using Kari's example, as a guide, determine your yearly and monthly budget. Find out how much you spend each month by keeping track of everything you spend for three months and writing down even small items like chewing gum, then dividing the total amount by 3. The result is your monthly budget.

Yearly Budget

YEARLY BUDGET ITEM	AMOUNT	
Tuition & fees		
Room & board		
Books and supplies		
Transportation		
Personal		
Clothing		
Telephone		
Recreation and entertainment		
Personal care (cosmetics, toiletries, etc)		
Other		
Total		

Monthly Budget

MONTHLY BUDGET ITEM	AMOUNT	
Tuition & fees		
Room & board		
Books and supplies		
Transportation		
Personal		
Clothing		
Telephone		
Recreation and entertainment		
Personal care (cosmetics, toiletries, etc)		
Other		
Total		

Subgoal 3: Devise a savings plan. Your first reaction to this suggestion might be, "How can I save anything? I'm only a college student." Some people with six-figure incomes also have trouble saving money. The issue is not how much money you have but your attitude toward money management. Here are two savings tips that you can start applying now. If you continue using these tips for the rest of your life, you will be more likely to avoid the financial problems that many people have.

●●●●●●EXERCISE 8.5

Setting Spending Priorities

Assume that you have money left over after paying for your tuition and fees, housing, food, and transportation. How would you spend the remaining money? Rank your spending priorities (on a scale of 1–5) over the next four years for the money you acquire.

CATEGORY	YEAR ONE	YEAR TWO	YEAR THREE	YEAR FOUR
Possessions—fashion clothes, stereos, etc				
Savings and investments				
Contributions to charities				
Entertainment—movies, sports events				
Cultural events—plays, concerts, lectures				
Personal growth—books, courses, seminars				

TABLE 8.4
Kari's Monthly Budget

MONTHLY BUDGET ITEM		AMOUNT
Books and Supplies		$ 53
Transportation		54
Personal		107
Clothing	$42	
Telephone	17	
Recreation and Entertainment	33	
Personal Care (cosmetics, toiletries, etc)	8	
Other	10	
Total		217

■ **Savings Tip #1:** Pay yourself first. When you get your monthly check for $217, put aside 10 percent, or $22, first in a savings account (credit union or bank), and try to forget that it is there. This growing amount will become your emergency fund.

■ **Savings Tip #2:** Save all of your spare change. When you make cash purchases, don't spend the change that you get. Put the money in a piggybank, and add it to your savings account when you have accumulated $10 or more.

Subgoal 4: Develop a plan to manage the use of loans and credit cards. Lending institutions pass out credit cards on campuses the way theaters sell popcorn. Stories abound about gullible students who run up thousands of dollars in charges with no plans for how they will pay off the debt. You need a plan to help you borrow and repay money in a responsible and timely manner. When you finish college, you will have to repay your loans. The most serious threat you face now is credit card debt. The steps you take to manage this problem will help you avoid bigger problems later on.

Let's assume that you have no credit cards at the moment but are open to the possibility of acquiring them. How should you respond to offers? Here are some suggestions:

1. Stay on a cash basis as long as you can. This approach will save you interest charges and establish a pattern of fiscal responsibility.

2. Before you apply for a credit card, understand what you are getting into. For example, the information in the accompanying box contains some common terms that apply to credit cards.

3. Use credit cards only for convenience.

Make charges when you have to, but pay off the entire balance each month. When you make a charge, do the following: Subtract the amount from your checkbook. Highlight this line in your checkbook. Then when the credit card bill arrives, you can add the amount back to your check register and write a check to pay the bill.

Terms Associated with Credit Card Use

- **Annual fee:** Some lenders charge annual fees; other lenders charge no annual fees but may charge higher interest rates and other fees.

- **APR:** The annual percentage rate (APR) is based on having the loan for one year. Some lenders offer fixed interest rates; others charge variable rates based on certain key financial market indexes.

- **Grace period:** This is a period of time between making a charge and when interest begins to accrue. This period applies only when there is a zero balance. If a balance exists, the interest starts from the moment the lender posts the new charge to your account.

- **Fees:** Lenders may charge fees for exceeding the credit limit, making late payments, taking cash advances, or submitting checks returned due to insufficient funds.

- **Introductory "teaser" rates:** Many lenders offer a low "teaser" interest rate good for only a few months. After the stated period ends, expect to pay a higher rate. For example, a company may offer an interest rate of 4.9 percent for the first six months. After six months, the rate might jump up to something like 21 percent.

Keep only one card for this purpose. Cut up all other cards, and send them back to the issuers with a note that says, "please cancel." If you already have a problem with credit card debt, consider the options in Table 8.5. Note that option 5 demonstrates the level of personal responsibility consistent with sound fiscal management.

OPTION	ACTION	DISADVANTAGE
1	Ask Mom and Dad to pay the bill.	This sets a pattern for continued dependence on your parents. When will you learn to take responsibility for your own behavior?
2	Ask the lender to reduce the interest rate.	The rate might still be too high to be consistent with prudent use of funds.
3	Consolidate debt into student loan.	This uses up money needed for education expenses.
4	Consolidate debt into lower interest credit card(s).	Interest charges could be used for more productive purposes.
5	Accelerate payments with funds from a part-time job during the school year and full-time in summers.	Little money will be available for recreation and entertainment.

TABLE 8.5
Options for Paying Off Credit Card Debt

Main goal: Develop a plan to manage financial emergencies. Every student will experience a setback from time to time. Perhaps your car will break down or your computer will crash. Or maybe you have to make a trip home for a family emergency, and your parents cannot afford the airfare. What will you do?

- **Emergency Action Plan #1.** Check with your financial-aid officer. She will know about the availability of emergency funds. Some campuses will make $50 to $200 available to students on a short-term basis, maybe a month. The funds might come from sources such as faculty or student associations. You repay the amount by the end of the loan period.

- **Emergency Action Plan #2.** Look for a part-time job. Jobs like tutoring high school students work well in these situations. You might also use this plan to pay back the emergency loan.

- **Emergency Action Plan #3.** Use some of your emergency savings. Use this plan as a last resort, since you will want your savings to grow to as large an amount as possible.

Main goal: Devise a plan for how to correct thought patterns that threaten your financial security. The examples and exercises at the end of this chapter will help you put together a plan of your own. As you gain skill and confidence in managing the money you have now, you will want to make plans for how you will acquire and manage larger sums of money in the future. You can set long-term goals to accomplish in the next five years or more. Examples of long-term goals might be buying your first house or visiting another country overseas. The next section will help you develop those plans.

Proactive Financial Strategies for the Twenty-First Century

*I*n the past, many people could develop a comfortable lifestyle just by working hard. Times have changed. Hard work alone is not the best choice. Here are eight proactive strategies that will put you on the right track to financial security. You can apply some of these strategies now while you are a student; others may be more relevant to your life after graduation.

STRATEGY ONE: TAKE CHARGE OF YOUR POTENTIAL FORTUNE

You have choices about how to manage your finances. You can choose to

- Rely on the government

- Rely on financial planners

- Follow the paths of your parents

- Leave money matters to chance

- Take charge yourself

Before you decide, think about this background information. Perhaps your parents are good role models for financial responsibility. But are your goals the same as those of your parents? Also, can you expect to use the same strategies that your parents did and succeed in a world that is changing more rapidly than when they were your age?

On the other hand, your parents might be poor role models for how to handle your money. Do you want to repeat their pattern? Will it take you where you want to go in life?

Government programs such as social security provide for basic food, shelter, and health care. The value of this system is that it provides for people who have little or no other resources. But will you expend the money and effort for college just to retire on social security? Will the money from this plan give you the kind of retirement lifestyle you desire?

Most financial planners derive their income from selling products that you may or may not need. Perhaps you can learn something from these professionals, but ask yourself this question: "Do I want to delegate responsibility for my fortune to someone else?"

The only sound choice for you is to take personal responsibility for your finances. You are the only one who you can count on to act in your best interest. Take charge of your finances in the same way that you take charge of your attitude, performance, education, and health.

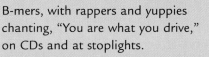

PROFILE FOR SUCCESS

Vince Brown

I guess for many people, the collection, display, and celebration of money is an end in itself, pursued with religious fervor. But when I have it, I like to use money to get the heck away from those zealots. My majors are history and film, and I enjoy traveling to all the places I've read about. It's nice, I've found, to use some carefully saved funds to leave home, pursue some personal curiosities, and escape the cult of accumulation. Ironically, I can do that only if I carefully manage my own money to my best advantage.

One of the best ways I know of to manage money is to ignore the summons of most advertisers and their legions of followers and instead save my money for my own long-term projects and plans. I don't buy new, or even nice, cars. I've had to live with noisy, ugly, automobiles for long periods of time in order to save for three-month trips to Central America, Europe, and India. That's not easy for a Southern Californian, raised in the exhaust of Benzes and B-mers, with rappers and yuppies chanting, "You are what you drive," on CDs and at stoplights.

Purposeful saving takes more fortitude than I trust myself to have, though. So I usually put some money away as soon as it comes in—almost before I've counted it—and pretend I don't have access to it. It's never disappointing to surprise yourself with money in your account that you haven't been thinking too hard about. Sometimes this strategy leaves tight margins on monthly bills and daily entertainment, but it's all worth it when I'm tasting the herbs and spices of a faraway land several months later.

Many young adults do not expect a prosperous future. They believe that they will not be as well off as their parents. Their concerns spring mainly from the changes that have taken place in our economy over the past decade including changes to social security. The pessimistic outlook of this large number of people leads to atitudes and behaviors that differ sharply from those of optimists. See Table 8.6 for examples.

Notice the item of "see diminishing opportunities" in the table. The irony of this issue is that many pessimists have comforts and options that most people in the world can only dream of. Then how can they see "diminishing opportunities"? Professor Richard MacKenzie provides some clues to this riddle in his book, *The Paradox of Progress:*[8]

- The mix of technological advances and economic success has given rise to the most abundant pool of opportunities the world has ever known.

- Increased opportunities have led to strong competition among businesses, resulting in reduced economic security.

- Strong business competition has also led to strong competition among governments, making governments less able to give their citizens the high level of security that they want.

- Vast opportunities and low security breeds pessimism among many people.

Thus, the main problem, MacKenzie contends, is too many opportunities rather than too few. In this sense, we will have even more opportunities than we have now because computers allow a person to tap into global networks that could lead to unlimited possibilities.

TABLE 8.6

Attitudes and Behaviors of Optimists versus Pessimists

PESSIMISTS	OPTIMISTS
Focus on the here and now; live lavishly with little concern for how this pattern might affect future needs	Long-term focus; live modestly; save and invest for future needs
Live by own set of rules; show no regard for societal codes of conduct	Conform to principles that reflect decent attitudes and behaviors
Exploit other people for personal gain	Seek win/win business deals with people
See diminishing opportunities	See unlimited opportunities
Support measures to limit opportunities to existing U.S. residents	Support measures to expand opportunities for everybody

Optimists will have advantages over pessimists in this scenario because they:

- Assume personal responsibility for their financial future

- Make the most of available resources and opportunities

- Create opportunities where none seem to exist

- Take rational risks

- Find ways to work around setbacks and defeats

Recall from Chapter 3 that optimism is the prevailing outlook among proactive people.

STRATEGY THREE: PAY YOURSELF FIRST

Paying yourself first is an old practice that still works. As discussed earlier, this plan calls for you to put aside a portion of your income before making any other payments. A good goal is 10 percent, but you can work up to that amount in stages. Pay yourself before taxes if possible. There are two main benefits of this approach:

1. You set the tone for financial discipline.

2. You develop a core savings fund that will grow over time.

STRATEGY FOUR: PREPARE FOR TWIN CAREERS

One observer states:

> *Each human being in the developed world is going to have to be largely self-reliant along the entire adult lifespan. In particular, the baby boom will be the first generation in the history of civilization whose members will bear individual responsibility for their own later-life income. Government will continue to play a role, business will continue to play a role, family will continue to play a role, but the buck will stop where it starts—with you and me.*[9]

One way to become self-reliant is to prepare now for twin careers, as follows:

- Get a job working for someone else as your first career.

- Learn as much as you can about the specialty or hobby that will become your second career.

- Take courses and read books to acquire or fine-tune the traits and skills you will need for your second career.

- Start your other venture on a part-time basis at first while you continue your full-time job.

- Continue part-time until you have enough experience and money to quit your full-time job in the first career and devote all your efforts to your second career.

STRATEGY FIVE: INVEST IN YOURSELF

Once a person earns enough money for basic needs, she thinks of making investments. The common route is through stocks, bonds, or real estate. She expects these assets to increase in value and thus return profits when she sells them to someone else. This plan has worked well for many people.

In the past, even a factory worker with little education could attain modest wealth using this plan. But it is more difficult in today's economy, even for someone with a college degree, to allocate much money for investments. Instead of, or in addition to, money, you will need to invest in your abilities.

The best opportunities now go to people with strong skills in the following areas:

- Problem solving

- Creativity

- Working in teams

- Leadership

In addition, a person will need to have the following traits:

- A passion for excellence

- Enthusiasm for learning

- Adaptability

These requirements make it clear that the key to wealth now and in the future is to increase your personal assets as well those that pertain to money. You will want to invest in yourself. Be generous with the money you spend for courses and seminars that will help you fine-tune your skills and keep them current. This approach will help you get the best-paying jobs and receive promotions, or succeed as an entrepreneur. With more money, prudent spending, and sound investments, you are more likely to have a secure financial future.

STRATEGY SIX: BALANCE WANTS WITH MAJOR GOALS AND OBLIGATIONS

As pointed out earlier, impulse buying can wreck a person's plans for a secure financial future. The most frequent causes of this pattern are tempting ads or a desire to compete with others in acquiring possessions. Perhaps no one would advise a person to deny himself all the things that could make life more pleasant. But when he gives in too often to present desires, he can threaten his long-term goals for a home, his children's education fund, or a secure retirement.

The answer to this dilemma is balance. Balance results from staying in touch with your values. You achieve a better balance between what you want and what you need when your spending choices reflect your values.

STRATEGY SEVEN: EXPAND YOUR MENTAL RESOURCES

Chapter 5 stressed how people have more than one type of intelligence. See Table 8.7 for ideas of how you can apply Sternberg's concept of multi-intelligences to managing your finances.[10]

ANALYTICAL	CREATIVE	PRACTICAL
Balancing bank statements	Visualizing yourself creating wealth	Paying bills on time
Maintaining a monthly budget	Visualizing lifestyle choices	Making investments
Tracking investments	Visualizing debt-free living	Identifying credible advisers
Setting financial goals	Visualizing wealth desired	Making contributions to worthy causes
Monitoring progress toward goals	Visualizing how to use money to benefit others	Keeping records of expenditures
Identifying problems that prevent you from reaching your goals	Visualizing solutions to problems that threaten goals	Following through on plans to meet goals
Planning for starting a business	Constructing financial scenarios (what if . . ?)	
Identifying strengths and areas where you need help	Visualizing ideas on how to be financially independent	
	Visualizing how to make the most of available finances	
	Visualizing how to increase income	
	Visualizing the kind of business desired	
	Visualizing how to balance desires with intermediate and long-range goals	

TABLE 8.7
The Sternberg Intelligence Model Applied to Financial Management

Your financial well-being will depend more on your spending habits than on your earning power. In a previous section you saw how a person could lose large sums of money through wasteful spending. You will want to review this section often. In addition, carefully record what you spend, and make it a goal to spend less than the amount you earn. Follow these suggestions and you will tap into a proven path to financial security.

Identifying and Correcting Thinking Problems

Thinking problems, such as self-defeating beliefs or self-defeating values, often lead to problems with financial security. Your task is to identify which of the problems apply to you and correct the problems using the Change Formula in Figure 8.3. In this process, you select a remedy (S) to change the self-defeating beliefs or values to productive beliefs or values. Remedies for correcting thinking problems appear in Figure 8.4. Recall that self-defeating beliefs (values) lead to self-defeating thoughts that lead to self-defeating behaviors, as shown in Figure 8.5. Figure 8.6 shows that you can correct self-defeating beliefs (values) by using one or more of the remedies. This process results in productive behaviors. Figure 8.7 shows the impact that values (or beliefs) can have on life outcomes.

Examples 8.1–8.4 and Exercises 8.6 and 8.7 will give you practice in working with the Change Formula as it applies to finances. With practice, you will become more proactive in how you manage your financial affairs.

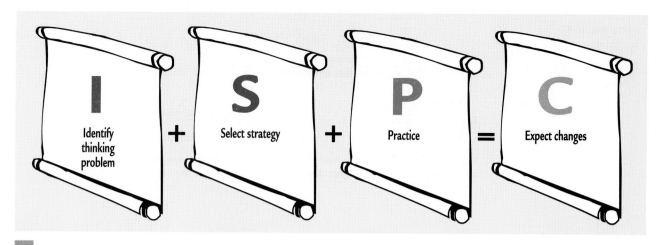

FIGURE 8.3
Change Formula for correcting thinking problems.

FIGURE 8.4
Remedies for correcting thinking problems.

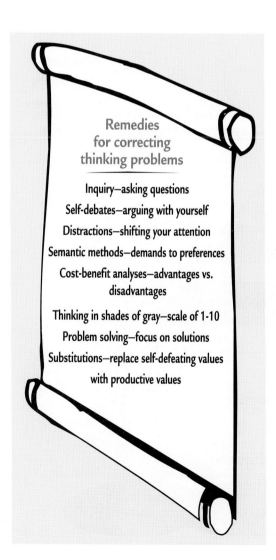

Remedies for correcting thinking problems

Inquiry—asking questions

Self-debates—arguing with yourself

Distractions—shifting your attention

Semantic methods—demands to preferences

Cost-benefit analyses—advantages vs. disadvantages

Thinking in shades of gray—scale of 1-10

Problem solving—focus on solutions

Substitutions—replace self-defeating values with productive values

FIGURE 8.5
How self-defeating beliefs lead to self-defeating behaviors.

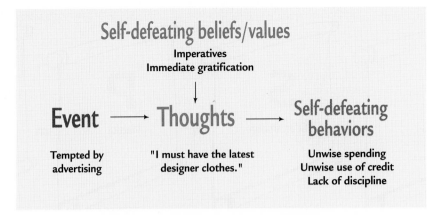

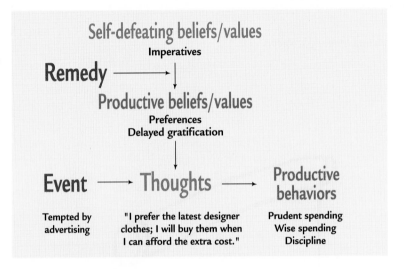

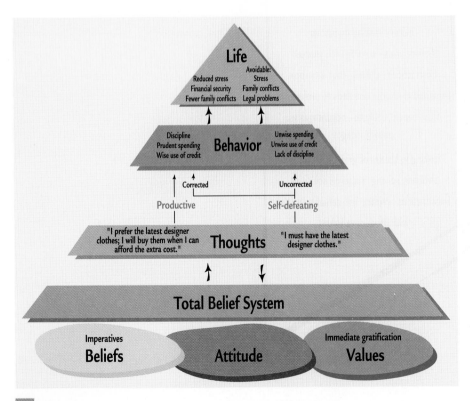

FIGURE 8.7
Impact of beliefs on life outcomes.

EXAMPLE 8.1

Event

Ruby ponders her lifestyle choices. Her parents have a good lifestyle, and she wants to live like they do. The problem is that her job pays her only enough to meet basic expenses.

Ruby's Self-Statement

I want to have a lifestyle like my parents'. The only way that I can do that is to run up my credit card debt.

(I) Identify the Thinking Problem

Value based on unsound principles

(S) Select a Remedy

Replace unsound principles with sound principles, as shown:

UNSOUND PRINCIPLES	SOUND PRINCIPLES
Impatience	Patience
Immediate return	Delayed gratification
Immaturity	Maturity
Wastefulness	Thrift

(P) Practice

Rehearse the alternate beliefs.

EXAMPLE 8.2

Event

Archie's mother owns a successful business. Since she provides him with plenty of spending money, Archie does not work himself. He uses some of his money to take his friends to dinner at expensive restaurants. Also, Archie often drives through the campus in his red German sports car with the top down.

Archie's Self-Statement

I must have the respect of my friends. I must conduct myself so that my friends will approve of me and respect me.

(I) Identify the Thinking Problem

Imperatives

(continued)

EXAMPLE 8.2 *(continued)*

(S) Select a Remedy: self-debate

1. Semantic methods: Replace imperative language. For example, change "must" to "prefer to" or "would like to."
2. Self-debate

Q. What makes me feel that my friends must approve of me?
A. I don't know. I just want them to.
Q. In what ways would it be catastrophic if my friends did not approve of me?
A. I would have low self-esteem.
Q. Is my self-esteem based solely on whether or not my friends approve of me?
A. No, it is not.
Q. What other factors contribute to my self-esteem?
A. My performance as a student, my optimistic outlook, and my ability to get things done.
Q. Would these other factors be enough to give me high self-esteem even if my friends did not approve of me?
A. Yes, they would.
Q. If these other factors would give me high self-esteem, would my friends' approval of me be nice to have, but not necessary?
A. I agree with that point.

(C) Productive Beliefs

Preferences

Productive Self-Statement

I would prefer that my friends approve of and respect me, but I would survive if they did not.

(P) Practice

Rehearse the remedy and revised automatic self-statement.

EXAMPLE 8.3

Event

Lillie grew up in an inner-city neighborhood with her single-parent mother and three younger brothers. The family's sole support is public assistance funds. Lillie works part-time to fulfill her responsibility to her financial-support program. Lillie's friends always wear the latest designer clothes when they go out. To avoid being left out, Lillie spends more on clothes than she or her mother can afford.

Lillie's Self-Statement

I must wear the latest designer clothes to stay tight with my friends.

EXAMPLE 8.3 *(continued)*

(I) Identify the Thinking Problem

Imperatives

(S) Select a Remedy: Inquiry

1. Do I really need this item or just feel that I want to have it?
2. What bad things will happen to me if I don't buy this thing now?
3. How can I achieve the same results by spending less money?
4. If I really need this item now, why didn't I need it three or four weeks ago?

(C) Productive Beliefs/Values

Preferences and choices

Productive Self-Statement

I prefer to stay tight with my friends, but I also choose to stay within my budget. I expect my friends to accept me for who I am and not what I wear.

(P) Practice

Rehearse the remedy and revised automatic self-statement.

EXAMPLE 8.4

Event

When Frank could not get into the lab classes he wanted, his response was to go out and buy ten new music CDs to comfort himself. Two weeks later, Frank did not have enough money left to buy food.

Frank's Self-Statement

I must do something to ease the pain of not getting what I want.

(I) Identify the Thinking Problem

Imperatives related to low frustration tolerance

(S) Select a Remedy: Self-Debate

Q. What makes me think that I can't stand the pain of not getting what I want?
A. Because I have always had my way.
Q. Is easing the pain in this case a life-or-death matter?
A. No, it is not.
Q. Will I survive if I don't get the classes I want?
A. Yes, I will survive.

(continued)

EXAMPLE 8.4 (continued)

(C) Productive Belief/Value

Patience

Productive Self-Statement

I would prefer to get all of the classes that I want, but it would not be catastrophic if I did not get them.

(P) Practice

Rehearse the remedy and revised automatic self-statement.

●●●●●●EXERCISE 8.6

Brainstorming for Events Associated with Thinking Problems

Give examples of money matters (events) from your own experience or the experiences of people you have known that reflect the thinking problems listed. Refer to Examples 8.1–8.4.

MONEY MATTER (EVENT)	THINKING PROBLEM
	Imperatives
	Imperatives
	Immediate return
	Immaturity
	Wastefulness

●●●●●●EXERCISE 8.7

Responding to Thinking Problems Related to Money

Choose one event that represents each of the thinking problems and develop a detailed response as shown in Examples 8.1–8.4.

Journal Activity

List the thinking problems that you think threaten your financial well-being. Use the Change Formula to correct them.

_____

_____

_____

_____

_____

_____

_____

CHAPTER SUMMARY

Most people have to discover on their own how to manage their finances. This knowledge comes, if at all, after they have made many mistakes. As we discussed in Chapter 2, change is more difficult as one gets older. The time to form good habits in money management is now. There are many books and other materials on the market that offer specific advice on how to handle your financial affairs. Most of these sources focus on the mechanics—loans, savings, investments, retirement planning, tax planning, and budgeting. We encourage you to seek out reliable sources of information on these topics as your needs may require.

The chapter you just finished takes a comprehensive approach to financial management, providing practical tips for the present, strategies for the future and remedies for how to correct the thinking problems that lead to financial difficulties. The other chapters in this book will help you be a strong student, have a productive career and life, and effectively manage your personal affairs and relationships despite your financial circumstances.

Keep this book as lifelong reference. Review it often. Use this book to work on those areas that you need to strengthen and to reinforce your existing areas of strength. The likely outcome is that you will join the ranks of a small number of people in our society who enjoy success not only in their career but in their personal relationships.

NOTES

1. R. Hulnick and M. Hulnick: *Financial Freedom in 8 Minutes a Day: How to Attract and Manage All the Money You'll Ever Need* (Emmaus, PA: Rodale, 1994). Used with permission of the authors.

2. O.S. Mitchell and J.F. Moore: "Retirement Wealth Accumulation and Decumulation: New Developments and Outstanding Opportunities," working paper 97-12, The Wharton School, University of Pennsylvania, pp. 63–64, table IA3.

3. M. Csikzentmihalyi: *Flow: The Psychology of Optimal Experience* (New York: Harper and Row, copyright © 1990), p. 44. Used with permission of Harper Collins Publishers.

4. I Timothy 6:10, *King James Version*.

5. Derived from concepts presented in A. Ellis and P. Hunter: *Why Am I Always Broke* (Secaucus, NJ: Carol Publishing Group, 1991).

6. Ibid.

7. M. Kantrowitz: http://www.finaid.org.

8. From *The Paradox of Progress: Growing Pessimism in an Era of Expanding Opportunities* by Richard B. McKenzie. Copyright © 1997 by Oxford University Press, Inc. Used by permission of University Press, Inc.

9. Ibid.

10. Based on concepts from *Successful Intelligence* by Robert Sternberg. Copyright © 1996 by Robert Sternberg. By permission of Simon and Schuster.

Post-Chapter
Self-Assessments

POST-CHAPTER SELF-ASSESSMENT

Read each statement and circle the number that best reflects your response.

NEVER   ALWAYS

1   2   3   4   5   6   7   8   9   10

1. When I encounter adverse circumstances, I assume that it is within my power to overcome them.

   1   2   3   4   5   6   7   8   9   10

2. When I make mistakes, I acknowledge, correct, and learn from them

   1   2   3   4   5   6   7   8   9   10

3. When faced with risky situations, I assess the worst and best possible consequences and my ability to cope with these alternatives, and then I make a decision.

   1   2   3   4   5   6   7   8   9   10

4. I choose constructive options to help me relieve stress.

   1   2   3   4   5   6   7   8   9   10

5. When I encounter a stressful event, my automatic thoughts are usually positive.

   1   2   3   4   5   6   7   8   9   10

6. When I encounter adverse events, I see them as temporary.

   1   2   3   4   5   6   7   8   9   10

7. I take responsibility for my behavior.

   1   2   3   4   5   6   7   8   9   10

8. I speak in terms that suggest that I have the power to overcome circumstances.

   1   2   3   4   5   6   7   8   9   10

9. When I experience complex events, I focus on issues that I can do something about.

   1   2   3   4   5   6   7   8   9   10

10. I take a step-by-step problem-solving approach to complex situations that I encounter.

    1   2   3   4   5   6   7   8   9   10

11. I read ahead for my classes, stay alert during lectures, and review notes after class.

    1   2   3   4   5   6   7   8   9   10

12. I spend time with people whose actions reveal their passion for what they believe.

    1   2   3   4   5   6   7   8   9   10

13. I make time in my schedule to maintain strong ties with family members.

    1   2   3   4   5   6   7   8   9   10

14. I take steps to cultivate my network of friends and supporters.

    1   2   3   4   5   6   7   8   9   10

15. I welcome opportunities to share ideas with people of different backgrounds such as those of a different age, race, culture, religion, or sexual orientation.

    1   2   3   4   5   6   7   8   9   10

16. I look for opportunities to help other people.

    1   2   3   4   5   6   7   8   9   10

17. I set aside time to relax and have fun.

    1   2   3   4   5   6   7   8   9   10

18. I seek out opportunities to learn and to broaden my perspective and add to my life experiences.

    1   2   3   4   5   6   7   8   9   10

19. I seek to balance my life by tending to my mental, physical, social, and spiritual needs.

    1   2   3   4   5   6   7   8   9   10

20. I can identify and fix the self-defeating thought patterns that lead to pessimism.

    1   2   3   4   5   6   7   8   9   10

Determine your relative degree of proactivity for this trait by using the following formula:

Percent Proactivity = Sum of Circled Numbers ÷ 200 × 100

(Note that 200 is the maximum sum possible. It would result in a score of 100 percent.)

Percent Proactivity = _____

For example, if you checked 5 for each question, your score would be

Percent Proactivity for Outlook = 100/200 × 100 = 50

POST-CHAPTER SELF-ASSESSMENT

Read each statement and circle the number that best reflects your response.

NEVER   ALWAYS

1   2   3   4   5   6   7   8   9   10

1. I feel that I have a high degree of control over my life.

   1   2   3   4   5   6   7   8   9   10

2. I feel that I am good at completing tasks.

   1   2   3   4   5   6   7   8   9   10

3. I have people in my life whom I love and care about.

   1   2   3   4   5   6   7   8   9   10

4. I have people in my life who love and care about me.

   1   2   3   4   5   6   7   8   9   10

5. I feel that I have a clear sense of what I think is important in my life.

   1   2   3   4   5   6   7   8   9   10

6. I feel that I know what I stand for and what I will fight for.

   1   2   3   4   5   6   7   8   9   10

7. I feel that the world will be a better place because of my contributions.

   1   2   3   4   5   6   7   8   9   10

8. I have a list of things that I intend to achieve by a certain date.

   1   2   3   4   5   6   7   8   9   10

9. I feel that I have a high level of enthusiasm for learning.

   1   2   3   4   5   6   7   8   9   10

10. I form mental pictures of what I want to do and achieve in life.

   1   2   3   4   5   6   7   8   9   10

11. I make sacrifices so that I can achieve my goals.

   1   2   3   4   5   6   7   8   9   10

12. My values—the things I think are important—do not conflict with my goals—what I want to achieve in life.

   1   2   3   4   5   6   7   8   9   10

13. I bounce back quickly when I don't achieve my goals.

   1   2   3   4   5   6   7   8   9   10

14. I can identify and correct thinking problems that hinder my performance.

   1   2   3   4   5   6   7   8   9   10

Determine your relative degree of proactivity for this trait by using the following formula:

Percent Proactivity = Sum of Circled Numbers ÷ 140 × 100

(Note that 140 is the maximum sum possible. It would result in a score of 100 percent.)

Percent Proactivity = _____

For example, if you checked 5 for each question, your score would be

Percent proactivity for Performance = 70/140 × 100 = 50

POST-CHAPTER SELF-ASSESSMENT

Read each statement and circle the number that best reflects your response.

NEVER   ALWAYS

1 2 3 4 5 6 7 8 9 10

1. I feel in charge of my education.

   1   2   3   4   5   6   7   8   9   10

2. I am able to focus on how I can use what I know and learn.

   1   2   3   4   5   6   7   8   9   10

3. The source of my motivation for learning is internal rather than from external sources such as grades and test scores.

   1   2   3   4   5   6   7   8   9   10

4. I use role models to help me learn and grow.

   1   2   3   4   5   6   7   8   9   10

5. I use a set of criteria for choosing the right role models for me.

   1   2   3   4   5   6   7   8   9   10

6. My behavior in the classroom promotes effective learning and shows respect for my professors and classmates.

   1   2   3   4   5   6   7   8   9   10

7. In addition to my private efforts, I spend some time studying with other students.

   1   2   3   4   5   6   7   8   9   10

8. I use my analytical, creative, and practical abilities when I study for courses and manage my personal affairs.

   1   2   3   4   5   6   7   8   9   10

9. I use mental rehearsal when I prepare for events such as taking exams and making speeches.

   1   2   3   4   5   6   7   8   9   10

10. I use study materials to strengthen my memory, and I also use higher thinking skills, such as comprehension, synthesis, and judgment.

    1   2   3   4   5   6   7   8   9   10

11. I have a notetaking system that lets me both recall facts and grasp concepts.

    1   2   3   4   5   6   7   8   9   10

12. When I read, I first preview the material, propose questions, and then read for answers to the questions.

    1   2   3   4   5   6   7   8   9   10

13. I have a task-organization system that involves breaking big tasks into smaller segments, setting priorities, and checking off items on To Do Lists.

    1   2   3   4   5   6   7   8   9   10

14. When I write a paper, I first identify the questions I want to answer.

    1   2   3   4   5   6   7   8   9   10

15. I solve academic and nonacademic problems using ordered rather than random procedures.

    1   2   3   4   5   6   7   8   9   10

16. During problem-solving exercises, I read the problem many times in the process of finding a solution.

    1   2   3   4   5   6   7   8   9   10

17. I view exam preparation as an ongoing process rather than as periodic all-night events.

    1   2   3   4   5   6   7   8   9   10

18. I am able to identify and correct problems in thinking that hinder learning.

    1   2   3   4   5   6   7   8   9   10

Determine your relative degree of proactivity for this trait by using the following formula:

Percent Proactivity = Sum of Circled Numbers ÷ 180 × 100

(Note that 180 is the maximum sum possible. It would result in a score of 100 percent.)

Percent Proactivity = _____

For example, if you checked 5 for each question, your score would be

Percent Proactivity for Learning = 90/180 × 100 = 50

POST-CHAPTER SELF-ASSESSMENT

Read each statement and circle the number that best reflects your response.

NEVER   ALWAYS

1   2   3   4   5   6   7   8   9   10

1. I feel that I am responsible for my health.

   1   2   3   4   5   6   7   8   9   10

2. My meals conform to a semi-vegetarian diet.

   1   2   3   4   5   6   7   8   9   10

3. When I cook, I look for ways to replace unhealthy ingredients with healthier choices.

   1   2   3   4   5   6   7   8   9   10

4. I get 30–45 minutes of moderate exercise each day.

   1   2   3   4   5   6   7   8   9   10

5. My weight falls within acceptable guidelines for my height.

   1   2   3   4   5   6   7   8   9   10

6. I get enough sleep.

   1   2   3   4   5   6   7   8   9   10

7. I respond to stress in constructive ways, not by getting angry.

   1   2   3   4   5   6   7   8   9   10

8. I use a system of relaxation to help me control stress.

   1   2   3   4   5   6   7   8   9   10

9. I reduce stress by staying current in my coursework.

   1   2   3   4   5   6   7   8   9   10

10. When I experience stressful situations, I seek the comfort of close friends or relatives.

    1   2   3   4   5   6   7   8   9   10

11. I wash my hands after using the toilet.

    1   2   3   4   5   6   7   8   9   10

12. I avoid sharing eating or drinking utensils with other people.

    1   2   3   4   5   6   7   8   9   10

13. I avoid risky practices such as body piercing and tattooing.

    1   2   3   4   5   6   7   8   9   10

14. I follow safe practices during intimate contacts with other people.

    1   2   3   4   5   6   7   8   9   10

15. I avoid using chemical substances for the purpose of getting high.

    1   2   3   4   5   6   7   8   9   10

16. I can identify and correct thinking problems that threaten my health.

    1   2   3   4   5   6   7   8   9   10

Determine your relative degree of proactivity for this trait by using the following formula:

Percent Proactivity = Sum of Circled Numbers ÷ 160 × 100

(Note that 160 is the maximum sum possible. It would result in a score of 100 percent.)

Percent proactivity = _____

For example, if you checked 5 for each question, your score would be

Percent Proactivity for Health Issues = 80/160 × 100 = 50

Read each statement and circle the number that best reflects your response.

NEVER   ALWAYS

1   2   3   4   5   6   7   8   9   10

1. When I encounter a conflict with my parents, I consider the interests of both my parents and myself in reaching an agreement.

   1   2   3   4   5   6   7   8   9   10

2. In resolving conflicts between others and me, I look for win/win solutions.

   1   2   3   4   5   6   7   8   9   10

3. I choose friends who have compatible beliefs, values, goals, and aspirations.

   1   2   3   4   5   6   7   8   9   10

4. I can resist pressure from others who to engage in negative and self-destructive behaviors.

   1   2   3   4   5   6   7   8   9   10

5. When I discuss issues with other people, I try to put myself in the other person's place and figure out how she might think and feel.

   1   2   3   4   5   6   7   8   9   10

6. When I engage in a dispute with another person, I do not label that person but instead seek to separate the issue of dispute from the person.

   1   2   3   4   5   6   7   8   9   10

7. I am honest about my feelings and emotions when I try to resolve conflicts with other people.

   1   2   3   4   5   6   7   8   9   10

8. I base my evaluation of a professor mainly on my own observations and impressions.

   1   2   3   4   5   6   7   8   9   10

9. I am open-minded when I listen to and consider the religious perspectives of other people.

   1   2   3   4   5   6   7   8   9   10

10. I feel secure enough about my own abilities to attend instructors' office hours and initiate conversations with them.

    1   2   3   4   5   6   7   8   9   10

11. I can ignore the ridicule of other students who might accuse me of "sucking up" to instructors.

    1   2   3   4   5   6   7   8   9   10

12. I have a detailed plan (including a list of questions to ask) for attending the office hours of each of my instructors.

    1   2   3   4   5   6   7   8   9   10

13. Most of my questions during office hours reflect a deeper understanding of the material rather than simple recall of facts.

    1   2   3   4   5   6   7   8   9   10

14. I can identify and correct specific thinking problems that hinder effective interactions with parents.

    1   2   3   4   5   6   7   8   9   10

15. I can identify and correct specific thinking problems that hinder effective interactions with peers.

    1   2   3   4   5   6   7   8   9   10

16. I can identify and correct specific thinking problems that hinder effective interactions with my professors.

    1   2   3   4   5   6   7   8   9   10

Determine your relative degree of proactivity for this trait by using the following formula:

Percent Proactivity = Sum of Circled Numbers ÷ 160 × 100

(Note that 160 is the maximum sum possible. It would result in a score of 100 percent.)

Percent Proactivity = _____

For example, if you checked 5 for each question, your score would be

Percent Proactivity for Outlook = 80/160 × 100 = 50

Read each statement and circle the number that best reflects your response.

NEVER   ALWAYS
1   2   3   4   5   6   7   8   9   10

1. I feel that I responsibly manage my financial affairs.

   1   2   3   4   5   6   7   8   9   10

2. I pay credit cards in full each month to avoid interest charges.

   1   2   3   4   5   6   7   8   9   10

3. I avoid late charges by paying my bills on time.

   1   2   3   4   5   6   7   8   9   10

4. I drive in a manner that lets me avoid spending money for fines, parking tickets, and high insurance rates.

   1   2   3   4   5   6   7   8   9   10

5. I resist impulse buying, such as buying something in response to a frustration.

   1   2   3   4   5   6   7   8   9   10

6. When I buy clothing, I take quality, versatility, and cost of care into consideration, and I don't necessarily pay extra for the labels and fashions.

   1   2   3   4   5   6   7   8   9   10

7. I manage my phone budget in a responsible manner by limiting long-distance calls and making use of night-time and weekend rates.

   1   2   3   4   5   6   7   8   9   10

8. I limit computer-time charges by monitoring the time I spend online or by using free education access.

   1   2   3   4   5   6   7   8   9   10

9. I save money on automobiles by buying used vehicles.

   1   2   3   4   5   6   7   8   9   10

10. I use public transportation as often as possible.

    1   2   3   4   5   6   7   8   9   10

11. I avoid or limit the use of substances such as alcohol, tobacco, and narcotics.

    1   2   3   4   5   6   7   8   9   10

12. I take a preventive approach to health and dental care.

    1   2   3   4   5   6   7   8   9   10

13. I understand the impact of ads that claim to help me look better, have a better social life, and feel more secure, and I make informed choices.

    1   2   3   4   5   6   7   8   9   10

14. Whenever I receive any money, I follow a well-planned method for allocating my resources, which might include saving a portion.

    1   2   3   4   5   6   7   8   9   10

15. I have a savings account, and I make deposits into it whenever possible.

    1   2   3   4   5   6   7   8   9   10

16. I can identify and correct thinking problems that threaten my financial health.

    1   2   3   4   5   6   7   8   9   10

Determine your relative degree of proactivity for this trait by using the following formula:

Percent Proactivity = Sum of Circled Numbers ÷ 160 × 100

(Note that 160 is the maximum sum possible. It would result in a score of 100 percent.)

Percent Proactivity = _____

For example, if you checked 5 for each question, your score would be

Percent Proactivity for Financial Affairs = 80/160 × 100 = 50

INDEX

values and, 134
  See also Connectedness; Family; Friends
Relatives, 24
Relaxation, 89, 230, 231
Religion, 24
  change in, 36–37
  prejudice and, 37
Resources
  finances and, 331, 333
  learning and, 145
  mental. *See* Mental resources
  optimism and, 331
Respect, 272
Responses, 10
  automatic, 15, 48, 49–52
  habit and, 13
  positive vs. negative, 11, 228–230
  relaxation, 230, 231
  to stress, 228–230
Retirement, 36
  finances and, 307, 308
Risks
  finances and, 331
  from infectious disease, 232–237
  optimism and, 64, 85–88, 93, 331
  rational, 63, 85–88, 93, 331
  from sexually transmitted disease, 234–237
Robbins, Anthony, 107, 129
Role model. *See* Modeling/models (role)
Romantic relationships, 251, 252, 274–278

S
Sacrifices, 129
Savings, 307, 325–326, 329, 331
  for emergencies, 328
Scholarships, 319, 320
Schuckit, Marc, 242
Scripts, 13, 15
Selective editing, 42
Self-assessment, 167. *See also* Assessment
Self-awareness, 162, 164
Self-debates, 50
Self-defeating attitudes, 38–44
Self-defeating behavior, 114, 135
Self-defeating beliefs, 38–44
  correcting, 49–57, 134–138. *See also* Correcting thinking problems

finances and, 308
health and, 242–247
Self-defeating thought patterns, 31–33, 38–44, 49
  correcting. *See* Correcting thinking problems
  optimism and, 65, 66, 92–98
  pessimism and, 63, 91
  stress and, 65, 66
Self-defeating values, 38–44
  correcting, 58–60, 134–138
  finances and, 306
  performance and, 134–138
  pessimism and, 91
Self-determination, 6, 104–107, 132–133
Self-esteem
  competition and, 154
  optimism and, 84
  relationships and, 272
  weight control and, 223
Self-evaluation, 112
Self-improvement goals, 122
Self-management, 196
  exercise and, 218–219
Self-motivation, 101, 102
  competence and, 104
  connectedness and, 104
  exercise and, 218
  external vs., 114, 143
  goals and, 133
  intelligence and, 162, 164
  mission and, 112
  performance and, 101, 133
  pillars of, 104–107
  values and, 102–105, 111
  See also Motivation
Self-statements
  automatic, 49–52
  productive, 94–95
Seligman, Martin, 68, 70
Selye, Hans, 227
Semantic methods, 50
Semi-vegetarian diet, 211–212
Senses (five), 11
Sexual behavior, 210, 275
Sexual orientation, 37
Sexually transmitted disease (STD), 234–237, 240, 275
Skills
  analytical, 159
  critical thinking, 49
  goals and learning new, 128, 129

imagery and, 170
listening, 270–271
mental resources and, 159, 160
practical mental, 157, 159
social, 251–301
types of, 160–163
Sleep, 195, 220, 222–223
Smoking, 241. *See also* Tobacco
Social security, 329, 330
Social skills, 251–301
Social support
  optimism and, 84
  stress and, 231
Social tolerance, 34, 37, 38
Society
  learning and, 148
  mental resources and, 159
Socrates, 172, 191
Socratic method, 172, 191–192
Socratic writing exercises, 157, 191–192
Sound principles, 39, 44–48
  values and, 107, 111
Spaced repetition, 194–195
Spatial intelligence, 161–163
Spiritual goals, 122
Spiritual needs, 89
Staples, Walter Doyle, 29
Status, money and, 311
STD. *See* Sexually transmitted disease (STD)
Stereotyping, 37, 555
Sternberg, Robert J., 160, 164–165, 333
Stimuli, 10, 12, 13
Strategy for Solving Mathematics-Based Problems, 193–194
Stress, 227–232
  anger and, 230
  exercise and, 216, 230–231
  learning and, 192
  men's vs. women's, 231
  optimism and, 64–66, 84
  relationships and, 258
  sleep and, 220
  social support and, 84
Stress cycle, 64–66
Stress management, 230–232
Student employment, 319, 320, 328
Students
  classroom behavior by, 153–154
  information about, 144